Feminist Perspectives on The Past and Present Advisory Editorial Board

Feminist Academics:
Creative Agents for Change

edited by

Louise Morley and Val Walsh

Taylor & Francis
Publishers since 1798

UK	Taylor & Francis Ltd, 4 John St., London WC1N 2ET
USA	Taylor & Francis Inc., 1900 Frost Road, Suite 101, Bristol, PA 19007

First published 1995

A Catalogue Record for this book is available from the British Library

ISBN 0 7484 0299 3
ISBN 0 7484 0300 0 (pbk)

Library of Congress Cataloging-in-Publication Data are available on request

Typeset in 10.5/12 pt Times
by Graphicraft Typesetters Ltd., Hong Kong

Printed in Great Britain by Burgess Science Press, Basingstoke on paper which has a specified pH value on final paper manufacture of not less than 7.5 and is therefore 'acid free'.

Contents

Contents

Feminist Academics: Creative Agents for Change

Louise Morley and Val Walsh

This book discusses feminist interventions in dominant organizations of knowledge production. As a feminist anthology, it attempts to be both a political and strategic act, bringing authors together through a shared commitment and purpose. In this it breaks the primary taboo of women being seen together, especially women congregating with intent. Feminisms are located as creative energy for change and critique, empowering women to apply political understanding to methodologies for teaching, learning, research and writing in the academy. Contributors demonstrate how feminist analysis of the micropolitics of the academy in terms of power, policies, discourses, curriculum, pedagogy and intra- and interpersonal relationships, provides a framework for deprivatizing women's experiences and influencing change. Academic feminism is also problematized and deconstructed, particularly in relation to the linkage of the two terms. For many, academic feminism is a contradiction in terms, an oxymoron (Elam, 1994), selling out feminists' commitment to everyday praxis. Yet, on the other hand, academic feminism is also frequently viewed by the establishment as being insufficiently academic. Using theoretical constructs, our own biographies and experience, as impetus, example and frame, women map present predicaments and inequalities, and identify sites and opportunities for strategic interventions. We notice the transformative possibilities of feminism as an oppositional discourse whilst acknowledging that all experience is mediated by a discourse. As multi-dimensional actors, feminist academics are conceptualized as innovative rather than reactive, creating optimism about the permeation and permanence of change. Feminist process acts as both politics and self-care.

As agents for change, feminist academics frequent a territory in which micro and macro processes are analytically related. The chapters are set against a backdrop of major educational reform, particularly in the UK, and the rise of New Right policies and practices. The transition from welfare to market values and the socioeconomic climate of recession, have resulted in a new economy of power (Ball, 1994). Now that the methods of managerial capitalism are entering and reshaping the academy, academics are beginning to experience increasingly coercive working environments, combined with escalating work-loads, long hours, open-ended commitment/availability, together with in-creased surveillance and control. It is debatable whether New Right policies have changed, or have simply entered and reinforced gender relations in the academy. Whereas previously a central concern for feminist academics was to document the specificity of how gender inequality permeates intellectual frame-works, more recently attention has also been drawn to organizational and policy contexts and conditions of the production of feminist knowledge. Government legislation, unfunded expansion and the new concept of managerialism have resulted in changes in the culture, values, ideology and structure of Higher Education in Britain. There is a discourse of opportunity, without the prefix of equality, suggesting that whilst the client group of the academy may be in transition, changes in the understanding of the connections between gender, knowledge and power remain slow.

A gendered deconstruction of the academy exemplifies the social and psy-chic labour involved in the daily negotiation of patriarchal power in the acad-emy. Feminist academics demonstrate how oppressive patterns from the private sphere have been reproduced in the public services, made more complex by Enlightenment values of objectivity and detachment in the academy. This book invited women to move beyond the limitations of Enlightenment role expecta-tions, and discuss aspects of work which trouble, excite, or enrage us. In so doing, contributors articulate feelings and ideas behind the organizational cul-ture of disembodiment. As members of subordinate groups, based on gender, social class, 'race', sexuality and disability, feminist academics in this book dem-onstrate how social and psychic development occur simultaneously, resulting in a coagulation between external structures of discrimination and women's inter-nalized oppression. Hence, feminist academics are required to perform and produce, with authority and excellence, in an organizational and social context which disempowers materially and psychologically. This book attempts to give a voice to the psychic narratives which run when maintenance of external pre-tence of authority and composure is required. It also decodes and disentangles gendered message systems and the matrix of power relations in the academy.

In a culture where emotional literacy is discursively located in opposition to reason, feminist academics frequently have to repress pain and anger, and hide the contradictions and tensions that arise from being members of subor-dinate groups in powerful institutions. Discrimination in the academy can rein-force and restimulate women's wider experiences of sexist oppression. Feminist consciousness can act simultaneously to sensitize and heal. In postmodernist thought, power can be both oppressive and generative. The creativity comes when one recognizes that this hurt can be transformed into knowledge, action, analysis and energy for change. As Audre Lorde (1984: 127) suggests:

> Every woman has a well-stocked arsenal of anger potentially useful against those oppressions personal and institutional, which brought that anger into being.

Every chapter has been written by women enduring, negotiating, resisting and reworking the daily realities which both provide our contexts for writing (speaking out) and our data (the evidence). These acts of writing are, in themselves, evidence that oppression, discrimination and victimization need not end in depression or despair, but can fuel women's creative and political energies and purposes. This repositions women from victims to change agents.

The issues of location, accountability, constituency and focus of feminist energy for change are reflexively considered. Complex questions are raised about the role the academy can play in producing wider socio-political changes for women. The question of women's visibility/vulnerability, and the points at which our visibility most ensures our vulnerability, are evident in these chapters. There is also a recurring preoccupation with the consequences for women of the splitting expected of western academics. So, whilst feminists can make themselves more vulnerable by drawing attention to themselves as women in the academy, we are paradoxically strengthened for being part of a wider political movement for change.

As a feminist anthology, this book attempted to incorporate feminist process into its own production. This involved dialogue and interaction between editors and authors, and a commitment to transgress institutional hierarchies, by bringing together a diverse range of women, at different stages of our academic careers, and feminist academics not attached to any one institution. The process of this anthology has heightened our awareness as editors, of the challenges academic feminists face and how women's writing and knowledge production are marked by our *contexts* of production — the enmeshing of health and confidence, domestic and personal circumstances, economic, social and professional constraints and opportunities, our multiple identities and feminist networking. The contributors are experienced risktakers: as they repeatedly make clear, the dangers are real, not imagined. Here they demonstrate that 'consciousness is the way out of the box' (Pinkola Estes, 1994: 71).

Chapter Overview

Celia Davies and Penny Holloway explore the relationship between gender and organizational culture in the British academy. The current underfunded expansion and the new enterprise culture, with an emphasis on income generation and cost effectiveness, is affecting employment conditions. The restructuring of Higher Education leading to commodification and fragmentation of educational provision and casualization of labour is evaluated in relation to the impact on women academics. Naz Rassool considers how the social construction of black women as gendered, 'ethnic' beings provides potent images around which cultural 'truths' are built. Black women thus are, generally, experienced as 'powerless' and 'passive' within the culture of organizations. This chapter analyses the personal life histories of a selection of black women academics and their perceptions of themselves as knowledge producers and practitioners. These are discussed in relation to mechanisms of day-to-day life, within both the academy and wider academic discourses, that serve to undermine the strength of their contributions. Utilizing biographical detail the chapter explores the multi-levelled strategies for individual and cultural empowerment developed by black professional women in their quest to transform their social experience. Barbara Brown Packer bases her chapter on her research in the US academy. Her central question was to inquire how association with women's issues had affected the career development of women academics in North American universities. In so doing, the author identified patterns and processes of women's engagement with organizations. Debbie Epstein suggests that anti-racism and lesbian and gay activism have been tied together in conflict during the late 1980s and early 1990s through discourses of the 'loony left', and, more recently, of 'political correctness'. This popular common sense constitutes an important, but usually neglected part, of the hidden curriculum of Higher Education. This is particularly the case for students in the 18–25 age group, who have grown up during the Thatcherite years. The chapter explores how, as a feminist, lesbian academic, who is committed to developing anti-oppressive pedagogies and curriculum, negotiating the hidden curriculum has affected her teaching life and relationships in both negative and positive ways. Mary Evans discusses how being an academic involves living a life devoted to the great gods of 'truth' and 'rationality'. The dominant verb is to 'think', and not to 'feel'. The academic world, it is assumed, is one of 'the mind'. The person, let alone the body, is given little presence in this construction and this chapter examines how abstract thought is gendered. Universities grew out of all-male communities, and this initial identification of men with knowledge remains one which is still powerful and destructive for women academics.

Val Walsh considers the practical, political and symbolic significance of feminists who teach in Higher Education. Women embody sexuality in an environment devoted to its official suppression and exclusion. The construction of woman as body marginalizes and denies women's intellectual and professional identities. Transgression involves crossing the boundary between rationality and emotionality, and establishing an integrated model of creativity, intellect and feeling. Tracey Potts and Janet Price write their chapter as two women with ME, and analyse how their experiences of being differently-abled have produced new, specific and situated knowledge. The question of access is clearly central to academic work and yet academic institutions have been slow to recognize that the privileging of the mind renders bodies absent. This chapter aims to produce a feminist rewriting of the academy that insists on the creative and disruptive presence of particular bodies as a necessary element in the processes of theorizing, teaching, writing and learning.

Louise Morley examines the tension between writing and research as major outlets for academic women's creativity, and their role as performance indicators for academic career development. She considers how 'coercive creativity' affects the process of writing and how feminism affects the process of publication and career success. This chapter identifies the strategies that women evolve to prioritize their creativity, and analyses internalized narratives that are activated when women claim authority to write. Lesley Kerman believes that women must show outstanding abilities if they are appointed to senior management positions in Higher Education. Once installed, they must take care not to be seen as a threat, to either subject identity or management style. The anthropology of witchcraft provides some illuminating resonances for the observer of academia. Heidi Safia Mirza examines the complexity of black women's status in Higher Education. On the one hand, there appears to be a mass movement from the bottom up, shattering the myth of low representation of black women students in university. On the other hand, the low representation of black women lecturers and staff demonstrates the insincerity of equal opportunity policies and the marginalization of black women from institutional and feminist agendas. The chapter concludes that black women survive the educational system through strategic negotiation of racism, rather than through any effective operation of equal opportunities or antiracist policies. Ultimately, by defining their space on the margin, black women do win through to find their place in Higher Education. Mel Landells and Avril Butler base their chapter on a pilot study into the sexual harassment of women teaching staff at a British university. The authors critically examine the effective potential of sexual harassment policies which are introduced into gendered organizational culture. This culture, the authors suggest, condones sexual harassment and silences women who are harassed. In describing the research, which deliberately coincided with the introduction of a Sexual Harassment Policy at the university, the authors reflect upon the degree of success in influencing organizational policy through feminist research. Ways are identified in which the research process itself contributed to challenging the culture of silence surrounding women's experiences.

Jo Stanley exemplifies how a powerful part of class oppression is to negate the intelligence of working class people. This chapter analyses how internalized class oppression becomes activated by academic conferences. The author draws on her knowledge of Gestalt theory and the experiences of art therapy work in conference settings, which enabled women to express their dis-ease in empowering ways and develop strategies for dealing with dis-enabling situations. Liz Stanley argues that western social scientists' dependence on, and contribution to, a canon which enshrines and masks its élitism, colonialism, racism and sexism, as 'objectivity' and 'rationality', has been exposed and opposed by feminist work which has identified these axioms of academic life as the gatekeeping practices of an educational élite. Acknowledging Geertz's set of binary 'switches' used to characterize ethnographic experience — 'us' and 'them', 'there' and 'here' — the writer adds in the switch of time, the move between 'then' and 'now'. Drawing on a collaborative project, called 'Our Mother's Voices', the author demonstrates the complexity and challenge of issues concerning referentiality and textuality, in particular for feminists like herself, working at the crossroads of self/other, auto/biography, reality/representation, fact/fiction. She shows how these processes enable us to focus on analytic themes which are fundamental issues, ethically, politically and epistemologically, for feminism, auto/biography, and feminist presence in the academy. The book finishes with Dinah Dossor's poem, Grievance, which acts as a warning. Evoking women's vulnerability inside the academy with painful intensity, the poem also mourns/warns the risks of complicity and/or defeat, in isolation or exhaustion — the latter being for women notably connected.

References

BALL, S. (1994) *Education Reform: A Critical and Post-Structural Approach*, Milton Keynes: Open University Press.

ELAM, D. (1994) *Feminism and Deconstruction*, New York and London: Routledge.

LORDE, A. (1984) *Sister Outsider*, Trumansburg: The Crossing Press.

PINKOLA ESTÉS, C. (1994) *Women Who Run With The Wolves* (Contacting The Power of the Wild Woman), London: Rider.

Chapter 1

Troubling Transformations: Gender Regimes and Organizational Culture in the Academy

Celia Davies and Penny Holloway

There was never really any doubt in the early 1980s that the pattern of Higher Education in the UK would have to change. The values which had underpinned the expansion of the university sector in the post-war era included a firm faith in degree-level education as among the social goods that merited public support, and a strong belief in the capacity of academics to deploy government funding wisely and to run their own affairs with wisdom, prudence and foresight. Such values came to sound hollow in the context of a Conservative Government which was facing deepening economic recession, was keen to limit the activities and spending of the State, and was committed to the power of market solutions. In one arena after another — in the health and welfare professions, in local government and the civil service, as well as in education at all levels — new style managerialism was brought into confrontation with old style professional values (see, e.g., Pollitt, 1990; Davies, 1995: ch8). And the transformations that were put in train, calling for unambiguous mission statements and clear performance indicators, and introducing the incentive of market competition, were far-reaching.

This chapter traces the contours of the new managerial changes as these affected the traditional universities, paying particular attention to the implications for women academics. While it is still too early to conclude with any certainty about the long-term implications of restructuring, and to distinguish between these and the effects of the change process itself, the chapter invites readers to begin to think in terms of a shift from an old to a new 'gender regime' in Higher Education.[1] It argues that the gender regime now emerging has to be set in the context of two factors. The first is the campaign to secure equal opportunities for women in Higher Education, which has gathered strength in recent years. The second is the growth of feminist academics and the establishment (some would perhaps now say the institutionalization) of women's studies in the academy. Pessimists are right to point to the limits of both of these as agents of transformation in the academy, and to ways in which sexual inequality is in danger of becoming further entrenched in the new occupational cultures and structures of managerialism in the universities. But we should also remind ourselves that the gender regime of the older universities was itself profoundly unwelcoming to women and that there are aspects of its passing which women should not mourn. What we need to understand, and what will help us to place in context some of the energy and creativeness represented by the contributors to this volume, are the specific forms that the transformation of the old gender regime is taking — the contradictions that these engender and the spaces for struggle that they open up — at a time when women have succeeded, however imperfectly, in keeping issues of gender on the agenda in Higher Education.

New managerialism disrupts the established order and positions women differently. The questions are 'how differently?' and 'with what potential results?' To offer a preliminary answer to these questions, and to set the context in which other contributors to this volume are writing, this chapter is divided into three sections. First, we discuss the changes which have occurred in the Higher Education sector as a whole in the last decade or so, paying particular attention to their impact on the autonomy of the older universities. Second, we consider the extent to which the twin questions of equal opportunities for women and women's studies remained on the agenda throughout this period. Third, we turn to a direct examination of the fate of women in the new structures and to the question of changing gender regimes.

Change in UK Universities during the 1980s

If past experience were to be anything to go by, the universities at the start of the 1980s had little to fear in the way of an attack on their autonomy and their traditional modes of conduct. While they were heavily dependent on government funds through the conduit of the Universities Grants Committee (UGC), the working arrangements of that body respected their freedom to take their own decisions. A single, block grant provided almost two-thirds of the total income of the universities. While the universities had regularly complained about receiving less than they requested, the UGC had no tradition of close examination of performance. Allocations were based on the assumption that the universities clearly needed support beyond the cost of teaching as such. There was a substantial component of the block grant designed to support research, for example (the dual support system), and further monies to help with the additional costs incurred from overseas students — elements which were certainly not built in for public sector Higher Education. And the universities were given full discretion to decide how best to allocate their funds and to motivate and develop their staff. As with funding, so it was with standards. The universities believed in end-point peer review; an external examiner would peruse the scripts of final year students, coming to a judgement that the quality was acceptable and broadly comparable across institutions. Not for them the paraphernalia of paperwork associated with course review, the detailed scrutiny of content of courses, up-to-dateness of reading lists, appropriateness of staff cvs.

Once through the entry gate, the assumption was that a university academic was competent to carry out the work; words like performance appraisal, assessment and review were not part of university vocabulary. A new lecturer might be advised to undergo a course of training in how to teach, but by and large it was research that counted. If you did not appear to teach well or to do research, more often than not, little would be said.

Universities, as these arrangements make clear, were considered to be independent, self-governing bodies, who rightly enjoyed a large degree of institutional autonomy. The gulf between the universities and the polytechnics, particularly from the élitist vantage point of the former, looked very wide indeed. University autonomy was not only longstanding, and sustained by the current funding arrangements, it was guaranteed by being written into Charters and Statutes. And from this point of view change looked a thoroughly daunting prospect.

A New Kind of Funding

It was the depth and severity of the cut in the UGC block grant that was initially so remarkable. On top of the removal of subsidy for overseas students (calculated at six per cent of their total grant income), the 1981 Public Expenditure White Paper announced a reduction of 20 per cent on Higher Education expenditure to take effect over the next three years (Williams, 1992). While up to £80 million was made available to finance a programme of enhanced early retirement in order to facilitate a contraction in the numbers of staff employed, cuts of this order were going to cause severe hardship. The consequences for individual institutions varied considerably, ranging from six to a massive 30 per cent. By 1984, furthermore, the Government was making it clear that these cuts were not to be a one-off measure; the only means by which the universities could expect level funding in the future was to increase efficiency, and the only way in which they would increase their funds was by finding new sources of income and becoming altogether less reliant on government sources. All this has had an obvious effect in increasing the pressure of work for academic staff. The past decade has seen an increase of 64 per cent in overall student numbers and a rise of only 11 per cent in staff (AUT, 1994). Further reductions in the unit of resource, running at two per cent per annum, have occurred each year since 1989/90.

The UGC's criteria for allocating the funding cuts were fairly crude. From 1984 onwards, it became more selective, separating out the components of the grant for teaching and for research and further subdividing the research component so that a systematic evaluation of research performance in each subject area could be made, with funding seen to follow successful performance. Evaluations of research performance were carried out in 1984/5 and again in 1988/9.[2] In 1992, the first Research Assessment Exercise (RAE) was completed. This will be repeated in 1996, concentrating a large resource on monitoring the output of 'research active' staff across more than 70 subject areas and tying funding very directly to performance. Change in support for teaching came a little later. Following the failure of the first effort of the then Universities Funding Council (UFC) to set guide prices in 1990, the new funding councils were instructed by Government to establish a Teaching Quality Assessment, the results of which are directly to influence allocations. In addition, the Higher Education Quality Council (HEQC) was set up in 1991 to regulate quality assurance and quality control in universities. Funding formulae for teaching and for research have changed repeatedly over the decade, but they have provided an increasingly tightly controlled system of rewards and penalties which ensures that Government policy and priorities in respect of expansion and contraction in both these areas are upheld.

The economic depression of the late 1980s resulted in a further squeeze on finances and resources. There was increased Government pressure to persuade the universities to seek a greater proportion of their income directly from the marketplace and thereby to tie in the academic programme more closely with the wealth-creation needs of society and the economy. The Higher Education sector institutions themselves have seen the benefits of this, and their success in taking this route has varied. In overall terms, however, the shift is very clear. An early 1990s' estimate was that, by mid-decade, direct public funding for teaching would have reduced to around 25 per cent of the total and for research to 11 per cent (Williams, 1992).

New Forms of Decision Making

Government pressure for change in the values and structures of the universities can be seen not only indirectly through formula funding, but also more directly, through a series of reorganizations of the funding bodies and particularly through the encouragement of organizational change at the heart of the delivery of higher education itself. For the universities, this was embodied and expressed most fully in what has come to be known as the Jarratt Report (CVCP, 1985). This report concentrated on how universities could best meet the Government's desire for increased efficiency in an era when expenditure on higher education was not going to rise and when the aim was to increase significantly the participation rate of 18-year-olds. The report focused on planning, resource allocation and accountability in the context of market-led demand.

Jarratt recommended that University Councils should become more involved in the strategic planning process and that mission statements should be developed. Universities should proceed to a system of devolved budgeting, whereby appropriate cost centres would be responsible for their achievements set against their budgets. Performance indicators should be developed alongside full cost charging for services provided. The new efficiency should extend to academic staff time. Jarrett proposed fewer committees involving fewer people with greater delegation of executive responsibility to senior staff. Corporate identity was to replace departmental sectionalism; universities had to ensure that their objectives met the requirements of industry and commerce as well as students in order successfully to compete for sponsorship and contracts.

Many staff believed that these proposals heralded the end of what they had seen as democratic and collegiate decision making. Differences would emerge between different types of academic managers and staff, researchers and teachers, income generators and non-income generators. But the Jarratt proposals were received with enthusiasm by a senior management coming to grips with the new funding demands, realising the need for streamlined decision making and an altogether quicker response. In their eyes, 'efficiency' was becoming not a suspect business term, but a necessity for their survival in the new climate.

Appendix 1, by way of summary, sets out a chronology of key events which have preoccupied universities in the UK during the 1980s, placing them in the wider context of the restructuring of Higher Education as a whole. Here, as elsewhere, Government kept the idea of restructuring on the table in a number of ways. While funding change was in progress, a legislative programme was in train. There was a rash of discussion documents; here the 'big issues' about 'academic freedom' and 'tenure' turned out to have less lasting impact than the intertwining of the debates about the universities and the polytechnics, together with the reorganizations of funding bodies in both sectors that ultimately resulted in the ending of the binary division between the independent universities and public sector higher education. At times, it seemed that the Government would lose on the 'big' issues. Instead, public opinion turned against a privileged group who seemed to demand and expect jobs for life.

It is profoundly misleading to see the 1980s only as a period of cuts in resources. The cuts, together with an increase in throughput, certainly intensified work levels and put staff under considerable stress, but the new pattern of resource allocation, alongside the unprecedented scrutiny of internal affairs, transformed both the structures and the value climate of the universities. What has this meant and what will it be likely to mean for women academics? To answer this, we first need to consider the ways in which women and a concern for women have figured throughout the period of restructuring of the universities. We also need to address the suggestion that what is at stake here is a shift from 'collegiality' in the way in which the universities allocate resources internally, to a greater attention to agreed criteria and formulae, as well as to increased efficiency in line with a market philosophy (Mace, 1993). There is an important truth in this. But it also has a tendency to mask the very gender relations that we wish to consider.

Women — Still in the Frame

It is tempting to regard universities as hospitable places for women — places where academic excellence and the merit of an argument are the overriding values, places where there is a detached and impartial consideration of issues, and where argument is least likely to be *ad hominem* or *ad feminam* (Davies, 1989, 1993; see also Walsh, chapter 6). Yet there has long been evidence to suggest that this is not so. Twenty years ago, when the idea of sex discrimination legislation was still under discussion, the universities were singled out for criticism for their low proportions of female staff and students (Home Office, 1974 paras 11 and 13). By the mid-1980s, a decade after the legislation was put in place, it was clear that the Higher Education sector had been slow to act. A questionnaire, devised under the auspices of the Commission for Racial Equality and addressed to both the universities and the polytechnics in the UK, revealed that while a small number of the polytechnics had begun to formulate policy goals and to experiment with forms of implementation, the universities were notable for their lack of understanding and the high moral tone and sheer complacency of some of their replies (Williams *et al.*, 1989: 14). A further enquiry, focused on public sector Higher Education, was able to cite some good practice, but also noted the frustration of staff and students at the lack of arrangements and resources for implementation (NAB, 1988).

A steady stream of work, from around the time of the legislative debate to the present day, has continued to document the absence of women in senior grades in the sector (see, e.g., Blackstone and Fulton, 1975; Acker and Warren Piper, 1984; Davies, 1989). Recent comparative figures show that overall, women still hold less than a quarter of academic posts, with the new universities doing somewhat better both in the aggregate and in terms of women in senior grades (Heward and Taylor, 1992). The failure of the universities to understand equal opportunity issues is also reflected in studies of women academics themselves, who report how much effort they need to make to be treated as colleagues (McAuley, 1987) and how difficult it is to come to terms with the 'equality mystique' in an institution apparently so open to them (Davies, 1993). Further evidence of inequalities is apparent in the experience of those involved in local grassroots action, both through the trade unions and by means of enquiries into gender segregation in particular institutions, devising and recommending local action plans.[3]

Since the beginning of the 1990s, the lobby for equal opportunities in universities has gained strength; critical comment has become more focused and more vocal, and has begun to enter the mainstream. The publicity surrounding publication of the report of the Hansard Society Commission (1990), with its biting criticism of the failure of areas such as business and the law, as well as the universities, to provide room at the top for women, was a significant galvanizing factor. On the question of the culture of the universities, it commented on the irony that 'institutions dedicated to the unravelling of truth are themselves still wrapped in the myths of the past' (Hansard Society Commission, 1990: 68).

It was in the wake of this report, and following pressure from other organizations, that the Committee of Vice-Chancellors and Principals (CVCP) published recommendations on equal opportunities in the university sector, in the hope that all universities would now implement equal opportunity policies and begin to address the very real problems of female academic staff (CVCP, 1991). The controversial and still contested nature of the terrain was indicated by the withdrawal of the initial code of practice and its replacement by guidance (see Heward and Taylor, 1992). Many universities, however, did welcome this CVCP initiative and have been influenced by the guidance that was set out. The theme was taken up by the Commission on University Career Opportunity (CUCO).[4] Enquiries of this body suggest that over 90 per cent of universities have formally adopted an equal opportunities policy; a little over half have examined their criteria on appointments, promotions and regrading, and only 37 per cent have devised implementation plans and are implementing them (CUCO, 1994). CUCO has now established a number of task groups which will examine particular issues, including appointments and promotions procedures with a view to developing good practice guidelines specifically tailored to the universities.

Equal opportunities, as all this makes clear, has developed in a sporadic way and still meets strong resistance. It has also been seen very much as an employment issue, and not as an issue which relates to the delivery of educational courses and research.[5] In these terms, however, there are a number of factors keeping it on the agenda. Among these are university involvement in the Opportunity 2000 campaign,[6] continued trade union pressure, and the real possibility of expensive and embarrassing Tribunal cases taken by women academics themselves.[7] The creation in some instances of equality units, equal opportunity officers and equal opportunity committees within the structure of the university indicate that, even if senior managers in the universities of the 1990s are not enthusiastic about action to improve the position of women, they will be likely to remain alert to it and to the possibility of negative outcomes for women from the managerial changes that have been put in train.

A further factor to consider is the growth of women's studies as a newly established disciplinary area within the universities and of feminist scholars and scholarship more broadly. The UK is said to be the country in Europe where women's studies first made an appearance, with as many as 30 universities teaching courses of some kind by 1980 (CEC, 1984). By the end of the decade, a survey was able to describe a number of well-established postgraduate programmes, to argue that women's studies in one form or another was established in most institutions, and to give details of ten centres for women's studies that had been given some formal status (Zmroczek and Duchen, 1991). The continuing development of courses is witnessed in the growing size of the listings produced by the Women's Studies Network (WSNUK, nd); the establishment of wider European networks and interchange is also now clearly visible (Brown *et al.*, 1993). The growth of feminist scholarship within disciplinary areas in the humanities and the social sciences is also of importance. The growth of new journals and the key attention given by publishing houses to work on gender attest to the success of women in this field. Growing numbers of individual feminist scholars are gaining positions in the gatekeeping institutions concerned with publishing and with funding for research and teaching, and some are now beginning to receive the recognition of professorships and are succeeding to higher level managerial positions in the newly unified system of Higher Education.

It does not do to present too optimistic a picture. Women's studies represents a 'radical oppositional culture' in the academy, and the difficulties it faces in gaining recruits, acceptance and resourcing within the universities are substantial (Aaron and Walby, 1991). The equal opportunities campaign similarly runs into resistance and the assessments of what Cynthia Cockburn, in a more optimistic account, calls 'transformative change' (1991: 227ff) are often strongly pessimistic (see Webb, 1988; Webb and Liff, 1988; Heward and Taylor, 1992; see also Walsh, chapter 6). While accepting the force of these criticisms, it is also important to emphasize the greater visibility for women in academia that has arisen from such developments, the excitement and energy that can come from new and more critical scholarship, and the opportunities for networking and for confidence building that can arise. Women are not, and have not been, in the foreground and the forefront of the key debates about restructuring in the universities, but they are in the frame in a way that was unthinkable even a decade ago. The old gender regime has not been totally transformed by these developments, but the parameters within which it can be recreated in the new managerial universities are now different and perhaps narrower. It is the nature of that difference, its potential for both sustaining old gender inequalities and creating new ones, that needs attention. We will discuss in turn the position regarding research, teaching and administration.

A Changing Gender Regime

Following the Research Assessment Exercise (RAE) of 1992, it has become commonplace for universities to divide their staffs into those who are 'research active' and those who are 'research inactive'. Research active staff are valued because their efforts can be openly and directly linked to income. The additional funding that a university secures for highly-rated research performance within the various units of assessment is used to plough back money to the group in order to enhance their research further or as seed money for new areas. Insofar as the former is the more likely overall strategy, the gulf between these two groups will grow. The response of a number of universities to the 1992 RAE has gone in just this direction. It has been to concentrate on those who have already demonstrated that they are research highfliers, to persuade 'inactives' to take early retirement, and to recruit new and young staff with a proven research record.

This is likely to have a particularly detrimental effect on those women academics who are mothers. With intensified pressure for research output, the continuing unequal division of labour in the home, which leaves women with primary responsibility for childcare and domestic arrangements, will be strongly felt. The limited response of the universities in providing childcare, the lack of recognition in the performance indicators specified by the RAE, for example, of maternity leave and the effect this will have, is further testimony to an adverse impact for many women which to date is being ignored.[8] The much vaunted 'flexibility' that academic work was said to offer women with children — for example, to do research in the long vacation (read school holidays) — often proved, in the past, to be a myth. The new arrangements, the intensification of teaching through use of semesters and modularization, can exacerbate matters, leaving weekends and evenings as the only realistic time when personal research can be carried out. The adverse impact here affects not only mothers, but also all those women who are without partners who are free and willing to carry out domestic responsibilities. There is a distinct danger too, that women, regardless of their personal circumstances, will find themselves locked more tightly into the teaching/pastoral care role that was often a feature of the sexual division of labour in the old regime. Thus, there are several reasons why it may be harder for women in the new regime both to make the jump into the 'research active' category and to sustain a position within it.

The problems of contract research staff — disproportionately women — have long been known. They include difficulties of building a career across a series of short-term contracts; the lack of time allocated within the contract to develop the academic publications that are needed for this; their treatment in the university policy process as second-class citizens. The effects of focusing on the RAE will vary across disciplinary areas, but in the main it will be likely to encourage greater dependence on contract income and hence will promote a rise in contract staff. Furthermore, incentive monies for research are already in some cases encouraging staff to bid for very small sums to employ researchers for a matter of weeks or hours to get the work done. Again, women are likely to be the ones available for this casualized form of academic labour (cf Aziz, 1991).

The drive for research activity is affecting posts in teaching. There have always been those who are called upon, often at short notice at the beginning of an academic year, to fill gaps in teaching. Postgraduate students of both sexes have found this a valuable way to build experience and sometimes supplement their incomes. Less noted, and rarely documented in any way, is the penumbra of locally based graduates whose labour is used in this way. The wives of male academics can often fit into this category; so too can women tied to the locality by the jobs of their male partners. We might also suggest that as access courses and part-time degrees are offered, and as women take up these second chance opportunities, there will be a bigger pool of women who go on to become such secondary academic workers. Following the RAE, there has also been a new development, the 'teaching associate' or 'teaching assistant', usually fixed term, low paid, and very often female. The low pay and poor conditions of this appointment, the lack of a clear route onto the permanent staff, all indicate this as a more formalized and recognized new underclass of academic labourer, not restricted to women, but again, likely to be taken up disproportionately by women. The terms and conditions of the post serve to devalue the teaching process, the area where women have so often concentrated their activity.

What of the position of women in relation to the more centralized structures of decision making? We have already seen that the new corporate management group is differently composed. Recruiting directors of services for planning, personnel, estates, catering and so on, is unlikely to change the gender balance significantly, but it does represent the influx of new values, guided more by business administration and by overt, visible and often finance-driven performance indicators. This could cut two ways. Insofar as these new men form an integrated team with a tightly forged business-oriented corporate identity, a new gulf is likely to open up between academics (men as well as women) and managers. Insofar as there is a blending of academic and business values in a system that is more formalized and transparent, however, those previously excluded by the informality and the club atmosphere of the old regime may find that they have access to more understanding of the demands on the university and the way in which they can respond to these.

The altogether steeper organizational pyramid is relevant here. Where a multitude of small departments are amalgamated into larger units to which financial responsibility can be devolved, there is a reduction in the number of positions of responsibility to which women can aspire. Yet at the same time it has become obvious that much delegated and coordinative responsibility is needed. This can represent an added burden of work and remain unacknowledged and unrewarded. On the other hand, where it falls to women, it can act as a further aid to transparency. The emphasis on individual performance and the exposure of staff to comparison can also challenge aspects of the gender regime. Developing junior staff in their own right may be more helpful to the RAE record than allowing the 'grand old man' of the department to continue to exploit their work without giving them due credit. Questioning the dramatic differences in hours of teaching among a staff group may also redound to the distinct benefit of women.

To date, there is little real evidence to document the transformations that have occurred. In some places, it is clear that reorganization has brought a higher ratio of women in senior positions; in others, as the number of such positions has diminished, the reverse has been true.[9] In a recent diary-keeping exercise, it was shown that academics already work an average of 53.5 hours per week, that administrative duties take up as much as 17–18 hours of this, and that the bulk of personal research, nearly 40 per cent, was being squeezed into evenings and weekends. It was also clear that women carried a greater administrative load than men. Furthermore, women at every level actually worked longer hours than men. The average working week of a woman professor was 64.5 hours compared with an average for male professors of 58.6 hours (AUT, 1994). When we add to this information from the salary studies of the AUT, there seems little doubt that women continue to be disadvantaged; if not actively discriminated against, then systematically disadvantaged within the sector. The growing number of Tribunal cases taken by women academics suggests a similar story (see note 7).

Concluding Remarks

There is no doubt that there is a great deal in the new managerial universities that should be of concern to those who seek to combat gender inequalities, and to ensure that Higher Education is not only open and accessible but is also contributing in all aspects to a questioning of the *status quo*, including the gender *status quo*. We have discussed ways in which rigid definitions of active and inactive researchers redounds to the disadvantage of women. We have drawn attention to an array of emergent forms of secondary academic labour which call upon the skills of women in a particularly exploitative way. We have also identified dangers in the more centralized hierarchies to do with the disproportionate allocation of a growing volume of teaching and of time-consuming administrative work to women in the context of a continuing devaluation of both of these activities in favour of an emphasis on research.

Yet we have also suggested that the new gender regime denoted by these arrangements is double-edged; its greater formality and the requirement to identify goals and monitor progress add a new and important element of transparency to university functioning. This, coupled with the drawing of women into the administrative process, offers a new opportunity for understanding and perhaps contesting the directions of development and change. Continuing campaigns around equal opportunity issues, the growth of women's studies and of feminist scholarship are important factors here. This is not solely a matter of the improvements in the 'gender count' in strategic places (though this is undoubtedly important), but a matter of raising consciousness about the nature and depth of disadvantage that women face, and countering, on an ever wider basis, the persistent myth that universities are kind to women and offer flexible freedoms unavailable elsewhere.

Universities at present are not comfortable places for academics of either sex. The pace of change and the accompanying intensification of work have made sure of that. But we would do well not to ally ourselves completely with those who set their faces totally against the new regime and hark back to a golden age of freedom and collegiality. To do this would be to ignore the disadvantages for women that that gender regime entailed. There is a potential, and we put it at no more than that, for a new and more inclusive debate to be had in the contemporary vocabulary of goals, missions, strategies and performance. To the extent that there are growing numbers of women in strategic places in Higher Education, to the extent that students are giving positive feedback for the work that women do, and to the extent that new feminist scholarship is enlivening and rejuvenating us, so we may find the energies to seize the opportunities presented by the new gender regime and to struggle against the ever present danger of deeper entrenchment of sex inequality in Higher Education.

Acknowledgements

The authors are grateful to officers of the Association of University Teachers (AUT) for their assistance in providing relevant information. The views presented here are those of the authors themselves, writing in a personal capacity.

Notes

1　The term 'gender regimes' derives from the work of sociologist R.W. Connell. He defines a gender regime as the 'state of play of gender relations in a given institution'. It involves a distinct sexual division of labour, 'an ideology, often more than one, about sexual behaviour and sexual character' and a set of practices that constructs notions of masculinity and femininity. Taking the specific example of the school, he points out that there are often conflicts going on over sexism in the curriculum or over promotion and prestige among the staff. He argues that gender relations are present in all types of institutions, and in most cases are a major feature of institutional structure (Connell, 1987: 120). The emphasis in this paper is mostly, though not completely, on the sexual division of labour.

2　This was the point at which a specific component of the UGC grant was set aside for research, using the four-part formula: SR (staff research), DR (direct research), CR (contract research) and JR (judgemental research) (see Williams, 1992: 9).

3　For examples of local enquiries and reports on the position of women as academics at individual institutions, see for example Bowey and Bamford (nd), Cambridge University Women's Action Group (1988), University of Ulster (1990). The journal *AUT Woman* is also a useful source documenting that union's action and initiatives in the university sector.

4　CUCO emerged as a CVCP initiative arising out of pressure brought about by the evidence of sex discrimination in the sector and the launch of Opportunity 2000 (see note 6 below). It has representatives from universities, the business sector and trade unions. It is currently chaired by Dr Ann Wright, Vice-Chancellor of Sunderland University.

5　It is worth noting that some of the polytechnics, in taking up the equal opportunity issue, saw it as a matter not only of employment but of the goals and mission of the institution itself. This broader thinking was reflected in the work of the National Advisory Board (NAB, 1988). It does not seem to have permeated into the latest phases of equal opportunity activity in the newly unified sector.

6　Opportunity 2000 is a campaign to give greater profile to the issue of equality of opportunity for women in employment and to encourage employers in all sectors to express their commitment by joining the campaign. Questions of women's advancement within organizational hierarchies and their proportions in senior management are given particular prominence. Launched in the autumn of 1991 by the Prime Minister, Opportunity 2000 has held a number of high-profile conferences and events. Its Third Annual Report in November 1994 showed a total of 275 members. Figures earlier that year suggested a total of 21 universities had joined.

7　Recent tribunal cases include *Hubbert* v *Cambridge University* (1986), *Smyth* v *University of Ulster* (1994), *Marrington* v *Sunderland University* (1994).

8　The length of the assessment period was increased for the 1996 RAE. Though the decision was not taken with the issue of maternity leave in mind, it should at least ease the situation somewhat.

9 The Universities of Manchester and Leeds are two examples where managerial change has resulted in an increasing number of women in senior positions. In Bristol, the increase in the number of female professors seems directly to have led to an increase in the number of women heads of department. Restructuring in the University of Ulster, however, has had a much less favourable effect and has actually reduced the proportions of senior women.

References

AARON, J. and WALBY, S. (Eds) (1991) *Out of the Margins*, London: Falmer Press.

ACKER, S. and WARREN PIPER, D. (Eds) (1984) *Is Higher Education Fair to Women?*, Guildford: SRHE and NFER-Nelson.

ASSOCIATION OF UNIVERSITY TEACHERS (AUT) (1994) *'Long Hours, Little Thanks': A survey of the use of time by full-time academics and related staff in the traditional UK universities*, London: AUT.

AZIZ, A. (1991) 'Women in UK Universities: the road to casualisation', in STIVER LIE, S. and O'LEARY, V.E. (Eds) *Storming the Tower: Women in the academic world*, London: Kogan Page.

BLACKSTONE, T. and FULTON, O. (1975) 'Sex Discrimination among University Teachers: a British-American Comparison', *British Journal of Sociology*, **26**, pp. 261–275.

BOWEY, A. and BAMFORD, C. (nd) *The Position of Women Employed by the University of Strathclyde*, Glasgow: University of Strathclyde.

BROWN, L., COLLINS, H., GREEN, P., HUMM, M. and LANDELLS, M. (Eds) (1993) *International Handbook of Women's Studies* (W.I.S.H), London: Harvester Wheatsheaf.

CAMBRIDGE UNIVERSITY WOMEN'S ACTION GROUP (1988) *Forty Years On . . . The CUWAG Report on the Numbers and Status of Academic Women in the University of Cambridge*, Cambridge: CUWAG.

COCKBURN, C. (1991) *In The Way of Women*, London: Macmillan.

COMMISSION OF THE EUROPEAN COMMUNITIES (CEC) (1984) *Women's Studies*, Supplement No. 18 to *Women of Europe*, Brussels: CEC.

COMMISSION ON UNIVERSITY CAREER OPPORTUNITY (CUCO) (1994) *A Report on the Universities' Policies and Practices on Equal Opportunities in Employment*, London: CUCO.

COMMITTEE OF VICE-CHANCELLORS AND PRINCIPALS (CVCP) (1985) *Report of the Steering Committee for Efficiency Studies in Universities (Chairman Sir A. Jarratt)*, London: CVCP.

COMMITTEE OF VICE-CHANCELLORS AND PRINCIPALS (1991) *Equal Opportunities in Employment in Universities*, London: CVCP.

CONNELL, R.W. (1987) *Gender and Power*, Oxford: Polity Press/Blackwell.

DAVIES, C. (1989) 'Women in Academia: A Chance for a Change?', in OLIVER, S.M. (Ed.) *The Psychology of Women at Work, International Research Conference Proceedings*, Worthing: P(SET).

DAVIES, C. (1993) 'The Equality Mystique, the Difference Dilemma and the Case of Women Academics', *UCG Women's Studies Centre Review*, **2**, pp. 53–72.

DAVIES, C. (1995) *Gender and the Professional Predicament in Nursing*, Buckingham: Open University Press.

HANSARD SOCIETY COMMISSION (1990) *Women at the Top*, London: Hansard Society.

HEWARD, C. and TAYLOR, P. (1992) 'Women at the Top in Higher Education: Equal opportunities policies in action?', *Policy and Politics*, **20**, 2, pp. 111–121.

HOME OFFICE (1974) *Equality for Women*, Cmnd. 5724, London: HMSO.

MACE, J. (1993) 'University Funding Changes and University Efficiency', *Higher Education Review*, **25**, pp. 7–22.

MCAULEY, J. (1987) 'Women Academics: A case study in inequality', in SPENCER, A. and PODMORE, D. (Eds) *In A Man's World*, London: Tavistock.

NATIONAL ADVISORY BOARD FOR PUBLIC SECTOR HIGHER EDUCATION (1988) *Action for Access*, London: NAB.

POLLITT, C. (1990) *Managerialism and the Public Services: the Anglo-American Experience*, Oxford: Blackwell.

UNIVERSITY OF ULSTER (1990) *Women as Employees in the University of Ulster: Report of a Working Party*, Coleraine: University of Ulster.

WEBB, J. (1988) 'The Ivory Tower: Positive Action for Women in Higher Education', in COYLE, A. and SKINNER, J. (Eds) *Women and Work*, London: Macmillan.

WEBB, J. and LIFF, S. (1988) 'Play the White Man', *Sociological Review*, **36**, pp. 532–551.

WILLIAMS, G. (1992) *Changing Patterns of Finance in Higher Education*, Buckingham: Open University Press/SRHE.

WILLIAMS, J., DAVIES, L. and COCKING, J. (1989) *Words or Deeds? A Review of Equal Opportunity Policies in Higher Education*, London: Commission for Racial Equality.

WOMEN'S STUDIES NETWORK (UK) (nd) *Course Listings 1991–92*, Lancaster: WSN (UK).

ZMROCZEK, C. AND DUCHEN, C. (1991) 'What *are* those Women up to? Women's Studies and Feminist Research in the European Community', in AARON, J. and WALBY, S. (Eds) *Out of the Margins*, pp. 11–29, London: Falmer Press.

Appendix 1: Key Events in the Restructuring of Higher Education

1980	Introduction of full cost fees for overseas students
1981	White Paper on public expenditure announces 20 per cent reduction in government expenditure for next three years across Higher Education
1982	Establishment of National Advisory Body for Local Authority Higher Education (NAB)
1982	Secretary of State for Education announces local authority contribution to university fees to be halved from 1982/83, with corresponding increase in institutional grants awarded centrally by UGC/NAB, in order to facilitate the management of the necessary restructuring of Higher Education
1984	*Strategy for Higher Education in the late 1980s and beyond* (published by NAB)
1985	Jarratt Report: *Report of the Steering Committee for Efficiency Studies in Universities* (published by CVCP)
1985	Green Paper: *The Development of Higher Education into the 1990s*, Cmnd. 9524

1987	First evaluation of university research
1987	White Paper: *Higher Education: Meeting the challenge*, Cm. 114
1988	*Education Reform Act*
1988	As a result of the Act, UGC becomes Universities Funding Council (UFC); NAB becomes Polytechnics and Colleges Funding Council (PCFC)
1989	*Shifting the balance of public funding of higher education to fees* — a consultation document (published by Department of Education and Science)
1990	Introduction by UFC of 'guide prices' and trading (in January)
1990	'Guide prices' abandoned by UFC in November
1990/91	Local authorities receive from central government 100 per cent of fees payable to HE institutions — up from 90 per cent
1991	Second evaluation of university research
1991	White Paper: *Higher Education: A new framework*, Cm. 1541
1991	CVCP establishes Higher Education Quality Council (HEQC), in response to White Paper
1991	*The State of the Universities* (CVCP)
1991/92	Further transfer of fee income
1992	Transfer of research element in funding to the Research Councils: dual support transfer
1992	First detailed research assessment exercise (RAE)
1992	*Further and Higher Education Act*: establishes Funding Councils, ends binary line
1992	*Quality Assessment*, a consultation paper (published by HEFCE)
1993	White Paper: *Realising our Potential: A strategy for science, engineering and technology*, Cm. 2250 — includes social science; special emphasis on promoting competitiveness and wealth creation and responding to users and beneficiaries
1993	Teaching quality assessment process, organized by funding councils, begins
1993	*Review of the Academic Year: A report of the Committee of Enquiry into the organization of the academic year* (Chairman: Lord Flowers, published by HEFCE)
1994	*Assessment of the quality of higher education*: a review and evaluation report for HEFCE and HEFCW (report on 1993 teaching quality assessment)

Chapter 2

Black Women as 'Other' in the Academy

Naz Rassool

Introduction

The social construction of black women as gendered, 'racialized ethnic' beings provides potent images around which cultural truths are built. Black women thus are generally perceived as 'powerless' and 'passive' within the culture of organizations — represented here by the academy as a context of work. Yet these institutional 'beliefs' contrast sharply with the reality of most black women's lives. Entering the academy as a professional is a landmark achievement for most black women intellectuals. It is so because by that time they would have triumphed against different kinds of oppressions and would have made numerous sacrifices in their quest to live their lives as women — according to their own definitions personally, socially and professionally.

This chapter provides a case-study account of the conscious (and unconscious) ways in which black women engage in struggle and resistance against domination and marginalization within the processes of the academy. Central to this analysis is Giddens's (1991: 244) concept of the 'reflexive project of the self', which refers to the process by which self-identity is 'constituted by the reflexive re-ordering of self-narratives'. Self-identity, according to Giddens, is not 'given'; it 'has to be routinely created and sustained in the reflexive activities of the individual' (1991: 52). Moreover, '(t)o be a person is not just to be a reflexive actor, but to have a concept of a person (as applied both to the self and others)' (1991: 53). In thus foregrounding the 'self' discursively in relation to the social world, the chapter explores the participants' subjective understandings of how their social roles have been determined, culturally and historically within society and their communities, and also how they themselves are constituted as knowledge producers within the academy. At the same time it also highlights their strengths in being involved actively in re-defining that experience in a reflexive and proactive way. Thus, it is argued that the positioning of women as change agents and centring on their creative reflexivity goes far beyond the issue of finding a 'voice'. Indeed, it is suggested here that in articulating their everyday experiences within the academy these women are illustrating their ability to reflect upon and re-order their 'self-narratives'

(Giddens, 1991). This particular concept of 'self', as suggested by Probyn (1993: 2):

> represents the process of being gendered and the project of putting that process into discourse. (. . .) the self is an ensemble of techniques and practices enacted on an everyday basis and (. . .) it entails the necessary problematization of these practices. The self is not simply put forward, but rather it is reworked in its enunciation.

Thus black women are engaged in everyday praxis. It is argued further that because this self-defining construction of the 'self' is often challenged, undermined and refracted within and through the processes of institutional power, it is never complete and is, therefore, always in the process of becoming.

Theorizing Black as 'the Other'

As the 'black experience' is embedded in different socio-cultural milieux, particular meanings have been attached to it historically in different societies. Because the concept is used here in a very specific way, it needs further clarification. The choice of 'blackness' as a category denoting 'ethnic otherness' relates, first, to the cultural relations that have shaped the consciousness and social experience of one of the interviewees who spent her formative years in apartheid South Africa. Within that social context, the notion of cultural pluralism provided a political metaphor for the racist practice of *eiesoortigheid* (ethnic purity) which formed the cultural basis of apartheid hegemony. The period of the Black Consciousness Movement during the 1970s saw the adoption of the term 'black' as a means of delineating the ethnic identity of *all* the 'non-whites' within that society. Blackness thus became a powerful means of subverting the state's attempt to fractionalize the diverse ethnic groups within the country. Moreover, it became a positive way of re-defining 'ethnic otherness' (as opposed to the pejorative term 'non-whites') and, as such, formed a significant part of a united counter-hegemonic struggle amongst oppressed groups to refract the imposed linguistic categories that were aimed at describing various hierarchical 'ethnicities'.

In the USA, on the other hand, the term 'black' denotes a specific cultural group whose history has been shaped by enforced geographical and cultural displacement, slavery, racial discrimination, poverty and unemployment. As such, blackness features as a strong and very distinct identity variable within that society. However, the social experience of racial oppression is not a clearly defined black/white issue in the USA. Other than the Afro-American experience, racial discrimination in the USA touches the lives of a diverse range of people, including the indigenous Indian population as well as immigrants from different parts of the world. The cultural 'melting pot', as is represented in American society, therefore also comprises numerous other disempowered ethnic groups amongst which 'Asian Americans' (immigrants from South-East Asia) are still engaged in a struggle for inclusion in mainstream multicultural discourse. The stereotype image of 'Asian American' women as 'submissive, subservient, ready-to-please and easy-to-get-along with' (Yamada, 1983: 37) perhaps still remains the most captivating and enduring image of 'Oriental' femininity.

In the UK, the 'black' experience involves the everyday lives of immigrants and political refugees from different parts of the world. The most significant presence in terms of mass immigration is that of the Caribbean population groups who were encouraged to immigrate to Britain during the economic boom period of the late 1950s and early 1960s to work mainly in the service industries. The 'Asian' population group largely comprises those who were expelled from Uganda during the 1960s and those who immigrated subsequently from Kenya and the Indian sub-continent during the 1970s. The common factor amongst these diverse groups of people is the central role that the divide-and-rule policies of colonialism have played in the shaping of their economic, social and cultural experiences — and, *de facto*, their self-identities. These immigrant groups, which now include second-generation citizens, still exist largely at the periphery of British mainstream society.

The women included in the case study below represent this broad range of socio-cultural histories. Unifying these diverse histories, is the key role that colonialism, diaspora, ethnic 'otherness' and the development of a cultural hybridity in exile have played in the shaping of their subjectivities, material reality, cultural experience and consciousness. The choice of the term 'black women's experiences' to describe these different sets of histories is therefore a conscious one. It makes distinct (from white society), and at the same time unifies, their experiences as 'marginals' within both the academic institution and metropolitan societies. Blackness thus features here as a signifier of social 'otherness' rather than as a racially descriptive term; it represents a diversity of social experiences within the margins of society. The term 'black' demarcates those 'who are not white' and 'who do not belong' socially; it describes the position of those 'looking in' on the real world of power within metropolitan society — and those who are allowed to participate only 'with permission'. It also provides a useful category to transcend a relativistic focus on ethnic particularities, on the one hand, and racial absolutism on the other. Moreover, in contrast to a taken-for granted, unproblematic association between blackness and powerlessness the concept is used here from a position of what Pecheux (1982) describes as *disidentification* — that is to say, it seeks actively to work on and against the prevailing ideological and social practices in which black and gendered subjection are constructed.

Disidentification, according to Macdonell (1987: 40) operates antagonistically 'with the effect that the identity and identifications set up in dominant ideology, though never escaped entirely, are transformed and displaced'. Blackness in this instance, then, does not denote passive acceptance; rather, it provides the *basis* of struggle against racial, gender and class oppression. The analysis seeks to lay bare not only that form of power which seeks to dominate and subordinate through coercion, but also to examine the subtle machinations of racialized hegemonic power which serve to render black women (and men) voiceless and invisible — and thus distanced from the locus of power in society. Racism, in other words, forms an integral part of social process — and, locating these changing histories within a context of ongoing struggle and contestation, allows the concept of a 'racialized ethnicity' as a social and ideological construct to lose its rigidity — enabling racial meanings to be examined:

> not as an autonomous branch of ideology, but as a salient feature in a general process whereby culture mediates the world of agents and the structures which are created by their social praxis. (Gilroy, 1987: 17)

Black Women Academics: A Case-study

The research drawn on in this chapter comprised a sample study of black female academics working within universities in the UK and USA. Semi-structured interviews were conducted with a selection of four black women academics at different stages of their careers and within a range of disciplines, which include Science, Humanities and the Arts. In order to obtain a wider perspective, the interview data were supplemented with a questionnaire similar to the interview questions, which was sent to ten additional black women academics working in the Arts, Humanities and Sciences. The basis of the enquiry was, first, to establish the perceptions that these women had of themselves as knowledge producers within the academy and how they perceived their positions both as professionals and as black women. Second, I sought to establish the nature of the barriers encountered as women within their own ethnic-cultural communities as well as their daily working lives, and the potential implications of these on their future career prospects. Third, I wanted to identify similarities and differences in their experiences and, fourth, to explore the range of strategies that they have adopted in order to overcome these barriers. Collectively, these aims would provide participants with the opportunity to engage in an exploration of their 'self-narratives' and through this to offer an insight into the process of re-definition and re-construction of their self-identities in relation to their everyday experiences within the academy.

Underlying these questions are deeper issues related to, for example, socialization processes and how the academy perceives the value of black women professionals in practice. They also relate to the discourses of 'otherness' constructed within the daily routines and ethos of the academy which serve to exclude and marginalize ethnic minority group experience. Moreover, they refer to the ways in which societal racism and sexism have impacted on academic structures and whether the actions of individuals can challenge racist and sexist structures within both the institution and in wider society. Theoretically, the chapter draws on Giddens's perspective 'that structures are produced by interactions which are constantly in the process of reproducing the overall characteristics of society; but that such reproductions are not exact' (Ackroyd, 1994: 291); that they are subject to change through human action. The ways in which these women draw on their own biographies, insights and personal abilities to articulate and redefine their own social experience as 'black' professional women is a recurring theme in this study.

Structuring Subjectivities

Providing an account of black women's experiences within the academy cannot take place outside an analysis of the ideologies and cultural practices that underpin class and racial oppression within society — and the historical relations in which social inequalities are reproduced. This relates, in a significant way, to the fact that (1) racism is materially grounded and transcends gender and class barriers, and (2) the gendered and racialized subjectivities documented here have, to a large extent, evolved within relations of dominance and subordinance structured within the context of colonialism, neo-colonialism and the 'black' diasporic experience. These variables counterpose with structured gendered subjectivities that are grounded in patriarchal inequalities and ultimately hegemonized in religious-cultural and ethnic social relations. The view of subjectivity presented below describes the values and meanings grounded in historically derived social and cultural practices which have shaped and influenced black women's perceptions of themselves in relation to others, the academy and the world in which they live.

All the women in the interview sample cited the need, in the first instance, to break the barriers erected within their ethnic-cultural and religious communities which have served historically to repress, in a very systematic way, female aspirations in terms of having and maintaining independence of thought and action. An 'Asian American' philosopher who was interviewed described her formative experience in this way:

> I grew up in a culture where women are not highly valued and basically you use your college education as a means to marry well. It's not your education that is valuable but the fact that it helps you to become a future wife . . . But I fought that . . . I fought the notion that Chinese women are submissive and obedient.

Yet, as we know, this phenomenon is by no means particular to Chinese society and culture; it has been an intrinsic feature of male hegemony in different parts of the world historically. The importance of education for minority groups generally is also more complex. The Chinese experience in the USA, as is the case for immigrant groups in the UK and oppressed groups generally, reveals high expectations for their children in terms of education. In the words of the same respondent:

> In my family, which is middle class, when you grow up you're always
> under pressure . . . it's like you never doubt that you're going to go to
> college or university . . . the whole course of your education has been
> laid out . . . you just go!

The primary view of education then is utilitarian-academic, that is, a belief that
participation in the meritocracy provides individuals with the opportunity to
escape from poverty and social marginalization. Yet, education is a double-
edged sword. Whilst, on the one hand, it is valued very highly within the
community as a primary means of improving life chances, on the other, it
serves a pre-defined sexual purpose for girls. Thus, rather than being a neutral
self-defining and personally empowering process, education for girls within this
context assumes the position of a cultural commodity with a high exchange
value. In terms of this, it objectifies knowledge and learning as an integral part
of a wider genderized political economy in which educational achievement is
exchanged for a 'profitable' marriage contract. Clearly then, individual consciousness is shaped, very powerfully, at the level of the family and cultural
community. The fact that gender expectations, subliminally present within
society, play an important role in shaping girls' attitudes towards different
school subjects has been reported in the Hoyles (1988) study into girls and
computers in the UK. The genderization of school subjects, it is argued,
influences their choice in career routes later — a factor which is echoed in
a comment by a woman scientist interviewed:

> We learned at a very early age that as women we were not as capable
> as males to become scientists; to engage in rational thought . . . you
> assimilated these meanings prevalent in the culture . . . the way teach-
> ers reacted to you . . . did not make it easy for you to take to these
> (scientific) concepts . . . and this erected barriers . . . I felt it to be a
> challenge for me too as a woman, as a black woman to overcome those
> barriers . . . to go into the sciences and to do just as well and even
> better.

So, despite the pervasive influence of these cultural meanings, what is
significant in both examples cited above is the fact that these forms of
socialization are resisted and re-defined within the framework of the individual's own goals and aspirations. Giddens (1984) terms this the actors' use
of 'knowlegeability' which enables them to draw consciously and discursively
on their understanding of the social world in order to challenge the hegemonic
powers of control that inhere within wider society and, in the process, to redefine the parameters of their world. Similarly, Cockburn (1985: 167) stresses the
importance of ever-present resistance:

> The ideology of groups that have power tends to be hegemonic — a
> vehicle of power. But always there are sets of practices and ideas that

run counter to these and resist them, setting up alternative ways of understanding things, of 'making sense'.

Black women's experiences also provide a basis for the possibility of exploring more universal forms of domination; indeed they concentrate and reveal the multi-levelled, matrix-like interaction of domination within wider society (Hill Collins, 1991). Black oppression is not a segmented experience. According to hooks (1989) the 'politic of domination' operates along inter-locking axes of 'race', class and gender oppression which touch the lives of everyone in the community. Thus the need to resist the hegemonic structuring of subordinated subjectivities extends beyond the immediate family and ethnic minority cultures, to incorporate also intercultural-group struggles against oppressive practices rooted in class exploitation within the wider dominant culture. Again, this forms part of a broader struggle taking place in, for example, metropolitan societies like Britain and the USA, as well as the erstwhile neo-colonialist South Africa, where institutionalized barriers had existed historically to exclude black males and females from full participation as workers, professionals, students — and, until very recently, as citizens. The black South African scientist interviewed — educated in the UK and now residing in the USA — underlined the importance that this experience has had on the shaping of her consciousness:

> growing up in South Africa meant that structures of 'race' were very important, every aspect of life was structured and defined in racial terms, you were socialized into the stereotype of your 'racial' group ... and my aim is to completely break down those barriers.

In reality this meant that as a 'black' woman she was educated in an under-resourced 'black' school and would not have been able to study at a 'white' university (the only place where her discipline was catered for) without special permission from the apartheid State. She contrasts this with her experience as a black political exile in the UK where she completed her studies:

> in Britain they 'othered' me in a colonial stereotypic way ... because of our phenotype we were immediately stereotyped as 'Asians' ... as 'Pakis' ... and as a woman, passive and non-threatening ... and that made me very aggressive because you were seen just as this reduced stereotype and nothing else ... and you spent most of your time breaking down those barriers before you could be recognized for who you really were as an individual. Over here in the States I am 'othered' in a very different way ... I am seen as this exotic 'Indian' woman because I have Eastern features.

This provides an interesting example of how 'racialized ethnic' meanings vary within different social contexts. Whereas this respondent had previously been self-defined as a 'black' in neo-colonialist South Africa, then defined as an

'Asian' in post-colonial UK, in the USA this has changed to her being socially classified as an 'Indian'. The latter group occupies a fairly favoured position within the 'ethnic hierarchy' in the USA as against 'Asian Americans' — that is, Koreans, Chinese, Japanese and Vietnamese, who occupy a lower social status than other immigrant groups. Clearly then, racial stereotypes change depending on the socio-historical and geographical contexts in which people are situated which, in turn, will influence their social experience in terms of the relative value and meanings attached to particular social groups within that society at that particular time. Two decades ago, before the influences of the Civil Rights Movement, black women in the USA would have been referred to formally as 'Negroes' in quite an unproblematic way.

This respondent's experiences also give an indication of the complex life-histories and the multi-levelled interaction of hegemonic discourses through which gendered and racialized subjectivities are structured within both metro-politan and neo-colonialist societies. At meta-level, it provides an insight into the 'black' diasporic experience: as people, for various reasons, migrate across the world they encounter overt and covert pressures to adapt to the language and cultural mores of their adoptive countries as soon as possible in order to minimize discrimination against their foreign 'otherness'. It is within this con-text that the conscious and subconscious development of a cultural hybridity obtains meaning as a strategic element of survival; it does not, as is often believed, necessarily constitute an unproblematic incorporation into the domi-nant culture. I will discuss below how some of the expectations of the dominant culture are structured into the discourses within the academy and the ways in which these influence the subjectivities of black women academics working within this context.

Subjectivity and the Academic Organization

Organizations are generally presented as rationally ordered systems of control into which individuals are incorporated coercively, and that their everyday reality is structured in relations of domination and subordination. Evaluating this orthodox framework Reed (1992: 222–223) suggests that:

> The development and diffusion of formal or complex organization is seen to signify the pervasive influence of rational systems of com-mand, coordination and control that eradicate all vestiges of human emotion, prejudice and subjectivity. Within this vision, organizations are seen as the primary institutional 'carriers' of a formal rationality based on logical calculation and control within modern and moderniz-ing societies.

Within the academy, these meanings can be associated with the bureaucratic forms of organization represented in the inter-locking, hierarchical and de-personalized processes of command inherent in departmental and faculty structures. However, this 'rational' view of management neglects consideration of the fact that organizations such as the academy are constituted primarily by people engaged in a continuous process of interaction; and that the network of relationships in which they exist is grounded in unequal power relations that are often ambiguous and contradictory. Indeed, Reed argues that organizational decision making, far from being rational–strategic consists of different systems of thought and action — dominated by 'cognitive, ideological and political practices' (1992: 223–224). The negotiation of meaning takes place, invariably, within a context in which contradictory and conflicting discourses traverse different arena of decision making. Collectively, these discourses and actions serve to shape the formal and informal culture of the organization. Some of the informal discourses that prevail in academic institutions are exclusionary and derive from the social meanings attached to particular groups of people within wider society. Although not formally present, they permeate the body politic where they construct 'commonsense' understandings of, for example, 'racialized ethnicity', gender and sexuality. Thus it is that concepts of 'racial otherness' may be constructed within the organization in terms of 'commonsense' or stereotypic understandings of 'ethnic or gender specific' behaviours, temperament and disposition which would ostensibly undermine individuals' ability to make rational decisions — and which, in turn, would influence their 'credibility' in positions of authority.

This was reflected by the experience in the UK of one of the respondents who, as part-time tutor responsible for in-service teacher training, also worked in an advisory role as acting head of a support service department in a Local Education Authority (LEA). Although appointed to restructure the department and to change staff and schools' perceptions towards a more integrative approach, and despite the fact that this had been successful in terms of the LEA's criteria, she was nevertheless not appointed as a permanent head of department when this position was advertised — even though she had been doing the job for eighteen months. She expressed her views in this way:

> The only reason that I can think of is that I am black . . . that within a Conservative borough I did not have the 'right' image to occupy such a public position of authority. When challenged as to whether I did not do the job properly, my line manager responded that, in fact, I perhaps had done it too well. . . . At this stage in the de-briefing I was so exasperated and bruised that I just gave up arguing. A follow-up 'informal' de-briefing took place in which the line manager came to discuss the issue 'as a friend' — and admitted the key role that 'internal politics' had played in the appointment . . . since we were to become sub-contractors in the future they had to consider my credibility with clients. How does one fight this sort of thing? If challenged he would just deny everything he had told me . . . I chose not to fight this battle . . . I left when a better job opportunity in the university came along.

Key issues that emerge from her experience relate, first, to the foregrounding of market principles in employment selection processes which here seemingly override concerns about equality of opportunity which have been formally inscribed into LEA policy. According to Reed (1992: 117), '(t)he actual courses of action followed by organizational actors will reflect the ambiguity which this multiplicity of circulating and competing discourses or rationalities generates'. As can be seen in this example, this reality is often revealed in the disparity that exists between policies formulated within the structures of the organization and the individual or group practices that prevail within the institution. Second, there is the unspoken criticism that she might have done her job too well — signifying perhaps a degree of 'over-zealousness'. And, third, the implied 'incredibility' of her as an authority figure evaluated chiefly in terms of the racial-stereotypic perceptions of prospective clients. Here then we have an example of marginalizing discourses of racial 'otherness' hegemonized within the internal structures of the LEA — and the routinized organizational strategies used to suppress potential challenges to institutional racial discrimination. These meanings operate in concert to exclude black people from positions of power within the academic organization and community.

Other pervasive signifiers of 'racial otherness' include ethnic dress, for example, the exotic sexuality and powerful image of docility that accompanies the sari worn by some East Indian women academics in the UK. Similarly, the meanings of 'passivity', 'foreignness' and, in the UK, also 'menial work' and 'under class' attached to a Sikh professional wearing the traditional shalwar-kameez. This was demonstrated in the case of one of the UK interviewees who, arriving at school early one morning to supervise a student teacher, was turned back from the gate by the caretaker who had mistaken her for a cleaner who had arrived too late for work. Clearly, the issue of dress in terms of ethnicity, sexuality, gender and the culture of the workplace takes on a more complex meaning for those women who choose to adhere to ethnic-cultural forms of dress as an important variable in maintaining their cultural identity. Moreover, one of the most powerful signifiers of 'racial otherness' is encoded in the accents and dialects spoken by ethnic minority groups which is often taken as a sign of stupidity and provides a great source of annoyance. The Asian-American philosopher, now an associate professor, described a previous experience in this way:

> when I was teaching in South Carolina, some students made comments such as . . . 'she doesn't speak English, we cannot understand her' . . . 'when I ask her a question she does not understand what I'm saying' . . . some of these are pretty cheap shots . . . it affected my confidence.

Racist discourse was used here intentionally not only to undermine her legitimacy as a professional authority in a very public manner, but also to weaken the strength of her contribution as a knowledge producer and so to erode her personal confidence. Her other experiences within the same institution also reveal how the exclusionary aspects of societal racism are sometimes reflected in staff relations within the academy:

> You assume some basic courtesy and respect in the university — and racial remarks or attitudes are generally not that blatant — but in South Carolina it was a different story . . . my colleagues would not acknowledge me. At parties they would talk to me but the next day they would not acknowledge me as a faculty member. One of my colleagues' explanation was that 'they don't know many Chinese . . . they don't know what to do with you . . . or what to say to you'.

Implicit in the comment made by her colleague is the view that those exhibiting this behaviour do so because they cannot deal with what they do not understand — although clearly well-meant, it nevertheless serves to underscore the idea of her 'foreignness' in a very powerful way. Again, these meanings of racial difference derive from wider social discourse which is grounded in notions of dominant ethnic group superiority. Incorporated subliminally into the meaning structure of the institution, in their effect they serve to render black people powerless and invisible.

Policy and Subjectivity

Since the 1970s, many organizations, including universities, have adopted equal opportunity policies in terms of both gender and 'race'. On the surface, these organizations have become de-sexualized and de-racialized with people being treated 'on merit'. Some of these policies, especially in the USA, incorporate the notion of affirmative action which became instituted under Title VII of the Civil Rights Act (1964). According to the US Civil Rights Commission, affirmative action plans 'should reduce the share of white men as a group to what it would roughly have been had there been no discrimination against minorities and women' (Sekaran and Leong, 1992: 119). Employment firms are encouraged to maintain standards by providing job training programmes to help those excluded to meet the job-criteria. According to US Government statistics in 1986, only 3.3 per cent of women working in universities were represented by ethnic minority groups (Sekaran and Kassner, 1992). Affirmative action has not been an uncontested concept in the US, especially in relation to the quota/numerical goals employed which, according to right-wingers in the Republican Party, discriminate against better qualified white males. The US respondents, although they could see some value in the principles of affirmative action, remained undecided. One interviewee expressed the view that:

> Here in America people are very sensitized to these issues . . . with affirmative action people will bend over to accommodate a woman or

an ethnic minority group . . . I feel very divided. I think that women and minority groups should be given a chance because they do not have the same starting points as white males have in society; but to certain degrees . . . that you would forgo a really talented white person just to have a minority who does not have the same qualifications . . . I feel very uneasy about it — what you do about it, I don't know.

The notion of affirmative action remains problematical also in a broader sense. If instituted to overcome racial disadvantage it would seem to be a paradox within a policy framework geared to equalize opportunity by rewarding merit. The notion clearly needs to be examined further in terms of its real value. Does affirmative action in reality overcome racial disadvantage? What is its relative value with regard to shaping the self-concept of the beneficiaries? A study conducted in the USA (Leonard, 1988) concluded that, whilst minority group productivity did increase significantly during the 1970s because of the enforcement of affirmative action policies in the work place, there was also evidence of more discrimination against women than against ethnic minority groups *per se*. With regard to the 1980s, the study concluded that 'the fact that more women are in the labor force owes more to a massive shift in the female labor supply, and perhaps the threat of lawsuits under Title VII, than to the impact of AA during the 1980s' (Leonard, 1988: 132). Moreover, it could also be argued that located as it is within the framework of discriminating practices and prejudice, affirmative action policy remains ameliorative and thus rooted within a surface perspective of racism and sexism which neglects to address the structural determinants of social inequality and other social practices that produce and reproduce racial and sexual inequality. A deeper exploration of these issues lies beyond the scope of this chapter. Davis (1989: 9), for example, is more sceptical and argues that the existence of these policies belies the reality of everyday life within many institutions. She maintains that:

> equal opportunity, affirmative action, and a new concern for occupational health and safety have all worked their way into the culture of most corporations. But for all the social change and new laws, the *pattern* remains the same. The guiding beliefs and root values of corporate cultures come from the top. (Emphasis added)

This view seems to hold validity if evaluated against some of the experiences discussed above as well as women's under-representation within the power structure of the academy generally. One US respondent, for instance, reported that in a department of twenty staff they have one full professor who is a woman. Out of the five associate professors (senior lecturers) who are women, perhaps only one would make it to professor level because, in her view:

> the decisions are still made by the men at the top . . . there are too few women at the top to influence decision-making . . . in most cases we

still require the patronage of those men in powerful positions . . . who would recognize us and promote us . . . very few women in my field get there purely by merit.

Indeed, Sekaran and Kassner (1992: 166) report that women academics in the USA hold only 12 per cent of tenured faculty positions.

Women's contributions as knowledge producers are also devalued in a variety of other ways in the academy. The majority of the respondents expressed the view that whilst women are highly respected as teachers, they are not valued and encouraged to do highly intellectual work within the academy — unless they are already well-established researchers and writers. One of the UK interviewees, a social scientist, stated that:

> I work in a department dominated by women . . . and still it's the men who get the plum jobs . . . who can somehow negotiate for themselves quality time to do research and have research students whilst we women are over-burdened with large classes to teach.

Within a context in which research and publication carry significant weight in terms of career advancement, the implications are clear — women are being disempowered within the organizational structure. These concerns extend also to the sacrifices that most interviewees felt they had to make because they are women. Many of their observations have already been documented elsewhere, for example, Cockburn (1991) and Sekaran and Kassner (1992) who have argued that men across ethnic and class boundaries benefit from having their families cared for by women and that inadequate child care facilities in organizations frequently inhibit many women's furthering of their careers. Indeed, Sekaran and Kassner (1992: 167) argue that in the USA 'some women are content to remain at the level of associate professor because juggling research productivity and family demands including child rearing is enormously difficult'. In addition, an assistant professor felt that she has had to work twice as hard to get where she is now because of racism:

> for example, my son . . . I felt that I was not really there for him while he was growing up . . . I was doing my PhD and building my career . . . and not only did I have to fight the competition and domination of men but I also had to deal with the racism sanctioned by the institutions in which I worked.

Similarly, a UK colleague currently working as a research assistant in education had to give up her first career in medicine in order to provide long-term support to her son who was experiencing racism in his infant school. As the only black pupil in his class, he was marginalized by his teacher who relegated him to the lowest stream in class even though it was proven, after much struggle, that he was in fact a very able pupil. His mother is only now (ten years later) beginning to think again of pursuing further studies within her own field. Clearly, racial and gender inequality intersect in poignant ways in many women's lives, which bear out the view expressed earlier that black women's lived experience reveals the multi-levelled interaction of domination in wider society.

Changing Subjectivities

Mills (1989) argues that the ambiguity inherent in organizational rules of control leaves open the opportunity for alternative interpretation and contestation which, in turn, creates possibilities for change to take place. He suggests that notions of femininity and masculinity constructed within the broader social terrain may be confronted, shaped and reshaped in interaction with a number of other organizational rules. The latter include legal rules which, in this instance, can refer to the relative success of equal opportunities legislation; strategic rules which serve the particular interests of the organization, for example, the provision of nursery care in the academy; and reproductive rules which refer to dominant views of women in relation to their roles as child bearers. To this end Mills (1989) advocates changing people's consciousness and emphasizes the need for organizations to adopt 'definite change strategies' as an intrinsic aspect of social change.

However, Mills's view neglects to take account of the ubiquity of racial and gender exploitation and discrimination within wider society which influence the shaping of power/knowledge discourses in institutions. As is evident in the experiences documented here, organizations will not change through appeals to individual understanding alone. Instead, we need to examine and make concrete the ways in which discourses of genderization, sexuality and racialized ethnicity are constructed within organizations and within society (Silverman and Gubrium, 1989). Nevertheless, the view that meanings are subject to contestation and therefore change remains an important issue to investigate. Exploring further Giddens's (1991) view of self-identity as constituting a reflexive, cognitive understanding of the 'self' in terms of the person's own biography, I will now examine the strategies adopted by some of the interviewees to re-define their subjective experiences within the academy.

Strategies Adopted to Manage Racialized and Genderized Subjectivities

People are not determined in a static way within the social structure — they are actively engaged in challenging and resisting the oppressive power relations which construct their reality (Cockburn, 1985). According to Pringle (1989: 168):

> Whilst resistance and struggle are intrinsic to the exercise of power, people also act as subjects whose actions are to some extent freely chosen from a set of alternative possibilities.

This was evident in the interviews that I conducted, as well as the information provided in the questionnaires. Whilst the participants were keen to discuss their negative experiences they, nevertheless, had a strong sense of how their self-identities have been shaped within their cultures and within the academy, what their roles were as academics within their particular fields and what their ambitions were in terms of the future. Moreover, they relied on a set of strategically devised actions, both conscious and unconscious, to re-define their social experience in terms of their own personal hopes, desires and aspirations. This serves to illustrate the ways in which they were engaged as reflective and reflexive individuals in re-ordering their 'self-narratives' within the context of their daily experiences within the academy — and thus to re-define their self-identities. Three key strategies being used by black women emerged in the interview and questionnaire samples. First, the important role that networking and mentoring played in their lives: two belong to professional women's networks which meet once or twice a year to discuss issues related to their particular fields and their careers. Others expressed their wish to develop supportive professional networks. This conforms to Berktay's (1993: 111) view that, in order to transform existing power relations, women need to 'communicate, to hear each others' voices, to learn about each other and to forge alliances'. Some also expressed the desire to support other younger black women within the academy and stressed the importance of role models for girls growing up. A UK scientist stated that:

> there is a very dire need for black women in the academy to be good role models for girls growing up — to show them that with hard work and good strategy . . . having a systematic long-term and short-term career plan, barriers can be broken because you challenge them.

This form of mentoring, also referred to as community 'othermothering' (hooks, 1989; Hill Collins, 1991), has been a long-standing tradition in Afro-American women's cultural experience. hooks (1989: 50) extends this to include the concept of 'mothering the mind' and argues that 'to teach in a way that liberates, that expands consciousness, that awakens, is to challenge domination at its very core'.

However, another interviewee who belonged to a university women's group had very strong reservations about its value as an inclusive support group. She argued that:

> although I was a founder member of the group I don't participate in their activities anymore because as whites they have a different

agenda . . . I think for many of them being a feminist is a very chic thing, it's a fashion; it's political correctness for the sake of being politically correct . . . their rhetoric is taken to extremes and very often they alienate . . . if you're going to change the sexual climate of the culture you need men as well as women. Also, for me feminism is about improving the lives of all women . . . I think they should listen more to minority women . . . respect the different cultures . . . not all feminisms are the same.

This view is shared by other black writers, including Hill Collins (1991), hooks (1989) and Davis (1989), who argue that black women within the Afro-American community have largely rejected notions of power based entirely on domination and have, instead, opted for a theory of power based on 'a vision of self-actualization, self-definition and self-determination' (Hill Collins, 1991: 24). Similarly, writers such as Berktay (1993) and Ramazanoglu (1989) argue for the need to take account of different cultures without necessarily condoning oppressive practices, for example, female circumcision or the sexual self-censorship implicit in the *chaddor* in some Muslim countries. Even these issues need to be examined within the context of the sexual, economic and political power relations that gave rise to these practices. Ramazanoglu (1989: 145) underlines the need to understand that:

Women in Muslim societies are also divided by class, ethnicity, nationality and sectarianism in ways which set women against each other. While we can ask why, how, and when relations between the sexes have become oppressive to women, and what forms such oppressions take, the answers to these questions are not self-evident.

In terms of this, Berktay (1993: 117) argues that 'a universal model for emancipation cannot arrogantly assume for itself a Western point of view'. The different socio-cultural histories that have shaped the individual subjectivities of the women interviewed in this sample study, and the social relations that circumscribe their lives, serve to underscore the views expressed by these writers. For black women in metropolitan societies, the issues of 'race', gender and class oppression form part of the same dialectic.

The second key strategy is that some women opt for strategic placement within their field. This played an important role in the careers of two respondents who consciously chose to work with women academics, irrespective of their 'ethnic origins', who are internationally renowned experts in their fields because they were their role models. This would seem to re-inforce the significance of mentoring strategies discussed above.

The third strategy was shown by one interviewee who opted for what Sheppard (1989) calls 'claiming a rightful place' by consciously challenging a predominantly male-dominated field:

I am more naturally inclined towards the arts but I wanted to overcome these barriers. I therefore felt it a challenge for me as a woman, as a black woman to go into the sciences. I see my role as very important; there are not many black women who are professors and not many who are scientists . . . we are the pioneers and it will take many generations of effort to clear the way for other black women who will come after us . . . so that they can be free to be themselves.

Most respondents also expressed the view that they wanted to contribute to knowledge within their fields but also wished to relate this to the way in which they experience their own lives as women and as members of minority groups. One of the scientists interviewed stated that:

I've fought against becoming masculinized . . . often you see women in the sciences becoming very masculine and brittle and brutish because the pressure is to become like the dominant group in order to succeed . . . but I've fought against that and I think that it helps me to understand who I am as a black woman . . . not to give in to the pressures and lose my identity.

This view conforms to Pateman's (1988) argument that 'women's equal standing must be accepted as an expression of the freedom of women as *women*, and not be treated as an indication that women are just like men' (1988: 231).

Conclusion

This study has argued that black women academics' experiences, because they draw discursively from meanings constructed within wider social discourse, cannot be analysed only in terms of the unequal relations that prevail within the academy. Thus the analysis focused also on socialization processes within the community and broader cultural practices. It also sought to highlight the 'multi-accentuality' of the term 'black' within different socio-historical contexts: the fact that 'racial' meanings are subject to change across time and space was illustrated in the terminology used to describe various ethnic groups within contexts of colonialism, neo-colonialism and immigration settlement. The potential for refracting dominant meanings and, in the process, to challenge them, was highlighted in the unifying self-definition of diverse oppressed ethnic groups in South Africa during the 1970s.

Focusing more specifically, then, on black women's experiences within the academy, the accounts provided in the sample study have shown that the different levels of racial and gender marginalization, as well as stereotyping that inhere within society also permeate the academic organization, however subliminally. These accounts have shown that by engaging in an organic process of revising and re-ordering their 'self-narratives' in terms of their everyday experiences within the institution and in society, black women do create opportunities to challenge attempts at social and professional marginalization. Although they may have been constituted as marginalized subjects within society and the power structure of the academy, they have not allowed themselves to be incorporated as 'powerless', 'passive' beings into the meaning structure of the academy — and thus to collude in their own dispossession. And, in the process of working against their structured 'racialized ethnic' as well as genderized subjectivities, they have been able to re-define oppressive social experiences in ways that can be individually self-empowering. In relation to this, the personal histories described here have illustrated the ways in which black women working in the academy re-interpret dominant racialized and gendered meanings within their own socio-cultural conceptual framework and encode their lives with their own meanings. Thus, they have been working from a position of *disidentification* (Pecheux, 1982) against racist and sexist practices that prevail within society. These strategies need to be seen as an intrinsic part of a broader counter-hegemonic struggle against racial and sexual domination, as well as social, cultural and institutional marginalization. In terms of this, although the relative success of the strategies adopted by these women does not detract from the fact that racism and sexism need to be confronted as ideological and cultural practices at both institutional and societal level, it does serve to illustrate the view expressed by Giddens (1991: 2) that:

> The self is not a passive entity, determined by external influences; in forging their self-identities, no matter how local their specific contexts of action, individuals contribute to and directly promote social influences that are global in their consequences and implications.

The study revealed differences in the experiences encountered by black women academics within the organization, which relate to their different social histories as well as the social meanings attached to their particular ethnic group within their countries of residence. On the other hand, it also highlighted aspects of their experience of oppression which are common to all women regardless of ethnicity. The women in the sample study all have middle-class family histories. This and the fact that they are extraordinary and dynamic individuals who are constantly engaged in a process of self-evaluation, as well as their obvious ability to articulate their views within the broader context of societal, sexual and racial oppression, obscure the perhaps different experiences of the women not heard in this sample study. Nevertheless, in sharing their experiences with us, these women have provided an 'account of the world and human relations as seen from the margins' (Berktay, 1993: 128). The importance of this refracted discourse is the possibility that it provides for 'transforming those margins into the centre, changing perhaps, the notion of the centre itself' (Berktay, 1993: 128).

References

ACKROYD, S. (1994) 'Re-creating Common Ground: elements for post-paradigmatic organization studies' in HASSARD, J. and PARKER, M. (Eds) *Towards a New Theory of Organizations*, pp. 269–297, London: Routledge.

BERKTAY, F. (1993) 'Looking from the "Other" Side: Is Cultural Relativism a Way Out?' in GROOT, J. DE and MAYNARD, M. (Eds) *Women's Studies in the 1990s: Doing Things Differently?* pp. 110–131, Basingstoke: Macmillan.

COCKBURN, C. (1985) *Machinery of Dominance: Women, Men and Technical Know-How*, London: Pluto.

COCKBURN, C. (1991) *In The Way Of Women: Men's Resistance To Sex Equality in Organizations*, Basingstoke: Macmillan.

DAVIS, A. (1989) *Women, Culture, and Politics*, New York: Random House.

GIDDENS, A. (1979) *Central Problems in Social Theory*, London: Macmillan.

GIDDENS, A. (1984) *The Constitution of Society*, Cambridge: Polity Press in association with Oxford: Blackwell.

GIDDENS, A. (1991) *Modernity and Self-Identity: Self and Society in the Late Modern Age*, Cambridge: Polity Press.

GILROY, P. (1987) *There Ain't No Black In The Union Jack*, London: Hutchinson.

HILL COLLINS, P. (1991) *Black Feminist Thought: Knowledge, Consciousness and the Politics of Empowerment*, London: Routledge.

hooks, b. (1989) *Talking Back: Thinking Feminist, Thinking Black*, Boston: South End Press.

HOYLES, C. (Ed.) (1988) *Girls and Computers*, Bedford Way Papers/34, Institute of Education, University of London.

LEONARD, J.A. (1988) 'Women and Affirmative Action in the 1980s', quoted in 'Legal Aspects of Women's Advancement: Affirmative Action, Family Leave, and Dependent Care Law', Carr-Ruffino et al, in SEKARAN, U. and LEONG, F.T.L. (Eds) (1992) *Woman Power: Managing in Times of Demographic Turbulence*, pp. 113–157, Newbury Park, London and New Delhi: Sage.

MACDONELL, D. (1987) *Theories of Discourse: An Introduction*, Oxford: Basil Blackwell.

MILLS, A. (1989) 'Gender, Sexuality and Organization Theory', in HEARN, J., SHEPPARD, D., TANCRED-SHERIFF, P. and BURRELL, G. (Eds) *The Sexuality of Organization*, pp. 29–44, London: Sage.

PATEMAN, C. (1988) *The Sexual Contract*, Oxford: Polity Press.

PECHEUX, M. (1982) *Language, Semantics and Ideology*, translated by Harbans Nagpal, Basingstoke: Macmillan.

PRINGLE, R. (1989) Bureaucracy, Rationality and Sexuality: The Case of Secretaries, in HEARN, J., SHEPPARD, D., TANCRED-SHERIFF, P. and BURRELL, G. (Eds) *The Sexuality of Organization*, pp. 158–177, London: Sage.

PROBYN, E. (1993) *Sexing the Self: Gendered Positions in Cultural Studies*, London: Routledge.

RAMAZANOGLU, C. (1989) *Feminism and the Contradictions of Oppression*, London: Routledge.

REED, M.I. (1992) *The Sociology of Organizations: Themes, Perspectives and Prospects*, Hemel Hempstead: Harvester Wheatsheaf.

SEKARAN, U. and KASSNER, M. (1992) 'University Systems for the 21st Century: Proactive Adaptation', in SEKARAN, U. and LEONG, F.T.L. (Eds), *Woman Power: Managing in Times of Demographic Turbulence*, pp. 163–192, Newbury Park, London: Sage.

SEKARAN, U. and LEONG, F.T.L. (Eds) (1992) *Woman Power: Managing in Times of Demographic Turbulence*, Newbury Park, London: Sage.

SHEPPARD, D. (1989) 'Organizations, Power and Sexuality: The Image and Self-Image of Women Managers' in Hearn, J., Sheppard, D., Tancred-Sheriff, P. and Burrell, G. (Eds) *The Sexuality of Organization*, pp. 139–157, London: Sage.

SILVERMAN, D. and GUBRIUM, J. (1989) *The Politics of Field Research: Sociology Beyond Enlightenment*, London: Sage.

YAMADA, M. (1983) 'Asian Pacific Women and Feminism', in MORAGA, C. and ANZALDUA, G. (Eds) *This Bridge Called My Back: Writings by Radical Women of Color*, pp. 35–40, New York: Kitchen Table: Women of Color Press.

Chapter 3

Irrigating the Sacred Grove: Stages of Gender Equity Development

Barbara Brown Packer

I overheard two professors talking. One told the other that she was having a difficult time getting women professors to serve on a status-of-women committee. She reported that the women they had invited declined because they were afraid that they would not get tenure if they were involved on a committee dealing with women's issues. It seemed as though those who were approached were interested, and wanted to be involved, but felt afraid to pursue their interest in women's issues.

Next I heard from a trusted source that a woman dean of a prominent university, who had written on women's issues, had decided not to do so any longer because she was afraid it would ruin her chances for a high-level appointment in Washington, DC. Later I talked to a college president and told her what I had heard about the dean. She relayed a story about being told by her advisor, while in graduate school, that she would never amount to anything if she pursued her academic interest in women's issues. His advice haunted her years later.

These events led me to become curious about the experiences of women professors at research universities in the United States of America. I wanted to know what they perceived as the relationship between involvement in women's issues and career advancement. To this end, I conducted 32 semi-structured interviews with women professors at three selected research universities in four selected departments in the behavioral sciences, humanities, natural sciences, and social sciences within the USA. I gathered from each professor information about her background, professional history, involvement or non-involvement in women's issues, attitudes and perceptions about women's issues and career advancement, and the attitudes she perceived that her colleagues held.

The ages of the women in the sample were spread between 28 and 63 years old. Though it was not part of the research design, most of the women in the sample were married with children. Thirty-one of the women were Caucasian and one was Mexican–American. One-third of them were in leadership positions. Most of the women were involved in women's issues on campus and considered themselves to be feminists, although the sample also included those who considered themselves to be anti-feminists, and those who preferred not to be labelled.

I found that women professors perceived that there was a relationship between involvement in women's issues and career advancement, but they did not alter their behavior because of it. For the most part, professors who were interested, were involved in women's issues. Although several women felt as though their involvement in women's issues had held them back, several others felt that their involvement in women's issues had been the reason for their advancement. In the latter cases their academic work revolved around women's issues.

Women in the USA historically have been outsiders to academia. Up until the early 1900s, US women were essentially denied the opportunity to receive doctoral degrees. With the exception of employment at women's colleges, women were not hired as professors at universities until the 1940s. The Women's Movement, which had its second wave of activism in the mid-1960s, paved the way for vast social changes with regard to equal rights for women (Rix, 1987). Title VII of the Civil Rights Act in 1964 and Title IX of the Education Amendments of the Civil Rights Act in 1972, banned discrimination on the basis of sex in federally funded educational institutions. At that time law suits sprang up, and changes in the gender composition of the professoriate began to occur. The changes have been slow, and even today there are relatively few women professors at colleges and universities.

According to the well-regarded US Task Force on Women in Higher Education, in 1989 women made up 27.1 per cent of all tenured and non-tenured faculty positions at colleges and universities in the USA. Women cluster at the lower ranks, in what has been termed the 'academic proletariat', non-tenure-track appointments, part-time, adjunct, and other temporary positions. Currently women make up 19 per cent of faculty at research universities, despite the fact that the percentage of women with doctorates doubled during the 1980s. Only 6.5 per cent of full professors at research universities are women. The number of women in academia is very slowly changing.

Georg Simmel argues that when numerical shifts occur within a group, interactions between people in that group are transformed. Simmel describes the introduction of a 'stranger' into a group saying,

> His [*sic*] position in this group is determined, essentially, by the fact that he has not belonged to it from the beginning, that he imports qualities into it, which do not and cannot stem from the group itself . . . His position as a full-fledged member involves both being outside it and confronting it. (Wolff, 1950)

How close this person is to the inside of the group will depend upon the proportion of others in the group who are similar to him/her, in relationship to the group as a whole. In a way, women are 'strangers' in academia because of their numerical proportion.

As there are so few women in academia, they constitute what Rosabeth Kanter calls 'outgroup members'. Kanter believes that an organization must have a significant number of outgroup people before they will begin to be viewed as individuals rather than symbols. Kanter describes the environment for women who are outnumbered in an organization:

> Those women who were few in number among male peers and often had 'only woman' status became tokens: symbols of how-women-can-do, stand-ins for all women. Sometimes they had the advantage of those who are 'different' and thus were highly visible in a system where success is tied to becoming known. Sometimes they faced the loneliness of the outsider, of the stranger who intrudes upon an alien culture and many become self-estranged in the process of assimilation. (Kanter, 1977)

An argument against Kanter's Critical Mass Theory is that by viewing women as a group, she essentializes women, suggesting that all women think and act in the same way.

Philip Mason also discusses the issue of numerical proportion, stating that patterns of domination may be related to the numerical proportion of groups within a culture. However, that is not always the case. For example, Mason mentions the situation in South Africa, where the numerical proportion of black Africans is much greater than that of the ruling whites. Mason concludes that in addition to looking at numerical proportions, one must consider the historical dimension of dominance (Mason, 1970). It is important, therefore, to look at the issue of women in academia within an historical context.

In discussing the historical climate of academia for women, Paula A. Treichler describes a contradiction:

> Historically, many women have found the academy compatible with their values, temperaments, and professional aspirations, yet few have been adequately recognized or rewarded for their achievements; with few exceptions, the academy has proved a thorny and inhospitable environment, making its concessions to women grudgingly, in the face of political, economic, and legal pressure. (Treichler, 1985)

In the American Council on Education's 1989 book, *Educating the Majority: Women Challenge Tradition in Higher Education*, a section entitled 'Transforming the Institution' discusses Cynthia Secor's 'Swiss Cheese Model' of social change:

> In the Swiss-Cheese Model, the individual 'finds a hole and keeps nibbling.' Its essence is to find a place where it is possible to act out of one's new values and understanding immediately, without requiring the rest of the institution to change . . . If enough people in an institution over a period of time adopt this approach, the configuration

of the whole changes. Furthermore, the hold of the old paradigm on an institution is loosened as more and more people experiment with alternative ways of thinking and behaving. The holes created in the whole allow, literally, for more openness. (Pearson *et al.*, 1989)

This model of social change may be used to explain how the research university is being transformed. My research generates the hypothesis that individuals and departments within research universities go through four transitional stages in their gender equity development. The holes in the Swiss cheese represent the enlightened individuals and departments within the institution, and the solid sections represent those in earlier stages of gender equity development.

This research suggests that it is the role of the department more than that of the institution or the discipline, which determines whether an environment is equitable for women professors.

Stages of Gender Equity Development

The department plays a crucial role in determining whether professors will be rewarded or punished for involvement in women's issues. Furthermore, merely being a woman may affect advancement, regardless of involvement or non-involvement in women's issues, depending upon the gender equity stage of the department. This can be true regardless of a professor's area of research, due simply to biases of decision makers. Four stages of gender equity appear to exist at research universities in the USA and are described below.

In two of the departments studied, both in the natural sciences, the classification of gender equity development was obscured by the fact that only one token woman held an appointment in each department. In both cases, she felt that she was treated fairly; however, no other women were making their way through the ranks. Neither of these women considered herself to be a feminist, and one described herself as 'unsympathetic to the women's movement'. None of the women professors in the natural sciences, including the two mentioned here, expressed concern about the lack of women coming through the pipeline. This attitude raises the question, can a department reach a state of gender equity merely through tokenism? I think not. Although the door remained effectively closed, the token served the specific purpose of legitimizing the department's denial of a closed door policy. Because of the conflict between the views of the token women and the apparent departmental discrimination, I did not classify the gender equity development of these departments.

The Closed Door

No departments in the sample refused employment to women. Title VII of the Civil Rights Act of 1964 and Title IX of the Education Amendments of the

Civil Rights Act of 1972 forbid such practices. Several professors remembered a time when career doors were closed for women, however. One full professor with tenure reflected upon the earliest years of her 30-year career when women had far fewer options than they have today. Reminiscent of stories told by Virginia Woolf, this professor explained that when she was a junior professor at a prestigious institution she was not allowed to enter the library because she was a woman, even though she had placed reserved readings for her classes there. The institution also would not, because she was a woman, allow her to march in commencement ceremonies. When she first started working at her current institution, the institution spent ten-times more on funding male athletic programs than they spent on female athletic programs. She also recalled that the Job Placement Office at the institution listed jobs separately for men and women.

She described an experience when she applied for a job in a department in the behavioral sciences and was denied the job, only to be consulted later about whom they should hire instead:

> I didn't ever used to think that it [my situation] had to do with my sex. They had women in my department, but the women didn't get voted upon. There was one point where I realized something was out of kilter. The department told me that the reason they did not hire me was because they weren't interested in my field. Then a couple of years later they called me up to ask my advice about the hiring of a man in that field. I was so mad I couldn't believe it. I just about flipped out I was so mad.

Another professor, 45 years old, also in the behavioral sciences, explained that she was explicitly told when she started her graduate program that women would not be hired for faculty positions at that institution. She said:

> Women were not allowed on the faculty when I was a graduate student. The women students were told explicitly when we arrived that in order to be admitted to the program we had to be considerably better than the men applicants they had. They would admit us under those circumstances, but they wanted us to understand that women would not be hired for our faculty and would not be recommended for positions elsewhere. I was told specifically once by a very famous professor that 'Everybody knows that women can't do [field in the behavioral sciences]. Nobody wants a woman in the laboratory.'

Although it is now illegal for institutions to openly discriminate against women on the basis of sex, many of these old attitudes, that women are not capable or welcome in academia, have remained. Thus, the behaviors toward women have necessarily changed because the law has changed, but some of the remaining negative attitudes toward women have created what may be called a revolving door phenomenon (Macaulay, 1980) in which women professors enter an institution but do not stay.

The Revolving Door Phenomenon

New women enter, experience an uncomfortable environment, or an environment in which they will never succeed, and leave, only to be followed by other women who will also leave. In this way departments are fulfilling their affirmative action goals in recruiting women faculty, but are not succeeding in retaining the women faculty they hire. Three, or one-quarter, of the departments studied fit this description. Two of these three departments each had a token woman who had received tenure, and who had stayed at the institution, watching the other women exit through the revolving door. These two survivors acknowledged that other women were exiting through a revolving door, and seemed confused about why they personally were treated differently. One felt that her department was hostile toward women and the other felt that women who were good enough would advance in the department.

Some professors and administrators argue that there is no such thing as a 'revolving door phenomenon' and claim that each case exists *sui generis* and cannot be considered as part of a pattern. In making this argument, they cite numerous reasons why each particular woman left the institution. Although specific, personal reasons influence a given professor's separation from a university, a general pattern has nevertheless emerged and ought not be ignored. A lecturer, in a department that had a revolving door for women professors, talked about her experiences in the department:

We have had a number of women leave this department. But, my male colleagues see no pattern in it, and they want to insist that each case is separate. Those of us who want to insist that this is part of a larger issue, in a feminist way, are always greeted with the response 'You can't generalize. This person left for personal reasons. This person left because she never properly adjusted to the Academy. This person was too ambitious.' They will not allow for the possibility of a pattern. They will not consider that they had something to do with it.

During the course of the interviews women professors related some experiences in their departments which I consider to be at the very least sexist, and in many cases discriminatory. Some of them took action as a result of the offensive behavior, and some did not. Some, in describing the behaviors, did not mention that they felt them to be offensive and accepted them as a fact of life in their departments. Some of this unfair treatment was in the form of unwritten rules that barred their future options, and some of the unfair treatment was in the form of a hostile environment.

An unstable future

All of the junior professors at one of the institutions believed that they would never get tenure there. They believed that it was nearly impossible to do so. Consequently, that institution provided an unstable future for those professors. They explained that tenure was difficult to achieve at that particular institution because of its high degree of selectivity.

In terms of retaining women professors, one particular department in the sample had the worst record. In this department, all three professors were leaving at the end of the academic year because of the unwritten rule that women did not gain tenure there. This type of mass exodus of women was not unusual in this department.

One professor in this department talked about the lower status of women faculty. She had recently been denied a promotion at the time of the interview. She said:

> Women on the faculty are much more articulate and outspoken because they are freed from the misconceptions of the possibilities [of tenure]. We know that we are the stepdaughters and will not legitimately inherit. We are not truly faculty, we are *women* faculty.

These data suggest that certain departments have unwritten rules that women will not gain tenure. One professor who had been hired with tenure at her current institution had been denied tenure at her previous institution. She told the painful story about how she perceived that being a woman apart from her family had influenced the tenure decision:

> The Chairman [*sic*] of the department, who happened to be a friend of mine, called me to tell me about the vote. He said that it was an unbelievable discussion. He said, 'You have no idea of the extent to which you, as a woman who abandons her family in [another state] . . . [are viewed as], in Mary Douglas's anthropological language, "taboo". You are unthinkable. They don't even want to think about a woman who would leave her husband and children.'

Professors who were not on the tenure track, as either adjunct professors or lecturers, felt a similar degree of uncertainty about their future. One professor not on the tenure track was an Adjunct Professor and Research Scientist. Her financial support depended solely upon her ability to get grants. Her situation seemed even more tenuous and powerless than that of the junior professors. She was 63 years old and had been at that university for 32 years with no job security. For much of her career, she conducted research on women, and felt very strongly that her choice of research topics had held back her advancement. In her case, she had not exited through the revolving door, but felt dizzy from her 32 years of job insecurity.

Uncomfortable environment

The environment created within a particular department has a tremendous impact upon a woman professor's experience in academia. Certain departments in the sample maintained pockets of discrimination within an institution, adversely affecting the women working in those departments. No institution studied was free of a pocket of this type. I had wondered if certain disciplines might be more hostile than others toward women, but quickly learned that the attitude of the department, as exhibited by the leadership of the department and department members, far outweighed that of the discipline.

Conducting research on topics related to women's issues emerged as an area of concern for women professors. Those in relatively tenuous positions worried about the topics that they were researching, and wondered whether those topics would be taken seriously. One professor from a particularly discriminatory department explained that her research on women was not considered a serious topic by her colleagues. Along with several others in the sample, she described feeling 'marginalized'. She noted with seriousness how deeply she felt that her colleagues were affected by their involvement in women's issues, and emphatically felt that the fact that some of her colleagues had a feminist perspective negatively affected their career advancement. She described a situation in which one of her former female colleagues had been publishing a lot. When one particular piece was published, she heard several male colleagues saying, 'Oh, well, she's probably just friends with the editor of the journal'. But she noted that when the male professors had some of their own work published, and they were friends with the editor, they called it 'collegiality' and 'professionalism'.

One Mexican–American woman professor in the social sciences talked about the lack of pay equity at her previous institution and different sexist and racist remarks that were made, especially by her department chair. She considered the department to be riddled with sexism and racism and described the unaccepting environment:

> It is a very anti-feminist climate with an anti-feminist president. Many women left [the institution]. Salary scales were very unfair . . . It was a very traditional department in which people without realizing it made sexist comments. And if you pointed it out, it was not appreciated. Then you were not one of the guys . . . It did not help that I brought up a sex equity grievance in my department. The chair of the department said to me, 'Yes, we hired this guy and we brought him in for $3000 more than you are currently making, even though he got his dissertation the year after you did and even though you've published more, because his wife doesn't work and he has two small children.' That's actually what he said. I looked at him and said 'You've just won yourself a trip to the Dean's office.' I won my grievance.

After three years she left that institution and has worked for four years at her current institution. She emphasized the role of the department as being of ultimate importance in influencing the experience of individual professors.

In many cases, women professors left intolerable environments and found other departments at other institutions that were more accommodating. The professors found themselves in a revolving door where they exited soon after they had entered, either because there was no chance of their gaining tenure or because of uncomfortable environments. While these women found new environments, it is not always easy or possible for professors to relocate.

The Door Ajar

Similar to the revolving door, the door ajar describes an environment which is not always friendly toward women, or understanding of any type of differences. The two stages differ in that, when the door is ajar, some women have been able to make their way through. In this stage the door is not completely open, nor is it entirely shut, but it is more closed than it is open. The departments in this stage were not so unbearable that women left shortly after having arrived. On the other hand, the women did not feel comfortable in the environment. This category included half of the departments in the sample.

Some of the women in the sample had positions which they described as being 'tantamount to having tenure'. In limited ways they had security of employment without officially having tenure. In one case, by virtue of being an administrator, a professor was guaranteed a teaching post. In other cases, policies had been enacted that protected the rights of those with the status of lecturer for three-year intervals. The women with these limited forms of security felt very strongly that involvement in women's issues might affect their chances for advancement.

A professor at the most selective institution in the sample, who was in a position she described as 'tantamount to having tenure' by virtue of an administrative appointment, described the environment in her department and her level of vulnerability:

> Women are not getting tenure at the rate they should. The percentage has stayed the same for a long time. There is a glass ceiling. Maleness is woven in, it is in the very fabric of so many of the traditions. The definition of quality work is imbued with male values. Anything outside of the mainstream is not accepted. Women often like to do interdisciplinary work, and that is not well received.

An associate professor with tenure in the social sciences described a prototype of some male professors in her department:

> This department is very backward compared to others . . . One category of male colleagues looks at a woman with hostility and assumes that

there are positions that obviously she takes, whether she does or not, and they see her as their enemy. You can say something to them about their field and they can be belligerent. They assume that you are critical of their field because it doesn't involve women. There is a tension, and a framework that is not positive. There are men in this department and other departments who provide this type of resistance towards women's issues. There are absolutely impossible, intransigent departments on this campus.

A junior professor in the behavioral sciences explained that the only reason she had not left her department was because she was able to avoid more than minimal contact with those in her department as a result of the location of her laboratory:

I haven't experienced the 'revolving door' phenomenon, but I spend most of my time here [in the lab] where it is comfortable for me. If I were in the department, I'd be looking for another job. I am a member of the department, but if I were housed there, it wouldn't be a very happy position for me. The resources in the department are miserable and the people in the department are small-minded.

A tenured woman from the same department talked about her department's resistance to her appointment when she was hired as an Assistant Professor in 1971:

They made me an Assistant Professor over a few dead bodies. It was a fight. A mandate was given to the department to hire women by the Chancellor's office. The department didn't want me. I was very lucky to get a job. I was the only woman I knew of to graduate with a Ph.D. and get a job. In 1968 women didn't get academic jobs.

Another professor, who had been appointed more recently, in 1986, also did not receive support from her department in the social sciences when she was hired in a joint appointment with Women's Studies. She said that her appointment was met with 'resistance and division'.

One behavioral scientist talked about some of the views of individuals in the department. She quoted one man as having said, 'We will never have ovaries in this department'. She summed up her feelings about being a member of her department by saying, 'I was in an isolated position in the department. I was marginal there'.

One tenured professor felt very strongly that involvement in women's issues holds women back from advancing:

My colleague who was the head of women's studies found that her leadership role didn't count as a major position . . . when it was time to consider her for a promotion. Informally these things are never recorded ... Being involved in women's issues has hurt me in my research, it has hurt me in my promotions, and it has hurt me in my interpersonal relations within the department.

Professors in some of the other departments scattered across the sample felt a certain degree of freedom if they had tenure even if they were in a department where the door was only ajar. For example, one professor who was chair of a program at the most selective university in the sample said:

At the stage at which you find me, I am very secure. I can do what I want to. I've been in that happy state for some years now. It's not only a question of security in terms of the fact that I've got tenure and no one can fire me unless I create great malfeasance or moral turpitude or some other such thing, but also that I've got a certain reputation, and so I'm not running scared, and don't have to.

The moments, days and, in some cases, years of antagonistic actions and attitudes that these women described in their departments were horrifying. In some cases the actions were subtle and in other cases they were blatant. The xenophobia of women as outsiders seemed equally strong across disciplines and institutions, with some departments containing pockets of more chauvinistic views than other departments across campus.

An Open Door

In the final stage of gender equity development, the door swings fully open. Men and women receive equitable treatment in their departments. In this stage women professors perceive that tenure and promotion decisions are handled fairly. It is interesting that women in these more enlightened departments acknowledged the existence of other departments with a revolving door and with a door ajar. They felt fortunate to be in a department with an open door. Only two of the departments in the sample approached this state of gender equity.

One such department included both a woman Dean and a woman department chair who were full professors with tenure. Three of the four women I interviewed in the department had tenure, and the fourth was under consideration for tenure.

The department chair talked about general advice she had for people who were just completing graduate school and were looking for tenure track positions in a research university. She felt that being a feminist or being involved in women's issues was not what keeps someone from advancing. Rather she felt that if a person was too narrow in her interests, this would keep her down. She talked about a woman in her department who had recently been awarded tenure because of her research on women:

She made a lateral move here in mid-career. It would have been the threshold of her career at another place. She chose to come to us and start the clock all over again and take the time to retrain herself in another line of critical enterprise. That line of critical enterprise proved in fact to be a feminist one, and that is precisely why we're interested in her. That's why we hired her away from [name of institution]. She has a book that is coming out next year. She is tenured starting this fall.

The other department in the sample which approached having an open door was in the social sciences. All three of the professors interviewed in that department had tenure. Two of the three professors described negative experiences they had undergone at previous institutions. They compared their previous experiences with their current experiences and were delighted by the equitable treatment they were receiving.

One professor talked about the open door atmosphere in her department:

My department is very, very supportive. It really varies from campus to campus. I've found the university to be very supportive. I've had very few problems. If I do have a problem, I go directly to the person and talk with them, and they listen. That's really important in creating a supportive academic environment.

In the two departments that were approaching an equitable state, there were a few notable qualities which made it appear as though the door was not completely open. In one case, a junior professor being considered for tenure felt uncomfortable posting feminist notices and felt as though her male colleagues in the department objected to her feminist approach in the classroom. The other department approaching an open door had not promoted two of their tenured professors to the rank of full professor. One of those two associate professors had been at the university for 12 years.

Conclusion

The four stages of gender equity, the closed door, the revolving door, the door ajar, and the open door represent stages in the growth of departmental attitudes of acceptance of, and accommodation for, gender difference. Cynthia Secor's Swiss Cheese Model of Social Change is an apt description of how change occurring in small segments of the whole can change the construction and complexity of the essence of the whole. The holes in the cheese represent the departments with open doors. Those departments create more light and more openness throughout the whole. They also create opportunities for advancement which women cannot find elsewhere, either simply because they are women or because of certain unwritten rules of conduct for women. Although not all departments necessarily transit all of these four stages, and do not necessarily do so sequentially, this description provides a useful structure for illuminating the experience of women professors in academia.

On the whole, women professors pursued their interests, whether those interests related to women's issues or not. Many women professors told stories about how their involvement in women's issues had adversely affected their career advancement. But those who became interested had remained involved nonetheless. A few professors in departments with open doors felt that their careers had been beneficially affected by their involvement. In most cases, merely being a woman had a greater impact upon a woman's career than her involvement or non-involvement in women's issues. In the perception of the women faculty I interviewed, male senior faculty resist the entrance and progress of women professors within the research university. Those senior women professors who were tokens in the natural sciences joined the male faculty through their silent acceptance of the *status quo.*

Unfortunately, in academia, the very process of educating young scholars indoctrinates them with only certain accepted theories and beliefs, and leads them down a narrow path. One consequence of this is that most scholars learn a tremendous amount about only tiny subjects. Exceptions to this certainly include Women's Studies and other interdisciplinary studies. I am concerned that this grooming process may actually narrow minds rather than expand or broaden them. Academia is producing individuals who have intensive training but who have not been taught to understand or even tolerate ideas, beliefs, or physical characteristics that differ from their own. Because prejudice can obscure excellence, the university must ensure that obstacles to equality are removed. Academia must embrace women within its fold rather than continuing to push them to the margins.

The experience of the older professors in the sample may differ from that of the younger professors simply because of historical and societal changes. Therefore, it would be interesting to study a given group of women professors throughout the course of their careers in a longitudinal study, noting changes in their views as changes occur in the numerical proportion and status of women in academia. A longitudinal study could also answer questions about patterns in the development of gender equity within specific departments.

It is because this research studies only one type of institution of Higher Education that I am currently distributing a survey which will study women professors and administrators at other types of institutions as well, such as comprehensive universities, liberal arts colleges, and women's colleges. Different academic environments might provide very different atmospheres. On the other hand, women might face obstacles regardless of the type of institution. Similarly, it would be interesting to study women professors at universities in other countries. It may be that American colleges and universities provide a different environment for women in terms of gender equity development.

The experience of a woman professor within the research university seems to be contingent upon the stage of gender equity development of her department. This appears to be true regardless of whether a woman is involved in women's issues or not. If proven to exist in future research, the stages of gender equity pose some interesting issues for women professors entering academia. The theory of gender equity stages suggests that women carry an extra burden unless they are in one of the rare departments with an open door. Most likely, opportunities will arise in departments in the other stages. Women professors must make keen observations during their interviews and ask pertinent questions of those they trust in their field. It is unrealistic, and would probably be counterproductive, for women professors to boycott departments with revolving doors or doors ajar. Perhaps prospective women professors can find clues to successful coping strategies by reading about the experiences and approaches of women interviewed in this research.

The research university is not an equitable place for women yet, but it is changing. It is time to irrigate the sacred grove. It is time to encourage acceptance of, and accommodation for, differences to grow. I am hopeful that in the decades to come women's voices, clear and strong, will ring throughout academia.

References

KANTER, R.M. (1977) *Men and Women of the Corporation*, p. 207, New York: Basic Books.

MACAULAY, J. (1980) 'The Revolving Door for Faculty Women in Higher Education', pp. 1–10, unpublished piece, University of Wisconsin, Madison.

MASON, P. (1970) *Patterns of Dominance*, pp. 54–65, London: Oxford University Press.

PEARSON, C.S., SHAVLIK, D.L. and TOUCHTON, J.G. (1989) *Educating the Majority: Women Challenge Tradition in Higher Education*, pp. 369–370, New York: Macmillan.

RIX, S.E. (Ed.) (1987) *The American Woman 1987–1988: A Report in Depth*, pp. 33–36, New York: W.W. Norton.

TREICHLER, P.A., KRAMARAE, C. and STAFFORD, B. (Eds) (1985) *For Alma Mater: Theory and Practice in Feminist Scholarship*, pp. 5–6, Urbana: University of Illinois Press.

WOLFF, K.H. (Ed. and trans.) (1950) *The Sociology of Georg Simmel*, pp. 402–408, Glencoe, IL: The Free Press.

Chapter 4

In Our (New) Right Minds: The Hidden Curriculum and the Academy[1]

Debbie Epstein

Introduction: The Auto/Biography of the Question[2]

I began my PhD in 1987. At that time I was a Teacher Adviser for Race Equality, working in majority white schools in a large industrial city, and my thesis was based on this work (Epstein, 1991a, 1993a). I was strongly committed to anti-racist struggle in schools and to feminism at both activist and theoretical levels. During the time which it took me to complete my thesis I came out as a lesbian and became active in lesbian and gay politics, moving rapidly from a position of keeping the closet doors well locked to proposing, as an out lesbian, the 1989 Labour Party Conference motion on lesbian and gay equality, and appearing on national television in the process. This shift was (like all such decisions) complicated and rested on issues such as the ages of my children as well as on my own confidence as a lesbian, but what really spurred my coming out process was the introduction of Section (then Clause) 28 of the Local Government Act 1988 and the massive Stop the Clause campaign that resulted from it.[3] In this I was not alone. Literally thousands of lesbians and gays came out of the closet through the Stop the Clause campaign. Indeed, Jackie Stacey (1991) suggests that Section 28 had the (unintended) effect of promoting homosexuality.

Because of my location within them, I was positioned as 'Other' in two of the major populist campaigns of the New Right in the mid-1980s: against anti-racism and against lesbian and gay activism. This involvement was more than theoretical. A colleague and I were the subjects of a minor moral panic about anti-racism in majority white schools in the late summer of 1987.[4] In the course of a flurry of attention to our project we were described in the national press as 'lunatics' guilty of 'indoctrinating young children' (see, for example, *Daily Mail*, 28 August 1987). As a lesbian mother I was one of those identified, in the words of Section 28, as having an unacceptable 'pretended family', while as a lesbian teacher I was amongst those seen as 'promoting homosexuality' and, thus, corrupting (potentially at least), childish innocence. In these ways, I could be seen as embodying two tied poles of what came to be identified as 'loony left' politics. Such struggles, around anti-racism, feminism, and lesbian and gay politics, have always influenced what has gone on in my classrooms both because of what I have brought into the class and because, as I shall be arguing in this chapter, the hidden curriculum of all teaching is in part constituted by events beyond the classroom.

It is a common sense of educational theory and politics that the hidden curriculum of schooling is at least as important as the taught curriculum. It is less frequent to find a discussion of the hidden curriculum in Higher Education (HE). Furthermore, the hidden curriculum in schools is commonly discussed in terms of the institutional arrangements and relationships in individual institutions. In this chapter, I will be arguing for an extended definition of the hidden curriculum, one which takes into account the popular common senses of the time as well as the micro-politics of particular institutions. I will also be turning my attention away from schools and towards HE, suggesting that the hidden curriculum is as important in this sector as it is in schools. I will suggest, furthermore, that the hidden curriculum for both schools and HE in the 1990s has been shaped, in part, by the experience of the years since 1979, not only in relation to government itself, but also in relation to the New Right more generally.

In my discussion, I will follow Richard Johnson (1991a: 88) in treating the New Right as a kind of 'new social movement' with its own theoretical frameworks, in much the same way as the women's movement, black politics, the lesbian and gay movement and eco/green politics have not only a politics of action but also theoretical frameworks. Indeed, as Johnson suggests, the theories of the New Right can be seen as having been formed in struggle with the ideas of the critical social movements of the period since the 1960s. However, unlike these latter social/political movements, the New Right has had, at its centre, much of the popular, tabloid press. These mass-distribution papers have not only represented the New Right, they have also been critical in its formation and in shaping it. They have had political alliances in the United Kingdom with the Right of the Conservative Party, but these alliances, as we can see in the attacks on Major's administration by such papers as *The Sun* during 1993 and 1994, have not always been solid and have assumed shifting forms. Nevertheless, I will show that the New Right, as represented both by the Thatcher, and now Major, administrations and by the right-wing tabloids, has had at its cutting edge, not only questions about the management of late capitalist economies, but also questions about 'race' and sexuality.

The Hidden Curriculum

The hidden curriculum is defined in the *Collins Dictionary of Sociology* as: 'A set of values, attitudes, knowledge frames, which are embodied in the organization and processes of schooling and which are implicitly conveyed to pupils' (Jary and Jary, 1991: 273). It has generally been taken to refer to the ethos or atmosphere of the school and what pupils/students learn from it. Kelly (1982: 8) describes it as:

> including those things which pupils learn at school because of the way in which the work of the school is planned and organized but which are not in themselves overtly included in the planning or even in the consciousness of those responsible for the school arrangements. Social roles, for example, are learnt, it is claimed, in this way, as are sex roles and attitudes to many other aspects of living. Implicit in any set of arrangements are the attitudes and values of those who create them, and these will be communicated to pupils in this accidental and perhaps even sinister way.

This description of the hidden curriculum is in line with sociological theories of 'socialization'. It assumes a one-way process in which those 'responsible for the school arrangements' socialize (teach) pupils into particular ways of relating and understanding the world. I have argued elsewhere (Epstein, 1995), that socialization theory is problematic in failing to see children as active makers of meaning rather than over-determined results of what is done to them.[5] If children are, indeed, active agents in producing themselves, then this would suggest that the hidden curriculum in schools is produced not just by those 'responsible for school arrangements' but also by those others participating in those arrangements, the pupils. What pupils learn within the school context, then, derives from each other and from the ways in which they make sense of their experiences in school as well as from the institutional arrangements and from adults.

This argument also applies, of course, to those young (and sometimes older) adults who come into universities as students. It is, in fact, commonly held that university students learn as much from each other as from the lecturers, but this is seldom described as constituting part of the hidden curriculum of universities. Indeed, the hidden curriculum is rarely mentioned in relation to HE and, as can be seen from the above definitions, is implicitly seen to apply specifically to schooling rather than to Higher Education.[6] However, it seems to me that the concept of the hidden curriculum can just as usefully be applied to the learning that goes on in institutions of Higher Education as it has been in the past to schools. University students do not learn only that which is specifically taught to them in the content of the curriculum (or syllabus). They also learn a whole range of other things ranging from exactly how to negotiate the academic hoops through which they have to jump to the value put on different kinds of knowledge by the institution (through, for example, the relative status of different departments). Furthermore, the ways they make sense of what they learn (whether it be by books, articles, lectures, classroom and bar discussions, their own observations or other aspects of university life), depends very largely on the ways in which they already make sense of the world.

Contemporary literary and critical theory assumes that intertextuality (that is, ways in which readers make sense of a particular text by reference to other texts) is crucial in understanding texts. We can think of the curriculum (taught and hidden) as a kind of text (in its extended sense) which students are required to read. In this context we can see that how students 'read' the curriculum (or what they learn) derives from a combination of what lecturers offer (and the way they offer it), the ethos produced by the institutional arrangements of particular classes and of the institution as a whole, and events and common senses from the wider society. In other words, the hidden curriculum can be seen as including the cultural referents available to students and staff alike.

If this is so, it means that any analysis of the hidden curriculum of universities must include a consideration of the world outside the university. The majority of students in Higher Education in Britain are aged between 18 and 25 years old. This means that the 1980s have been a key period in their growing up (an 18-year-old in 1994/5 would have been 4 or 5 years old in 1980). This means that for the majority of students, their cultural common senses would have been constructed almost entirely within or against the dominant discourses of the New Right. So powerfully have these discourses taken hold, that this is also true, to a greater or lesser extent, for those of us who grew up during the 1960s and 1970s. Indeed, this is the meaning of the initial 'my' in Richard Johnson's (1991a) chapter 'My New Right Education' in which he points out that the New Right has:

> Produced its own knowledges — in a strenuous, collective and accumulative work of analysis, polemic and prescription . . . It colonizes the academy. It invents intellectual traditions for itself. It recruits 'big names' (Locke, Hume, Adam Smith, etc), over their dead bodies so to speak.
>
> Second, it educates opinion more widely. It wins consent, makes yesterday's heresies desirable, puts pressure on dissenters like me. It campaigns in the press and other media. (pp. 87–88)

In the rest of this chapter, I will be looking at the specific aspects of New Right policy, theory and popular common senses which have made a difference to me in my teaching and to my students in the ways they have read what I have tried to teach.

The Entrepreneurial Right

A key issue for the New Right has been marketization of public services. I have discussed elsewhere (Epstein 1991a, 1993a,b) the influence of the philosophy of the market on social justice issues in schools. There are strong parallels between what happened in schools during the late 1980s (and is still developing) and what started to happen a little later in relation to HE. Like schools, the HE sector is increasingly being forced into and, in some cases, has willingly adopted the entrepreneurial spirit of the market. There has been an expansion in student numbers — but one which has been driven, on the part of HE institutions, by the need for money rather than a commitment to an expansion of educational opportunity, and, on the part of students, by the paucity of job vacancies for school leavers.[7] One consequence of the move toward entrepreneurialism, which most of us are experiencing, is a shift towards the stronger 'managerial' culture within HE (see Johnson, 1991a,b).

Beverley Skeggs (1994) has written about the impact that marketization, research selectivity exercises and inadequate resourcing have had on the teaching (and learning) of Women's Studies. The picture she draws is one which is easily recognizable, not only to Women's Studies lecturers, but to others in the academy and, perhaps especially, other feminist academics:

> Time for staff to do anything other than required teaching, administration and writing is very limited (especially if sleep is required). The teaching only institutions are still measured through the Research Selectivity Exercise but the format has been established in such a way that they cannot fail to loose (*sic*). The more teaching, the less research, the less funding, the more teaching. (pp. 9–10)

Teachers working under pressure are able to give less to students who, in what Skeggs calls the 'entitlement culture', demand more. Thus, marketization makes its impact on what goes on in the classroom through dissatisfaction, on the one hand, with conditions of work in the academy (and often simple lack of time for adequate preparation) and, on the other, with the struggle to be a student with virtually no money and the feeling that the lecturers are not giving enough to compensate one for living on and beyond the margins of poverty. Skeggs (1994: 6) comments on a student who said to her 'I can't afford to carry a 64 [as a mark for course work]' and suggests that this is illustrative of the instrumental way in which students are likely to regard their Higher Education in the current context.

Ken Jones (1989) points out that if education is subject to the push and pull of market forces rather than being about personal development and egalitarianism, then this changes the way in which we, as educators, think about what educators do. It also changes the contexts of education and the expectations and experiences of students. For example, in the training of both teachers and social workers there has been a distinct shift, which actually began in the mid-1980s and was reinforced, rather than introduced, by the Education Reform Act 1988 and other legislation pertaining to education. This shift has taken the form of a pressure to focus on the purely 'practical' in these vocational subjects without any thought about the theoretical frameworks involved in making practical judgements — a pressure which has come not only from government and other institutional sources, but which has also been taken on, to a large extent, by students. Within these vocational areas, there has, it seems, been an inexorable demand for the 'practical' (at the expense of the 'theoretical') both from students and from government. Within the academy, lecturers may struggle to provide a theoretical framework for the understanding of practical issues, but this is often resisted by students who barely have the time to think about anything but their immediate situation. One day on a Post-graduate Certificate in Education course on 'equal opportunities' cannot equip students with the tools to deconstruct the common senses about inequalities which surround them, or to develop strategies to combat them in the classroom in all their complexity.[8]

There are other contradictions produced by the extension of Higher Education. For example, when I was working at the University of Central England, we were very successful in attracting students to the sociology BA on which I taught. Many of these students were black (and often women) and/or working class and/or mature and/or single parents and had not reached university through the conventional routes. At the point of access to entry to HE, therefore, it could be said that the university was successful in promoting equal opportunities. However, once these students were in the university, we did little to support them and ensure their successful progress through our degree courses.[9] This was not primarily because of lack of good will or even because of a failure in individual commitment to equal opportunities amongst the majority of the academic staff, but because of the very pressure of numbers resulting from the market success of attracting and accepting these students.[10] To what extent can an extension of access to Higher Education be said to have improved equal opportunities if many of the students entering HE for the first time lack the tools which will enable them to succeed in gaining degrees and are not enabled to gain those tools? Indeed, as Skeggs's student who was unhappy with a mark of 64 might have pointed out, current graduate unemployment has led to a situation in which the desired (and necessary) degree class, even for those not intending to continue with graduate studies, is an upper second. There are consequences of this situation which arise for us as individual (and especially feminist) tutors. How can we survive and give the time we know is necessary to help our students achieve their degrees? How can we balance the demands (reasonable and unreasonable) that students and institution make on us, survive *and* promote equality? And how can we respond to the rising tide of individualism inside and outside the academy? Is it possible for us to develop a framework from within which we can do all these things rather than simply lurch from demand to demand and from crisis to crisis?

Thus, it is clear that the marketization of education and, more generally, discourses of market and entitlement constitute an important part of the hidden curriculum of HE. As Skeggs (1994: 7) points out in relation to Women's Studies:

> students enter . . . courses with beliefs in their entitlement to education and their entitlement to judge the provision (be it by feminist and/or consumerist criteria). They also speak a language of commodification. The investments they have made — both economic and personal —

generate a desperation for an education which will produce success. . . .
[T]he political conditions of the 1980s appear to have influenced the
educational responses of the 1990s students.

These political conditions are comprised not simply of marketization and
commodification but also of broader discourses surrounding the construction of
national identity.

Constructions of 'Us' And 'Them'

One of the projects of the New Right has been the construction of a British/
English national identity. The National Curriculum is, as Johnson (1991a: 70)
says, in part an attempt to produce a sense of national British/English identity
which:

> Implements years of campaigning around 'sociology' and 'social sci-
> ence', peace studies, sex education, religious instruction, anti-racist
> and multicultural education and around 'progressive education' and
> 'second-order subjects' more generally. It is the culmination of the
> Black Paper campaigns, many themes of which were revived in the
> formative period of 1985–7. Like these campaigns, the curriculum
> favours conventional subject categories to exclude what it disapproves
> of. It imposes its 'standards' negatively; it stops the rot.

For neo-conservatives within the New Right, anti-racism represents a threat
to national identity and traditional values, particularly in its incorporation of
'alien cultures'. For neo-liberals there is a denial of racism as a cause of
inequality. Their radical individualism indicates that the 'achievement' of black
people is a function of individual effort and virtue and they draw attention to
the success of some black businessmen[11] as an indication that the market is
open to all to enter in the same way. Similarly, for neo-conservatives 'deviation' from the norms of institutional heterosexuality (whether through lesbian,
gay or bi-sexuality, or through single parenthood), represents a danger to ideas
of 'family values' and, therefore, to national identity, while the breakup of
traditional nuclear families provides an economic problem for neo-liberals.

Consequently, both anti-racism and lesbian and gay activism have taken
their place in the pantheon of folk-devils evoked by the right-wing tabloid press
and have been incorporated into what Ball (1990: 31–42) has tellingly labelled
'discourses of derision'. As Ball comments:

> The social-subject of neo-conservatism is the loyal, law-abiding family
> man (or housewife/mother), holder of and believer in traditional values
> and sober virtues. Over and against this ideal citizen/parent is set
> an alternative subject: the carrier of alien values or alien culture, the

agitator/trade unionist, sexual deviant, or working, single-parent mother, permissive/liberal, and progressive teacher — in other words 'the enemy within', the traitor. (Ball, 1990: 40)

The position of teachers, whether in schools or universities, in relation to the 'discourses of derision' has been complex and contradictory. On the one hand, they are held to be the cause of many of the nation's ills, while on the other, they are themselves summoned to be 'upright citizens' in the way that Ball describes. Increasingly academics, especially those engaged in social sciences and humanities, have been subject to similar discourses of derision to those applied to school teachers from the publication of the *Black Papers* (Cox and Dyson, 1969; Cox and Boyson, 1977) onwards.

These discourses of derision were built up, in part, through major campaigns against initiatives to promote equality which centred around attacks on Labour-controlled Local Authorities, such as Brent, Haringey and ILEA, in the mid- to late-1980s. The particular foci of these attacks were usually anti-racist policy developments and attempts to develop 'positive images' of lesbians and gays (particularly in education), and the support offered by these Local Authorities to community development for ethnic minority groups and for lesbians and gays. Such attacks served to split off different minority groups from each other. On the one hand, there was an interpellation of white lesbians and gays, through their identifications with Englishness/Britishness, to racist popular discourses and of straight black people, through their identifications as family members and (often) Christians, to homophobic discourses. Contradictorily, these attacks served also to connect these two groups through the appellation of 'loony left'.

Associations between anti-racism, anti-heterosexism and the so-called 'loony left' were made in a number of places: in some right-wing books with a relatively small circulation (for example Palmer, 1986); in right-wing journals such as, for example, the *Salisbury Review*; in specialist weeklies like the TES (see, for example, 10 January 1986); in statements by (usually) Conservative politicians; and, extensively, in the popular press. These attacks peaked in the run up to the London local elections of 1986 and the General Election of 1987, and immediately after that election, and coalesced around two particular campaigns: that against the development of policy for 'positive images' of lesbians and gays in Haringey, and the establishment of the Development Programme for Race Equality (DPRE) in Brent. I will discuss the press coverage of positive images in Haringey and anti-racism in Haringey and Brent in some detail for three reasons. First, the coverage was very extensive. Barely a day went by during the period between autumn 1986 and spring 1988 without an article about either Brent or Haringey or both represented as the epitome of what it meant to be 'loony left'.[12] Second, the extensiveness and nature of this coverage meant that discourses employed in the popular media around the dangers of both anti-racism (and, by implication, black people) and lesbian and gay sexuality became well established as common sense and have, therefore, become part of the hidden curriculum of Higher Education in the 1990s. In particular, 'loony left' discourses have become transmuted into the now fashionable discourses of 'political correctness' which, it is popularly supposed, originated in the (American) academy and are the result (according to tabloid and broadsheet press alike) of the damaging effects of feminism, lesbian and gay activism and anti-racism.[13] Third, these events and the coverage of them can be seen as key moments in the construction of popular support for two major pieces of legislation affecting education: the Education Reform Act 1988 and Section 28 of the Local Government Act 1988.

Events in Haringey and Brent[14]

The moral panic around the impact of the 'loony left' on education began early in 1986.[15] Throughout this year and the next the tabloid press regularly published articles which ridiculed anti-racism with largely apocryphal stories about, for example, the banning of black bin bags and the introduction of 'Baa, baa, green sheep' into nurseries. These articles ran alongside a number of articles attacking Labour Local Authorities for their adoption of non-sexist, non-racist language as a result of feminist and anti-racist intervention — such changes being represented as self-evidently ludicrous.

The particular spark for the campaign in the popular press against Haringey was the alleged use of a photostory book called *Jenny Lives with Eric and Martin* about a day in the life of a young girl with her gay father and his male lover. Part of the context for the scandal was the disturbances on the Broadwater Farm Estate in October 1985 following the death of a black woman, Cynthia Jarrett, in a raid on her home, and media attacks on Bernie Grant (now an MP but then leader of Haringey Council) and on Haringey's 'loony left' anti-racist policies.[16] Thus, when the availability in Haringey of *Jenny Lives with Eric and Martin* became known, it made excellent copy with which to follow up press attacks on the Council. At this time, *Today* published the following editorial comment:

> There was a time, in the dawn of the permissive society, when enlightened liberals campaigned for an end to the laws which made homosexuality illegal — on the grounds that they were a vicious discrimination against a minority. But by a law of human nature, once this reasonable concession was granted, some homosexuals could not stop there. Next they wanted homosexuality to be regarded as socially quite acceptable. Then they wanted actually to crusade for it, by having it taught in schools and written about in books for children as something quite admirable. (2 September 1986)

What can be seen at work here are a number of discourses which characterized much of the coverage of lesbian and gay sexuality, particularly in relation to education. First, there is an implicit attribution of the perceived ills of society to the 'permissiveness' of the 1960s. The second sentence, with its appeal to 'human nature', establishes that, while limited decriminalization of homosexuality might have been 'a reasonable concession', there is an inherent unreasonableness in demands for equality. The implicit assumption of the third sentence is that homosexuality is self-evidently unacceptable, while the final sentence hints at the spectre of the corruption of the innocence of vulnerable children. Here we have, in a nutshell, virtually all the arguments which were used in favour of Section 28 in Parliamentary debates: children are vulnerable; education is inherently capable of being subversive and needs to be controlled; teachers (especially lesbian and gay teachers) are likely to subvert children; homosexuality is unacceptable and certainly should not be taught about in schools.

During the following month, the establishment of the DPRE in Brent hit the news. Under the banner headline 'RACE SPIES SHOCK', the *Mail on Sunday* ran a front page story which began:

> Race commissars in a Left-wing borough are recruiting 180 Thought Police to patrol schools for prejudice . . . Brent plans to put a race adviser in every school from January. They will be backed by project teams who will move in at the first hint of prejudice. The 180 advisers will have the power to interfere in every aspect of school life, from discipline to the curriculum. (19 October 1986)

Page 13 carried a further banner headline, 'COMMISSARS OF THE CLASSROOM', with the subheading '"Loony" war on racism may hit future of our children'. In a small inset piece we read: 'BY THE LEFT: Baa, baa black sheep has been branded a racist nursery rhyme by Haringey Council. Children must sing "green sheep" now'.

In this coverage we see a similar set of common sense assumptions: children are inherently vulnerable and their innocence may be corrupted by unacceptable versions of education; teachers (especially black and white anti-racist teachers) are likely to subvert children; education (and teachers) must, therefore, be controlled. In addition there is the use of language which suggests an enemy invasion ('race commissars') and draws on the language of George Orwell (1949) in *1984* ('Thought Police'). This idea was picked up by most of the rest of the press, an achievement for which the *Mail on Sunday* claimed credit the following week when, on page 13, it reproduced headlines from the *Evening Standard* ('Classroom spies like Nazi Era'), the *Daily Mail* ('This most evil force in Britain' and 'Today this is Brent. Tomorrow it could be Britain.') and the *Independent* ('Political board games'). In so doing, white and black anti-racists and, by implication, black people in general, were established as 'the enemy within' and a threat to society. In this construction of Englishness, these groups were definitely 'them' rather than 'us'.

On 20 October 1986, at a meeting of Haringey Council, Conservative

Councillors used almost identical language to denounce the positive images policies of the Labour-controlled council, equating this policy with fascism and communism (see Cooper, 1994: 114), while the leader of the Conservative group on the Council referred to the policy as containing 'an element of George Orwell's thought police' (cited in Cooper, 1994). Around the same time, Tottenham Conservative Party issued a press release about the establishment of Haringey's lesbian and gay unit, denouncing it as '. . . a bigger threat to family life than Adolf Hitler' (published in the *Hampstead and Highgate Gazette*). Here again we see the invocation of images of the foreign Other, the alien tyrant and the linking of anti-racism, anti-heterosexism and the loony left. This was, I believe, a key historical moment in the formation of the Education Reform Act, Section 28 of the Local Government Act and the more recent changes that we have seen in Higher Education and in the construction of popular support for these legislative moves. It was, perhaps, Margaret Thatcher who made the most explicit links between anti-racism, anti-heterosexism and the 'loony left' when, at the Conservative Party Conference in 1987, she said that:

> Children who need to be able to count and multiply are learning anti-racist mathematics — whatever that may be. Children who need to be able to express themselves in clear English are being taught political slogans. Children who need to be taught to respect traditional moral values are being taught that they have an inalienable right to be gay.

Here we have quite explicitly the notion that education (through the actions of teachers) is inherently subversive; that vulnerable children need to be protected against the dangers represented by anti-racism, politicized teachers and lesbians and gays; and that education needs to be controlled for the good of the country (and, implicitly, national identity). As so often in her speeches, the 'them' and the 'us' are clearly identified.

Anti-racism and Lesbian and Gay Activism in Conflict

While the popular media have tied anti-racism and lesbian and gay activism together through discourses of the loony left, they have nevertheless been tied in conflict. While, on the one hand, homophobic headlines were often mediated through racism (for example, by the placing of photographs of Bernie Grant looking aggressive next to articles about Haringey's lesbian and gay positive policies), on the other, racism was often mediated through homophobic attacks on Haringey's policies. In this context, Haringey was equated with Bernie Grant who bore the burden of representation as the dangerous black man. Furthermore, both racism and homophobia as expressed in the tabloid press share metaphors of invasion and swamping. In both we see certain reversals within which marginalized groups are attributed with the power to damage substantially the *status quo*.

Nevertheless, there has been an interpellation, particularly through appeals to (and from) black churches, of black people in the cause of homophobia. In Haringey the Parents' Rights Group, formed with the explicit purpose of opposing the Council's lesbian and gay positive images policies, drew its membership from a combination of members of Tottenham Conservative Association and black and white members of a number of different churches. There were also several moments during the period when the demands for scarce resources for ethnic minority groups and lesbian and gay groups, not only in Haringey but also in other parts of the country such as ILEA and Manchester, came into direct conflict with each other and the 'Rainbow Alliance'[17] turned into a 'Rainbow Competition'. Another problem for any kind of 'Rainbow Alliance' was that among white liberals there are discourses of multiculturalism which require a kind of relativism which obviates any critique of those perceived as religious or 'community' leaders (see Sahgal and Yuval-Davies, 1992; Bard, 1992/3). Furthermore, just as there was (and is) homophobia and heterosexism within the black (as well as the white) straight community, so too is there racism amongst white lesbians and gays (as well as straights). Thus, we get a situation where, although they are tied, anti-racism and lesbian and gay activism are tied in conflict. This is a pattern which has been repeated in 1994 in the 'scandal' surrounding the decision by Jane Brown, the head of Kingsmead School in Hackney, to refuse subsidized tickets to the ballet of *Romeo and Juliet*.[18]

Contexts for the Academy

All this provides the context within which we, as feminist academics, have to work. This makes a difference to what we can actually achieve within our institutions. The context is very powerful. It provides strongly held 'common senses', not only for readers of *The Sun* and other tabloid papers, but also for our students, our colleagues and even ourselves. For example, a couple of years ago, I was interviewed as a lesbian mother by the *Birmingham Evening Mail* and was shocked when I read the article to realize that they had quoted me, quite accurately, as saying that my children had turned out to be 'normal', thus implicitly accepting that being a lesbian was, in some way, 'abnormal'. Although I have not made that same mistake again, this incident was evidence to me that, where certain views/discourses/ideologies have become naturalized, it is almost impossible not to fall back on them in moments of pressure. Thus, if we are put on the defensive in our teaching as feminist lecturers, then we are likely to make similar slips — and, indeed, being on the defensive is in itself a form of marginalization.

Furthermore, when the cultural referents used to make sense of the curriculum are those popular common senses which I have described above, then the readings of our teaching are often not what we intend or would prefer. For example, three years ago I was responsible for three lectures on the concept of patriarchy in a first-year undergraduate course on 'Sociological Concepts'. I was shocked to discover that a group of students (albeit a small group) had complained that having lectures on patriarchy from a lesbian meant, inevitably, that they were 'unbalanced'. Their complaints did not take the form of any particular criticism of the actual content or delivery of my lectures or of the fairness of my marking. The fact that I was an out lesbian was enough. These students had clearly not heard what I thought I had delivered — that is, a carefully constructed account of different theories of patriarchy and of the strengths and weaknesses of each of them. Rather, they had 'heard' or 'read' me as a stereotypical 'man-hating lesbian' who was out to 'promote homo-sexuality' rather than teach them a small part of feminist theory. Similarly, there are a few students among my current group of Women's Studies MA students (including at least one of the lesbians) who have suggested that the problematization of heterosexuality as an institution undertaken as part of the Feminist Theory course is uncomfortable for, and therefore unfair to, the heterosexual students.[19] There is also a strong take-up of those contemporary discourses of 'political correctness' which have replaced the 'loony left' discourses of the 1980s. Many students want to distance themselves from being 'PC' or will express some embarrassment if and when they express an opinion which might be interpreted as being PC. Many students have accepted as common sense, the notion that political correctness is a substantial problem, an acceptance also seen in and reinforced by liberal broadsheets such as *The Guardian* and *The Independent*.[20] They are also inclined to make equivalences between actions and events which are not equivalent. Thus, in a recent session on sexual violence with my Women's Studies MA students, one group seriously discussed the possibility that women might 'rape' men and, when I asked for an explanation, one of them suggested that a relationship between a 30-year-old woman and an 18-year-old man was abusive and could be seen as rape. While accepting that abuse of children by women does occur, the actual example given seemed to me to be bizarre and in line with the kind of equivalences made in attacks on feminism, on anti-racism and on lesbian and gay activism.

Conclusion

Much of this chapter has been concerned with exploring the construction, particularly in relation to education, of discourses of the market and of the loony left/political correctness mediated through attacks on anti-racism, on lesbian and gay activism and on feminism. I believe that the ground has shifted so far towards the acceptance of these discourses as common sense that it is sometimes difficult even to be aware of how far we ourselves have moved. It shocks me when, in all seriousness, I find myself counting how many refereed papers I have had accepted in the last six months and wondering if this will be enough to help me keep my (fixed-term contract) job. Sometimes I find myself believing that the hidden curriculum of the market and onslaught of the backlash against so-called 'political correctness' is overwhelming. But then I am reminded of the letter that one of my male ex-students wrote to me when I left the University of Central England. This student was one of two men who had walked out of my class when I had called attention to the fact that fifteen minutes had passed since any of the women (who were in a majority in the class) had spoken. He wrote that:

> your way of teaching has illuminated not only academic aspects of life, but also aspects of my own and other people's lives in reality. This is indeed a rare thing for students to learn and to be able to apply what they learn. (Sidhu, 1994)

When I feel at my most depressed, I pull out that letter to remind myself that feminist pedagogy and theory can (sometimes anyway) reach the parts that other academics do not!

Notes

1 This chapter has been developed from a paper given to the Network for Equal Opportunities in Higher Education at the University of Wolverhampton in 1993. I would like to thank Mary Kehily for the help she gave me in working on that version of the paper.
2 I take this phrase from a session on auto/biography as method taught to my Women's Studies and Education MA students in December 1994 by Anne Turvey.
3 Section 28 of the Local Government Act 1988 prohibited Local Authorities from intentionally promoting homosexuality or, within maintained schools, teaching about homosexuality as an acceptable 'pretended family' relationship.
4 See Epstein (1991a, 1993a) for further details of this.
5 See also Walkerdine (1981) and Davies (1989, 1993) on this point.
6 I take the word 'schooling' in the context of this definition to refer to primary and secondary schooling. It would be unusual, in a British produced dictionary, for universities to be subsumed within the category 'school' (although North Americans talk about going to 'school' when a British person would use the word 'university').
7 With the loss of money related to student numbers, particularly in the humanities and arts, being given to universities that expansion is now being put into reverse. Expansion of full-time HE will, of course, also be limited by the situation in relation to grants: the freezing of grants, followed by a further 10 per cent reduction over each of the following three years, and those measures which prohibit students from claiming benefits of all kinds, from unemployment benefit or income support during vacations, to free prescription, to housing benefit.
8 See Epstein, 1993a, ch 1 for further discussion of this point. For a discussion of the demand for 'tips for teachers' in In-Service Education of Teachers, see Epstein, 1991a,b.
9 Indeed, attention was drawn by our external examiner to the large proportion of black, working-class women amongst those who failed the degree or had to resit part of it.

10 However there were institutional failures, illustrated in the Faculty's refusal to allow one of the black secretaries, who was doing the sociology degree part-time, to have leave to study or time to attend courses!

11 I use the suffix 'men' deliberately here, although I recognize that there are (a small number) of businesswomen too. However, neo-liberals invariably talk about and interpellate 'men'.

12 Davina Cooper (1994: 128) comments that, 'during this period well over 100 items appeared in the press [about Haringey's positive images policy] and more than 20 television and radio programmes were devoted to the issue'.

13 See Epstein (forthcoming) and Epstein and Johnson (forthcoming) for more detailed discussions of political correctness in relation to sexuality and education.

14 For a detailed discussion around the events in Haringey, see Cooper, 1989, 1994. For a full discussion of the history of attacks on the DPRE in Brent, see Richardson, 1992.

15 When I did a media search for my PhD, the earliest use of the term 'loony left' which I could find was in the TES on 10 January 1986. This particular issue devoted several pages to exploring the alleged 'domination' of the NUT (especially in London) by the hard left and included a full page article by Geoffrey Partington in which he discusses the origins of the 'loony left', which he identifies as having emanated from Birmingham University's Centre for Contemporary Cultural Studies. As a PhD student in what had been the Centre, but was now the Department of Cultural Studies, I was delighted with this discovery!

16 See National Council for Civil Liberties (now Liberty) (1986, 1988) for a full discussion of events at Broadwater Farm.

17 The term 'Rainbow Alliance' became popular in the American context during Jesse Jackson's campaign to be nominated as Democratic candidate for the Presidency. It was used to indicate an alliance of different groups all of whom suffered some form of discrimination, for example, African-Americans and other People of Color, women, lesbians and gays, disabled people.

18 See Epstein (forthcoming) and Epstein and Johnson (forthcoming 1996).

19 Although this is the view of only a small group of students, I think it is significant that it exists at all within a Women's Studies MA course.

20 For example, *The Guardian* on 21 December 1994 carried, as its 'cover story' for the tabloid section, the latest in a number of articles that it has run about the damage done to men by universities' sexual harassment policies.

References

BALL, S.J. (1990) *Politics and Policy Making in Education. Explorations in Policy Sociology*, London: Routledge.

BARD, J. (1992/3) 'The Priests Have It', *Women Against Fundamentalism Journal*, **4**, Winter, 12.

COOPER, D. (1989) 'Positive Images in Haringey: A Struggle for Identity', in JONES, C. and MAHONY, P. (Eds) *Learning Our Lines: Sexuality and Social Control in Education*, pp. 46–79, London: Women's Press.

COOPER, D. (1994) *Sexing the City: Lesbian and Gay Politics Within the Activist State*, London: Rivers Oram Press.

Cox, C.B. and Boyson, R. (Eds) (1977) *Black Paper 1977*, London: Temple Smith.

Cox, C.B. and Dyson, A.E. (Eds) (1969) *Fight for Education: A Black Paper*, London: The Critical Quarterly Society.

Davies, B. (1989) *Frogs and Snails and Feminist Tales*, St Leonards, NSW: Allen and Unwin.

Davies, B. (1993) *Shards of Glass: Reading and Writing Beyond Gendered Identities*, St Leonards, NSW: Allen and Unwin.

Epstein, D. (1991a) *An Examination of Anti-racist Pedagogy, INSET and School Change in the Context of Local and National Politics*, unpublished PhD thesis, University of Birmingham.

Epstein, D. (1991b) 'Inservice Fairy Tales? The Role and Limitations of Antiracist Inset', *Multicultural Teaching*, **9**, 3, 36–39.

Epstein, D. (1993a) *Changing Classroom Cultures: anti-racism, politics and schools*, Stoke-on-Trent: Trentham Books.

Epstein, D. (1993b) 'Defining Accountability in Education', *British Educational Research Journal*, **19**, 3, 243–257.

Epstein, D. (1995, in press) ' "Girls Don't Do Bricks." Gender and Sexuality in Primary Classrooms', in Siraj-Blatchford, I. and Siraj-Blatchford, J. (Eds) *Educating the Whole Child: Cross Curricular Skills, Themes and Dimensions*, Buckingham: Open University Press.

Epstein, D. (forthcoming) 'Corrective Cultures: Jane Brown, *Romeo and Juliet* and the press', submitted for journal publication.

Epstein, D. and Johnson, R. (forthcoming) *Schooling Sexualities: Lesbian and Gay Oppression, Identities and Education*, Buckingham: Open University Press.

Jary, D. and Jary, J. (1991) *Collins Dictionary of Sociology*, Glasgow: HarperCollins.

Johnson, R. (1991a) 'My New Right Education', in Cultural Studies Birmingham, *Education Limited: Schooling and Training and the New Right Since 1979*, pp. 87–113, London: Unwin Hyman.

Johnson, R. (1991b) 'A New Road to Serfdom? A Critical History of the 1988 Act', in Cultural Studies Birmingham, *Education Limited: Schooling and Training and the New Right Since 1979*, pp. 31–86, London: Unwin Hyman.

Jones, K. (1989) *Right Turn: The Conservative Revolution in Education*, London: Hutchinson Radius.

Kelly, A.V. (1982) *The Curriculum: Theory and Practice*, 2nd edition, London: Harper & Row.

National Council for Civil Liberties (1986) *The Broadwater Farm Inquiry*, report of an Inquiry chaired by A. Gifford, QC, London: NCCL.

National Council for Civil Liberties (1988) *Broadwater Farm Revisited*, Second report of Inquiry, London: NCCL.

Orwell, G. (1949) *1984*, London: Secker and Warburg.

Palmer, F. (Ed.) (1986) *Anti-Racism — an Assault on Education and Value*, London: Sherwood Press.

Richardson, R. (1992) 'Race Policies and Programmes Under Attack: Two Case Studies for the 1990s', in Gill, D., Mayor, B. and Blair, M. (Eds) *Racism and Education: Structures and Strategies*, pp. 134–150, London: Sage/Open University Press.

Sahgal, G. and Yuval-Davis, N. (Eds) (1992) *Refusing Holy Orders*, London: Virago.

Sidhu, K. (1994) Personal communication.

SKEGGS, B. (1994) 'Women's Studies in Britain in the 1990s: Entitlement Cultures and Institutional Constraints', paper given at the Women's Studies Network (UK) Association Conference, University of Portsmouth, 8–10 July.

STACEY, J. (1991) 'Promoting Normality: Section 28 and the Regulation of Normality', in FRANKLIN, S., LURY, C. and STACEY, J. (Eds) *Off-Centre: Feminism and Cultural Studies*, pp. 284–304, London: HarperCollins Academic.

THATCHER, M. (1987) Speech to Conservative Party Conference.

WALKERDINE, V. (1981) 'Sex, power and pedagogy', *Screen Education*, **38**, 14–24.

Chapter 5

Ivory Towers: Life in the Mind

Mary Evans

In Jane Austen's *Persuasion* Anne Elliot, the central character, remarks that 'Men have had every advantage of us in telling their own story. Education has been theirs in so much higher a degree; the pen has been in their hands. I will not allow books to prove anything' (Austen, 1965). The quotation might well, and usefully, be placed above the entry to every university, to remind the incoming students, both female and male, that what they are about to study is not 'natural' knowledge, but constructed knowledge. Moreover, because what is studied in universities has been constructed by long years of male domination of academic life, the very assumptions of the academy — its claims to universal and generally applicable knowledge — have to be challenged.

So much for the opening attack on the patriarchal academy. Readers are no doubt familiar with the statistical material about women and men in British universities: women and men are almost numerically equal as consumers of higher education and women make some contribution as relative junior teachers. But a tiny percentage of women occupy the heights (if that is the correct expression) of the profession: about 4 per cent of professors are women and there are very few women Vice Chancellors or Registrars (Aziz, 1990). Control, rather than consumption, is in the hands of men. The implications of this monopoly for the organizational and institutional culture of universities has been explored elsewhere, what concerns me here is the way in which the sexual politics of the academics affect the curriculum and the way in which students are taught about their subjects, particularly in the social sciences and the humanities (Evans, 1994). Although my own work has crossed boundaries between the social sciences and the humanities, I have never worked on, or in, the natural sciences and thus can say little about science or technology. I am especially interested in the person, and the gender of the person, at the heart of debates in the social sciences and the humanities. This vague person, essential to the human sciences, has a singularly ill-defined presence, and when that presence is defined, the person is generally assumed to be male. 'People in all societies have wives', began one study of the Mediterranean by a man who is now a distinguished scholar of Oxford University.

But before this argument gallops off in the direction of an all-out attack on the 'male' academy, some powerful and important qualifications have to be made. The argument (which could have stood on its own in the early 1970s) has to be very firmly contextualized within changing assumptions about the production of knowledge. Two qualifications are of particular importance: the first is the growing translation of the universities in the United Kingdom from élitist institutions offering an education (and a ticket to social privilege) to a very small section of the population, into teaching machines for a much larger part of the 18- to 21-year-old age group. It is not, of course, that having a degree does not still carry very significant importance in the job market or that Oxbridge, as a nursery for the social and political élite, has declined in importance, but that the *mere* acquisition of a first degree no longer carries the immediate cachet and promise of occupational privilege as it did 30 years ago. What has happened during the last decade in Britain is that higher degrees and professional training have become increasingly significant and crucial to job-market prospects. As was (and is) the case in the United States of America, it is now in graduate school that students acquire the specific skills which will enable them to move into well-rewarded professional and managerial positions. The relationship of the first degree to the occupational structure has been challenged.

That this change has occurred has in part been a result of policy decisions by the British government to adopt a policy of mass education. By 'mass' in this context what is meant is a much larger proportion of the middle class, and a very much larger proportion of middle-class women. The working class (defined here as the children from homes in which the parents are in low-skill, low-paid occupations) remains under-represented, as do children from ethnic minorities. To put this shift simply: British universities now have more middle-class women in them as students, but not as academics or senior administrators.

This new 'teaching machine' university, in which in some institutions the old supermarket slogan of 'pack them in and pile them high' seems to have been adopted as the institutional motto, is an essential part of *any* discussion of women and higher education (Spivak, 1993). There is simply no point in writing of universities, and 'male' domination of them, without making it clear that what is happening now is a particular kind of domination, no longer based simply on the ascriptive status of universities but located within a context in which 'the market' (as defined by a right-wing government) has come to play a major part in academic thinking. Attracting students, and most of all high fee-paying overseas students, has become an ever-present gleam in the eyes of all Vice-Chancellors. In this sense, of course, the market has not recognized gender differences: as in other areas in which the market rules, the biological sex of the consumer has no importance. Equally, as in the case of mature women students, universities can recognize a lucrative, *gendered* market but then ignore the particular, gendered needs of that group (Edwards, 1993).

Thus it is that universities in Britain during the past 15 years have come to appear more inclined to accept women as students. The old barriers of discrimination against women as students have largely disappeared: in a degree factory it no longer matters who the student is. Yet, as the sex ratio of students (particularly undergraduate students) has changed, so little has changed in terms, as yet, of the organization and content of the curriculum. But — and this brings me to the second important qualification that I would make about contemporary British (and to a certain extent western) Higher Education — there are many indications that the curriculum does not remain unchallenged. To say now that British (or North American) universities *only* teach the history, or literature, or philosophy of 'Dead White Males' (DWMs), is a glaring inaccuracy and a distortion of the changes which have occurred in all western societies in the past decade. The DWMs are undeniably still there (and History and Philosophy remain, in Britain at least, largely dominated by male concerns and interests) but in all subjects, and on all levels, there has been a concerted challenge to the orthodoxies of the past. In very large part this challenge has come from feminist academics, working within the general framework of Women's Studies, but there have also been massively influential interventions from women and men working outside western assumptions. Of these interventions Edward Said's *Culture and Imperialism* and Audré Lorde's various essays are instances of a rich and vital challenge to western patriarchy (Lorde, 1984; Said, 1994). What both these individuals express is the inter-connectedness of cultures; as Gyan Prakash has argued:

> It is difficult to overlook the fact that . . . third world voices . . . speak within and to discourses familiar to the 'West' . . . The Third World, far from being confined to its assigned space, has penetrated the inner sanctum of the 'First World' in the process of being 'Third Worlded' — arousing, inciting, and affiliating with the subordinated others in the First World . . . to connect with minority voices. (Prakash, in Bhabba, 1994, p. 247)

These comments are made about the impossibility of isolating cultures by defining them as 'First' or 'Third' world. As Prakash points out, anti-colonialism itself was initially formed by fear and suspicion of the colonized 'other'.

Yet, just as many radical male academics have had little trouble in identifying with post (and anti-) colonialism, it is often more difficult for them to see that the very inter-connections which they accept with relative ease between colonizers and colonized also exist between men and women, and between masculinity and femininity. It is not, as Said and others recognize, that the relationship between colonizers and colonized is simply one of domination. The colonizers were more powerful, often brutal and almost always exploitative, but this very catalogue of inhumanity was structured by its own internal fears and weaknesses. Between women and men, femininity and masculinity, there exists, I would argue, a similar kind of dynamic and one which has informed relations within academic life quite as much as in other areas of social and political life.

In this dynamic, with so many similarities with other forms of cultural domination, certain key characteristics of the colonized are identified by the colonizers as negative and unacceptable. It is thus that I arrive at the main theme of the paper: that the western academy, in order to be effective and to maintain its authority within western society, has defined a certain way of studying the world and has proscribed others. The acceptable way has included a concentration on the public world, a search for universal explanations and universal patterns of human behaviour and a rigorous separation between 'thought' and 'feeling'. Hence, the academic stress on the importance of maintaining distinctions between the subjective and the objective. Marginalizing the world of the emotions, and emotional work (as Arlie Hochschild has described it) has the implicit effect of marginalizing women (Hochschild, 1989). As in relations between the colonizers and the colonized, it has not necessarily been the case that all the colonized have been excluded from membership of the exclusive club of the colonizers; membership does not always depend simply on given physical characteristics but can be earned by the colonizer adopting the habits and the mind set of the colonizers. The familiar figure who appears at this point is 'Uncle Tom'; the loathed traitor to his race who became a symbol for all those members of all subject peoples who are prepared to take on the behaviour of the rulers. That generation of British male writers who challenged British imperialism (for example Leonard Woolf, George Orwell and E.M. Forster) all recognized the over-enthusiastic servants of the Empire, and recognized in themselves their own suspicions and prejudices about the appropriate boundaries between races and cultures. Orwell's *Burmese Days* is replete with examples of his dislike of Burmese officials and his resignation from Imperial service was clearly related to his own dissatisfaction with his role as a policeman and as a representative of a particular culture (Orwell, 1934). In the same way, feminist academics have fought to refuse the possibility of the academy as masculine imperialism. The example of Orwell serves to illustrate particularly clearly that process of cultural assimilation and the imperialism of western culture which Fanon summed up so vividly in the title of his book, *Black Skin, White Masks* (Fanon, 1986). What we have to ask is the extent to which women in the academy have learnt the ways of the more powerful to the detriment of the less powerful. Thus, we might argue that women have internalized, both to their own disadvantage and ultimately to the disadvantage of understanding *per se*, certain key assumptions of male academics.

High on the list of assumptions made about the social world by male academics is that the social world is divided into the public and the private. The social world is not, therefore, according to this tenet, social in the fullest, inclusive sense. The worlds of the household and the home, despite their central importance in the legitimation of the bourgeois project, are marginalized by this distinction and with them, of course, women and children. Feminists have done much to open the doors on the 'private' world of the family and the household, but the integration of this understanding and knowledge into theories about the social structure remains to be made. We *know*, and it has now been demonstrated more times than feminists have had hot dinners cooked for them, that women's domestic responsibilities (an agenda which includes the care of the aged and infirm as much as of children and the household), effectively inhibits many women's access to and performance within the public world, but we do little with this information in any theoretical sense. Nor do we emphasize that even when women do not have domestic responsibilities they are frequently subjects of discrimination. (We also do little with the information in any political sense, but that is another issue and another question.) Political theorists such as Carol Pateman are beginning to de-construct the un-gendered social and political contract of liberal democratic theory, but this project remains in its theoretical infancy, largely because of the refusal of male political theorists to begin to think through the issue of gender in political terms (Pateman, 1988).

In challenging the universalistic assumptions of liberal democratic theory, Carol Pateman has taken on — as Carol Gilligan has done in the case of morality — a western tradition which claims that one of its greatest strengths is its uniformity and its universalism. (Gilligan, 1982). Indeed, in this claim western traditions have much to recommend them: part of the Enlightenment project was to give to all male citizens equal treatment before the law and within civil society (Lorch, 1990; Sapiro, 1992). Given its random authoritarianism and autocracy the *Ancien Régime*, I would argue (despite Foucault's attack on the notion of social change as progress), had little to recommend it (Foucault, 1971). Yet just as Leonard Woolf, George Orwell *et al.* had mixed feelings about the Imperial justice which they were dispensing, so I have mixed feelings about the western traditions of universality and uniformity which I now question (Orwell, 1934; Woolf, 1928). As Carol Gilligan has so rightly pointed out, a morality without subjective understanding has little human credence. As feminist critics of western law are now beginning to argue, 'equality' before the law is often an impossibly difficult goal (Nussbawm, 1993).

It is within this tangled web of assumptions and implicit values that I exist as an academic. As mentioned above, the academic world which I entered as a student in 1964, and as a lecturer in 1971, has changed. It is tempting to say here that it has changed simply for the worse (more students, more pressures and so on) but I do not think that the changes have been uniformly negative. There *are* more students and fewer resources, but at the same time the curriculum has broadened and has become less rigid in its subject demarcations. Against this, I would set the shifts in university management which have produced a more centralized management structure and a largely unresisted movement towards crude measurements of academic success. (Let me say in parentheses here that in my view academics have barely fought their case at all against government intervention. In contrast to the school-teachers and the doctors, university teachers have voiced little public resistance to the changes imposed upon universities from 1979 onwards.) In this changing world (in which the pressure to publish sits like an ever increasing burden on the shoulders of all academics) women have an even more complex set of problems to face: the academy is no longer 'male' in the simple, chauvinistic sense of the period 1945 to the mid-1970s, it is now an institution of *managerial* masculinity, rather than masculinity *per se*. A different kind of creature inhabits this world from those of British Campus novels of pre-1970; a world in which a new language of 'line management' and increased institutional surveillance (teaching quality audits, for example) have replaced informal and *ad hoc* arrangements.

In what I will describe as the 'old' university (not to be confused with the 'old' non-polytechnic university), it was simply taken for granted that students and academics were male. Certainly there were women's colleges (largely, though not exclusively, at Oxbridge) but in the main the culture, and the inhabitants, of Higher Education were masculine (Leonardi, 1989). The impact of this pattern was that it was inevitable that the world outside the university was seen in traditional terms of male interests and male careers: what universities were for was training middle-class men for the professions. The function of the universities was not in any doubt, nor was the fit of this function with its population. When the universities began to question their function (as they did in the liberalization of the curriculum and internal organization in the 1960s) they became more sympathetic places to many women. At the same time, resistance to liberalization was increasingly organized in Thatcherite, managerialist terms. Thus I would argue that, at least in part, the enthusiasm with which some universities adopted 'market models' of organization was derived from a sense of the erosion of the traditional 'toughness' of academic culture. As degrees were reorganized and new subjects, such as Cultural Studies, Women's Studies and Black Studies, began to appear, so those opposed to these intellectual shifts moved their ground from intellectual opposition (which was very often impossible given the nature of the emergent consensus) to political and institutional opposition. Liberalization, feared because it seemed to threaten the absolute authority of given knowledge, was therefore fought not in the journals or in the classrooms but in the committee rooms and the funding councils. One of the inevitable consequences of this — given the under-representation of women in power structures — is that women have often been left free to choose what they teach, but with fewer resources to do so.

Within this culture it is often hard for women to find a place, and to find a place in which to claim that 'voice' about which so many feminists have written. In a sense the 'old chauvinism' was an easier enemy to deal with than the new managerialism, and the tactics employed by women of earlier generations were remarkably similar in their attempts at accommodation. One pattern was that of becoming a 'chap' just like any other 'chap'; the divorce of some women academics from femininity was total and chosen by them as a means of distancing themselves from the negative implications of the secondary status of women. But as a strategy, it was often self-defeating, in that women were labelled as 'blue-stockings', defined as 'gradgrinds' and somehow distant from the 'real' intellectual originality and inspiration of their male peers. The history of women in the academy is replete with examples of women who have been marginalized and/or discriminated against not because of their academic competence but because of their perceived failings as women. In this, the audience was always male, and it was always men — as in the infamous case of James Watson's comments on Rosalind Franklin — who had the institutional power and intellectual credence to make the judgements which made or, more often, marred women's careers (Sayre, 1975). Another possibility with the 'old chauvinism' was simply separation, and the Oxbridge women's colleges attest to that particular response to male domination. It is ironic that many women's colleges now admit men, on the grounds that 'discrimination' has disappeared.

In all these strategies, the problem that academic women are addressing is that of how to achieve (and assess the value of) integration into academic communities. Universities, unlike the majority of schools, are distinct and separate communities. They rightly belong not to a particular community, but to a wider world. But in this lie two problems for women academics, and indeed for any person who wishes to live a life with less traditionally defined distinctions between public and private, home and work. The first is that for the majority of women, the reference group of their experience is local and is community based. The world is not, even in the late-twentieth century, women's oyster and it remains organized around local institutions. The second problem is that, whilst the empirical experience of the world for most women remains local, the interpretation of the world (and indeed any part of it) remains part of the wider, traditionally male world of abstract thought and theory. The early years of Second Wave feminism saw much work on the divisions between theory and the academy and activism and experience; this work remains as relevant today because, although feminist theory has become immensely more sophisticated than in the late 1960s, women's experiences have remained remarkably similar. It is still important, therefore, to state that 'care' (whether for children or adults) remains largely the responsibility of women, that women still earn about three-quarters of the pay of men and that women are concentrated in the low-paid, low-skill jobs in the service sector which have made up the new manual occupations of the consumer society.

The re-iteration of these facts of life remains, I would argue, important in the intellectual climate of postmodernism, in which it is sometimes supposed that no social structure exists, and the construction of a social identity depends upon choice and personal decision. Clearly, codes of dress, behaviour and morality have diversified and on the streets of the cities and towns where most women now live there is to be seen a wide range of possible urban identities. But alongside this diversity remains a high degree of remarkable similarity and it is representing and adequately theorizing this range of difference and similarity which remains a central problem for feminist academics. So giving voice to this diversity, and similarity, is one task for feminist academics, doing it in a way which does not emphasize difference at the expense of similarity seems to me to be quite as important. But — and it is a very important but — the question then arises of *how* to theorize, of *how* to analyse description and experience in a way which does not de-vitalize and de-racinate the material (Stanley, 1990). These are not new questions for feminism, but they do remain important ones, and especially so as the pressures on women in the academy to become appropriate members of the 'teaching machine' increase. This machine demands high research productivity (which in effect means the production of a great many publications) and it accords little status to excellence in teaching or in academic innovation of any kind.

As women are still only a minority of the total number of academics, it is impossible to assess adequately the impact of women as a group in the academy. Indeed, despite some successful networks (particularly around Women's Studies) women do not act as a group within the academy. But all of us, whatever our subject, are part of a world which validates the 'heroic imperative' quite as much as any other profession. What I mean by this idea is the compulsion which our society constructs for individuals to lead and to be in all respects outstanding. This 'heroic imperative' was rightly identified in psychoanalysis when Freud noted (and no doubt had his own experience to draw on) that any male child adored by his mother could do no wrong (Freud, 1905). A short step, therefore, in many cases from being the adored son to being the 'outstanding student' with 'original' ideas. As reports on the performance of female and male students at Oxbridge points out, men do better in final degree examinations because they have no difficulty in expressing their own opinions and in daring to put forward unusual ideas. Socialized into a heroic mode, they find that a flamboyant performance in final examinations comes as naturally as any other kind of theatre might allow. For women, on the other hand, trained in order and neatness, in the careful consideration of the views of others, advancing novel ideas is far more strange and far more antithetical to an entire process of socialization (Spurling, 1990).

Hence, women in the academy face, endlessly, the double bind of enforced originality (the 'hero' of the academic world) and the expectations of appropriate womanhood. The male/doctor and female/nurse is now well-known in all literature on career choice, but the mere increase in the number of women who now train as doctors should not be allowed to lead us to suppose that women have crossed the 'abstract knowledge' barrier in medicine. Merely, in fact, that as medicine becomes more specialized (as does the academy) the heights of what is supposed to be abstract speculation and theorization change and shift. To employ a male metaphor: the goal posts shift. Thus, to assume that improving (that is, increasing) the number of women who are academics will necessarily shift the nature and the process of the construction of knowledge is simply naïve: it will give, fairly, more women jobs in the academy, but it will not in itself do anything to change our expectations about what constitutes 'knowledge'. As ever, problems remain here between the value of increasing the number of women in any context (the critical mass theory) and the implicit essentialism of the idea.

For the discourse on knowledge to shift, I would argue that feminists have to confront the issue which I have defined above as 'the heroic imperative'. To do this, feminists have to challenge the nature of originality and innovation. This is not to deny the possibility of shifts in knowledge, but to articulate the part which collective changes play in formulating radical advances. The whole process of the academic career structure (as any other) pushes towards the individual: once within the structure it is extremely difficult to refuse to participate in that system and the temptation (in the sense of promotion and institutional gain) to do so is considerable. But there may be ways in which these pressures on the individual can be reconciled with the de-construction of the hero model. First of all, there is now a wealth of material on which feminists can draw to demonstrate that the very processes of both the natural sciences and the social science are intensely social as much as intellectual. Sandra Harding, Donna Haraway and Hilary Rose are amongst those who have built upon a sceptical consideration of the history of science (the work, for example, of Thomas Kuhn) to demonstrate that the boundaries in science between 'pure' knowledge and social needs are sometimes not all that clear (Kuhn, 1962; Harding, 1986; Haraway, 1988; Rose, 1994). Indeed, as Hilary Rose has recently argued, not only are the boundaries not clear, it is actually often the case that it is social (and material) need which dominates the production of knowledge (Rose, 1994).

The question which critical and sceptical writers on science have long asked, therefore, is one which might well be replicated elsewhere: what is this system of knowledge actually for? What, indeed, are the desired end results of the process which creates heroes out of theoretical innovators but assigns a serf-like status to those who do not 'innovate' in the same way? It is not necessarily anti-theoretical to question the nature of theory; asking questions about what, and who, constitutes theory may well be more theoretical than the random interventions of apparent liberality. In a cartoon of the early 1970s, a woman cleaning the floor of a university building remarked that women would be more careful about long words if 'they had to clean up after them'. The cartoon was directed, in this case, against women and it was published within the context of attacks on excessive, and incomprehensible, theorizing by academic women at the expense of women outside the academy. Discussing whether or not housework constituted productive or non-productive labour was quite another thing, as many women pointed out, from actually doing it. The disappearance of this debate, or questioning of academic practice, in the 1980s tacitly led to the acceptance of feminists within the academy of the 'high' theoretical model, advanced in the work of Judith Butler and others (Butler, 1990). This work, ground-breaking and innovative as it was, was nevertheless often inaccessible to many women and part of a distinct theoretical space and practice which assumed a high degree of intellectual sophistication. In this work, feminism could be seen, in traditional academic terms, to have come of age, in that it embraced both sophistication and theoretical innovation. The academic heroine, in fact, had arrived.

In the work of Judith Butler (and others) there lies an enormous commitment to the cause of sexual libertarianism and pluralism. Butler is clearly *for* change in aspects of our lives and as such she rightly occupies a special place within academic practice. But the tendency of work of this kind (although not necessarily this work) is towards making of feminism, and feminist, a mirror image of some male scholarship. That is to say, that what is not integrated into the new, sophisticated, feminist theory, is a sense of the interconnectedness of the academy and the world (Brown *et al.*, 1993). When I was an undergraduate we were encouraged to read (for I was fortunate enough to be a student at a cosmopolitan university and taught by critical academics) Robert Lynd on *Knowledge for What?* and C.W. Mills on power (Lynd, 1939; Mills, 1956). Neither of these authors is likely to appear on a feminist book list, but both made important contributions to thinking about the links between universities and the rest of society which are too easily forgotten. Feminists rightly question 'male' knowledge and 'male' understanding; that critique of the academy is firmly in place. But what tends to be over-looked is the connection, or connections, between the academy and the social world as a whole — precisely the connections that Lynd and Mills in the United States of America, and the Frankfurt School in Europe, attempted to isolate and define. Feminists have made connections between male domination in the universities, and the domination of our lives by models of rationality and objectivity, but the detail of these inter-relationships remains, in many ways, mysterious. We know, and it has been demonstrated endless times in critiques of our built environment, that when men design houses, urban space and transport systems they often fail to accommodate the needs of women and children and people with disabilities (McDowell and Pringle, 1992). But what we have yet to demonstrate is the connection between the apparent rationality of abstract knowledge and the equally apparent irrationality of much of male behaviour. That is, that the very values of the system which is about producing knowledge actually tend towards the failure to produce knowledge — of the kind which enables an understanding of human experience.

The comment which is often made about women's academic work is that it tends towards 'the descriptive'. Since, as suggested above, the impulse and the motive of the academy is towards the analytical, the word 'descriptive' acquires a negative meaning. But we might equally say of men's academic work that it is descriptive, in the sense of being an endless discourse on power, and power relations. Male sociologists, for example, write at length about the state, and its composition and its organization. Much of the work may be said to enhance our understanding of the political processes of contemporary western society, and there is no denying the range and complexity of the work. Yet at the same time we might ask what the work is *for*. In a famous and much quoted and cited paper Mary McIntosh discussed the state and the oppression of women, and in doing so she gave to the study of the state a political stance and a politics which is often absent in the work of men (McIntosh, 1978). The point of Mary McIntosh's paper was not to produce a complex model of the state, but to show how the state is an active part of human agency. The concept of *agency* was central to the paper; the model used was not one of static theory, or even dynamic (in the sense of ever changing) theory, but of understanding and intervention. This distinction, between the author's audience being academic, and the author's audience being activists of all kinds, seems to me to be crucial:

who is the audience, and what is the nature of intervention assumed are central questions.

In the late-twentieth century, these issues of audience and agency become increasingly important and complex for feminist academics. Women are allowed into the academy (albeit a changed academy) and inter-disciplinary work is permitted. At the same time, monolithic patriarchy no longer exists in all its glory in universities (though many tattered remnants remain) and so how to intervene in the policies and ideologies which shape our lives becomes a more complicated issue. Again, women have been allowed access to the 'rational' world, but since the form of rationality now expected in universities is that of managed-rationality, this creates a new set of problems for feminist academics. The old world has shifted and in part disappeared, but what has taken its place is full of ever changing shifting sands. What remains the case is that it is still difficult for women to identify themselves as different without being either inferior or falling into that kind of essentialism of which most academic feminists are wary.

Looking back over the years that I have spent in universities (almost 30 including time as a student) I cannot profess to great optimism about the future of Higher Education for anyone, let alone women in particular. This, then, is a pessimistic conclusion, but it is based on what appear to me to be increasingly oppressive conditions of participation in universities, for both students and academics. At the same time, I am not encouraged by what I see as the lack of opposition or resistance or debate within universities: the new pluralism of postmodernism, coupled with the new managerialism, creates a situation in which even if dissent is possible, there is little proper target for it. In this world, a major priority for feminist academics might be the politics of the academy, in the same tradition as that established by Lynd and Mills in the 1930s and enriched by E.P. Thompson in the 1960s (Lynd, 1939; Mills, 1956; Thompson, 1968). Yet, Warwick University Limited is now one of the most successful of the new 'old' universities and a study of its success would reveal that the university has negotiated very successfully the lure of mass expansion and quasi-populism. Within this context, Women's Studies has been able to flourish simply because resources have been available and academic debates, rather than managerial decisions, are still possible. A note of conservatism, therefore, along with the pessimism that the cause of the feminist agenda with radical possibilities is often best served by the more élitist institutional policies and patriarchal assumptions.

Institutional politics, then, have to be part of any academic agenda in the 1990s. The 'head' within which feminist academics have to live, therefore, is an understanding of lower case politics as well as pressing questions of global concern. It is, as ever, a double shift. Few women would expect otherwise, for such is the nature of our ordinary experience. The point, therefore, is to identify very clearly the nature of the contemporary academy — that it is not simply patriarchal, but is patriarchal in particular kind of ways, some of which come disguised with managerialist or expansionist labels. Thinking about gender and sexual politics in this context involves thinking not just about questions of access and promotion but also about questions of knowledge, precisely the kind of questions which the new university factory is too often disinclined to consider. It is only through identifying these issues that women can avoid being disempowered by them. Yet paradoxically, the disappearance of many patterns of academic control in the universities allows feminists precisely the opportunity which they have long coveted: to begin to construct alternative models of rationality and critical inquiry which do not depend on the assumption of male power.

References

AUSTEN, J. (1965) *Persuasion*, Harmondsworth: Penguin.

AZIZ, A. (1990) 'Women in U.K. Universities', in LIE, S. and O'LEARY, V. (Eds) *Storming the Tower: Women in the Academic World*, London: Kogan Page.

BHABBA, H. (1994) *The Location of Culture*, London: Routledge.

BROWN, L. *et al.* (1993) *The International Handbook of Women's Studies*, London: Harvester.

BUTLER, J. (1990) *Gender Trouble: Feminism and the Subversion of Identity*, London: Routledge.

EDWARDS, R. (1993) *Mature Students*, London: Taylor & Francis.

EVANS, M. (1994) *Agenda for Gender*, Canterbury: University of Kent at Canterbury (Women's Studies Committee).

FANON, F. (1986) *Black Skin, White Masks*, London: Pluto.

FOUCAULT, M. (1971) *The Order of Things: An Archaeology of the Human Sciences*, London: Tavistock.

FREUD, S. (1905) *Three Essays on the Theory of Sexuality*, Harmondsworth: Penguin.

GILLIGAN, C. (1982) *In a Different Voice*, Cambridge, MA: Harvard University Press.

HARAWAY, D. (1988) 'Situated Knowledge: The Science Question in Feminism and the Privilege of Partial Perspective', *Feminist Studies*, **14**, 3, pp. 575–599.

HARDING, S. (1986) *The Science Question in Feminism*, Milton Keynes: Open University Press.

HOCHSCHILD, A. (1989) *The Second Shift*, New York: Viking.

KUHN, T. (1962) *The Structure of Scientific Revolution*, Chicago: The University of Chicago Press.

LEONARDI, S. (1989) *Dangerous Degrees*, New Brunswick: Rutgers University Press.

LORCH, J. (1990) *Mary Wollstonecraft*, Oxford: Berg.

LORDE, A. (1984) *Sister Outsider*, New York: The Crossing Press.

LYND, R. (1939) *Knowledge for What?* Princeton: Princeton University Press.

MCDOWELL, L. and PRINGLE, R. (Eds) (1992) *Defining Women: Social Institutions and Gender Divisions*, Cambridge: Polity.

MCINTOSH, M. (1978) The State and the Oppression of Women, in A. KUHN and A. WOLPE (Eds), *Feminism and Materialism*, pp. 255–289, London: Routledge.

MILLS, C.W. (1956) *The Power Élite*, New York: Oxford University Press.

NUSSBAWM, M. (1993) Justice for Women, *New York Review of Books*, 8 October **4**, 3, pp. 328–340.

ORWELL, G. (1934) *Burmese Days*, New York: Harpers.

PATEMAN, C. (1988) *The Sexual Contract*, Cambridge: Polity.

ROSE, H. (1994) *Love, Power and Knowledge*, Cambridge: Polity.

SAID, E. (1994) *Culture and Imperialism*, London: Vintage.

SAPIRO, V. (1992) *A Vindication of Political Virtue*, Chicago: University of Chicago Press.

SAYRE, A. (1975) *Rosalind Franklin and DNA*, New York: Norton.

SPIVAK, G.C. (1993) *Outside in the Teaching Machine*, London: Routledge.

SPURLING, A. (1990) *Report of the Women in Higher Education Research Project*, report available from King's College, Cambridge.

STANLEY, L. (1990) *Feminist Praxis*, London: Routledge.

THOMPSON, E.P. (1968) *Warwick University Limited*, Harmondsworth: Penguin.

WOOLF, L. (1928) *Imperialism and Civilization*, London: The Hogarth Press.

Chapter 6

Transgression and the Academy: Feminists and Institutionalization

Val Walsh

This chapter considers the position and significance of women and feminists who teach in Higher Education. With Virginia Woolf (1928, reprint 1972) we can identify the language, concepts, codes and conventions of academia as recognizably 'a man's world', which *constitutes* the very masculinity it honours. Acknowledging the roots of the academic and the scholarly within the psychosocial world of men has generally been resisted by male scholars, and there is now the added problem that women seeking to enter academia may feel that they have to 'pass' as men, as middle class, or as heterosexual, and, as a consequence, by contributing to 'social frameworks which reinforce domination' (hooks, 1989: 14–15), oppress other women. In examining academia as both patriarchal institution and object of its own critical scrutiny, we discover our dilemma as 'women' and as feminists, and face the contradictory nature of Women's Studies. What does it mean to be effective as feminist academics, while also challenging the roots of our complicity in our own and other people's oppression? This is the practice of revolt, against how we are positioned historically and socially *in relation to each other as women*, which bubbles at the heart of any feminism.

Language like 'oppression' and 'revolt' may be seen as 'emotive' in academia, and as speaking openly from a specific class position. Delphy has described all intellectual practices as being 'rooted in a class position' (Delphy, 1984b: 150). Historically, this has often been disguised by those within the academy, and academic values have too often been purveyed as ahistorical, universal, 'scientific', and not the product of any particular period, culture, or dominant class. By contrast to my 'unruly' speech, academic discourse conventionally seeks 'order': in its theories (which are conceived of as an ordering/explaining/tidying of the unruly world of nature and experience); and in its exercise, which should be 'gentlemanly', 'objective' and sober, i.e. scholarly and dispassionate. But this rhetoric masks, for example, the aggressive competitiveness and emphasis on winning, which characterize the male academy (Silverstein, 1974; Morgan, 1981; Richards, 1986). It denies the emotional, even sexual investment made by men in their 'intellectual' and 'cultural' productions. For more than 20 years, Women's Studies has established itself at least in part as a consequence of engaging men in the defence of the indefensible: for example, their right to monopolize the construction and production of knowledge, and to deploy it to their own ends, against, by definition, the oppressed majority in society. Women academics who research, write and teach, infringe this monopoly.

Transgressers as Responsible Citizens

Transgression connotes infringement, non-observance, non-performance, deviation, nonconformity, trespass, violation (*Concise Oxford Dictionary*; *Roget's Thesaurus*); the 'movement against and beyond boundaries' (hooks, 1994: 12) conventionally secured in law and via circumstance, sanction and taboo. Within the patriarchal gender binary, transgression is bound into both normative femininity and any oppositional female identities. Hence for 'women', conformity is not really realizable, being itself replete with (derogatory) transgressive connotations. It is suggested, therefore, that women move from transgression consequent upon our identity as not-male (woman as Other); transgression contingent on women's sexual, racialized and sexualized identities (woman as Prey); transgression as a consequence of feminist identities and activism (woman as Witch); towards transgression as an aspect of personal, professional and social creativity, necessary to and part of organizational and cultural order.

Valuing diversity and dialogue go together in this process, which reconceives transgression as productive for organizations, as it has been shown to be for individual thinkers, makers and doers (see Kuhn, 1962; Vernon, 1972; May, 1976; Walsh, 1989). Within this framework, transgression is no longer pathological and associated with 'deviance' and 'disorder', 'criminality' and 'insanity'. Yet it need lose none of its political power in the shift from being experienced as threatening, to becoming part of an organization's responsible response to its internal and external environments — the matrix of communities and contexts which, to achieve ecological, environmental and social sustainability, have to weave together (in) a minimum measure of working mutuality. The alternative is power routinely used against rather than for: power as control rather than as a creative act.

Transgression linked to diversity is not a technical matter, but is a function of, and activates, social and political values which erode the pre-dominance of the hierarchical, adversarial, competitive, authoritarian, control model, as norm and ideal in the male academy. Challenging hegemonic masculinity is fundamentally a process of *sexual* transgression, which queries, deconstructs and resists prevailing sexual boundaries and gender power relations. This prepares the ground for flexible coalitions of change-agents within organizational culture, without their having to be assimilated, silenced or fatally compromised. Instead of academics being polarized in terms of conformity/transgression, this more holistic approach focuses on the process of maintaining conditions for renewal, both in terms of the academy's role in knowledge production, and the academy as a sustainable and fair working environment. The academy is not just an organizational setting, but is an institution specifically concerned with 'the very signifying practices that establish, regulate, and deregulate identity' (Butler, 1990: 147). Academic renewal must at least aim 'to disrupt the foundations that cover over alternative cultural configurations of gender' (Butler, 1990). In our performances as academics and as 'women' and 'men', taking up our responsibility for what comes next means examining how we got to where we are now, and practising ways of doing gender (Butler, 1990: 24) differently in order to forge forms and occasions of sufficient mutuality to support our diversity in action. Transgression as creative practice means making as well as breaking:

> The point is not to stay marginal, but to participate in whatever network of marginal zones is spawned from other disciplinary centers and which, together, constitute a multiple displacement of those authorities. (Butler, 1990: xi)

The importance of our feminist purposes as academics is brought sharply into focus by the commonplace that when a woman says 'no', she really means 'yes':

> Women's refusal is reinterpreted as 'yes' ... Enforced submission continues to be interpreted as consent ... (If) discussion, speech and deliberation are seen as central to democracy, (then) how are women to join in the debate between citizens if their words are meaningless? How can there be participatory democracy when consent is the prerogative of one sex? (Pateman, 1989: 13)

This fundamentally sexual polarity should not be overlooked because it is a familiar and popular assumption, a 'joke' even, about women. It is reiterated here because of its particular significance in the academy, an institution theoretically preoccupied with the preeminent role of language and speech in constituting citizenship, democracy, debate, and *power*. However, speech and sex are functionally connected in patriarchal environments: two poles of a power struggle enacted within academia with increasing vehemence as women's presence has increased (see Brodribb, 1994).

Sex and the Academy

> All I want is to get out from under
> (Segerman-Peck, 1991: 11)

Many women working in Higher Education, perhaps especially feminists, have been driven to feel like Segerman-Peck's client (see Bagihole, 1993; Burrage and Walsh, 1994). In her book on women's networking and mentoring, Segerman-Peck encourages women to make better use of our talents, develop more confidence, and head for the top, wherever we are. Women are simply urged to conform — 'it is vital to adopt the company style' (Segerman-Peck, 1991: 88) — and are warned that 'no amount of competence and good behaviour will help you if you don't follow the *right* rules for promotion' (Segerman-Peck, 1991: 28). However, 'competence' and 'good behaviour' are not neutral terms, but contextually specific and gendered. These organizational imperatives are *sexual* scripts (Fineman, 1994) covering performative and dress codes, for example. Whatever our 'choices', we cannot altogether escape the consequences of the semiotic frame within which our 'decisions'/appearance will be decoded in terms set by the 'epistemic regime of presumptive heterosexuality' (Butler, 1990: viii). For women, there is a lot to consider before breakfast (see Williamson, 1987).

Specific and additional 'workloads' — in this case, a feature of emotional labour (Fineman, 1994: 3) — accrue to women in the academy. There are many organizational nuances which must be attended to. One woman, moving from industry to university, failed to realize the difference in values, and had concentrated on developing her students, and neglected to establish a power base among academic colleagues (Segerman-Peck, 1991: 135). Yet, 'networking with the powerful' (Segerman-Peck, 1991: 94) and the idea that 'to use your networks successfully you have to be go-getting' (Segerman-Peck, 1991: 53), are not easy to reconcile with my political understanding of gendered power relations in society, and my potential role as a feminist academic in the UK (see Marchbank *et al.*, 1993; Wilton, 1993; Walsh, 1995). Advocating deference and conformity to organizational and professional codes requires us to disguise 'precisely these marks of womanhood that place women in opposition to, or, at best, in a paradoxical and contradictory relation to, citizenship' (Pateman, 1989: 14). But 'pretense has never brought about lasting change or progess' (Lorde, 1985: 57). Like so many other women, 'I don't feel like being strong, but do I have a choice?' (Lorde, 1985: 4). Audre Lorde — black, lesbian, feminist, and cancer survivor for 13 years before her death in 1992 — acknowledges the dangers that women face in a racist, misogynist society, and the importance of both individual responsibility and collective testimony:

> I do believe not until every woman traces her weave back strand by bloody self-referenced strand, will we begin to alter the whole pattern. (Lorde, 1985: 3)

It is notably women historically marginalized within feminism — black women, disabled women, lesbians, women from working-class backgrounds — who are providing inspiration for feminist process, inside the danger zone we call society. As academics, certainly in the UK, these women remain damagingly isolated, token and/or hidden figures. The sexual politics of racism, and the perceived 'threat posed by all dimensions, degrees, and manifestations of women's personal and political movement toward and for each other' (Raymond, 1986: 18), that is not just the taboo on lesbianism, but men and women's ambivalence even fear of single women and non-monogamous women (Rosa, 1994), are perhaps key cultural indicators, outside and inside the academy, of women's safety, status and opportunity. The position of black women, for example, is inextricably bound up with 'the problem of women' in the academy. If women in academia are defined in sexual terms, in opposition to a model of intellectuality and creativity which is white and masculine (Battersby, 1989; Walsh, 1990; 1991; Morrison, 1993), black women have an intensified relation to this ideology, in view of the stereotype which defines them, even more than white women, in terms of nature and sexuality (Hallam and Marshall, 1993; Marshall, 1993).

Many lesbian academics in the UK have been cautious in claiming lesbian identity (Marchbank *et al.*, 1993), balancing confidence, activism, and a sense of privacy, with a recognition of the possible consequences for the quality of daily life and career prospects, and, therefore, economic and social self-determination. Lesbians (whatever age, class, ethnicity or disabled status) are still less visible in British society than gay men; visibility here functioning as a marker of acceptability/safety. Whether 'out of sight' as a result of self-censorship or, if 'out', as targets for marginalization, ridicule, or abuse (and not just by men), lesbian identity, together with 'single' women's identities, encapsulates society's fear of women who live independently of men, be it economically, domestically, intellectually and/or sexually (perceived as a hierarchy of both resistance and transgression).

The sexual categorization of women, in terms of the demands of male heterosexuality, imposes a hierarchy of acceptability and vulnerability, within which for example, black women, disabled women and older women are visibly exposed. They cannot protect themselves by hiding or disguise, in the way that a feminist may keep quiet about her feminism, or a heterosexual woman may signal she is not available, or a lesbian may disguise her sexual preference, all to reduce day-to-day harassment and/or censure.

Woman as Sign and as Body in Academia

In understanding how masculinity constitutes itself and its power through exclusions and dominance, it is not just a question of what is excluded but why the exclusion takes place (Pateman, 1989: 3). We are now familiar with the idea that '"the public" rests on a particular conception of the "private" and vice versa' (Pateman, 1989: 3):

> Women, womanhood and women's bodies represent the private; they represent all that is excluded from the public sphere . . . 'The disorder of women' (Rousseau's phrase) means that they pose a threat to political order and so must be excluded from the public world. (Pateman, 1989: 4)

This helps us see why, as women and as feminists, we have been so difficult to accommodate in Higher Education, and I am not speaking quantitatively, though I take our overall scarcity and clustering in lower paid, temporary and part-time posts as tutors as evidence of resistance to our physical presence. If, as embodied women, we represent danger and disorder, the potential undoing of men and masculinity, the question of our access, status and influence in the academy exceeds the reach of any Equal Opportunities policies. The recent controversy over 'consensual' relations (mainly) between male tutors and their female students, is a sharp reminder of how central men's sexual desire is to both their sense of power and their academic identity. Noting the intensity and unanimity with which a proposal for guidelines on consensual relations was rejected at the 1994 UK National Association of Teachers in Further and Higher Education Annual Conference (including, presumably, by large numbers of men on the Left), participants at a workshop on 'consensual' relations (Carter, 1994) during the first National NATFHE Women's Conference later the same year, concluded that male tutors must either all be 'at it', or wish they were, or want to keep their options open in case they get lucky (see Carter and Jeffs, 1995).

Historically, men have projected their sexual preoccupations and anxieties, sublimated their desire and sexual energies, in the form of Culture — for example, painting, poetry, philosophy, political economy, politics — declaring this process a *self-discipline* (need?) and exercise of will, of which women are incapable. It is therefore both impossible and damaging for women to frame our aspirations in terms of incorporation within this cultural space. Women's bodily presence is believed to contaminate the public domain of convention and culture: women are associated with the private world of sex and nature. Within the gender binary 'woman' represents the object of male heterosexual desire, as well as men's suppressed 'femininity'; a reminder of what has been denied and controlled, in order that dominant masculinity can function as it should (Metcalf and Humphries, 1985; Stoltenberg, 1989; Jackson, 1990; Seidler, 1991; French, 1992). And just as the meaning of 'political' and 'democracy' in Rousseau's theory depends upon the meaning he gives to manhood and womanhood (Pateman, 1989: 6), so the values, 'academic', 'scholarly', 'scientific', 'objective', 'authoritative' and 'professional' are all words for the public consequences of this denial and fear: words of containment, demarcation. Words of approval for proving 'masculinity', and therefore *unavailable to women*, and oppressive and damaging for the majority of men. We need new words, new ways. But as bell hooks's friends reproached her: 'Do we have to go that deep?' (hooks, 1989: 1). And the answer is yes.

Feminist academics cannot simply aspire to 'the master's tools' (Lorde, 1984: 110). The fate of the academy is our fate as women too. Moving from transgression as a function of oppression (our status as victims), towards transgression as a sign and function of our creativity as women/citizens/knowledge producers, women shake the sexual and epistemological foundations of the old academy, and rattle the hegemonic masculinity it embodies. Whether as academics or activists, as *knowledge producers* we loosen the grip of the gender binary, and interrupt and resist the essentializing of women as sex/body/ nature/'female', and become change-agents with power and influence.

Making it Possible to Face the Dangers Together

The development of feminist conscience is fraught with risk, as before it contributes to our well-being and confidence, it destabilizes and threatens to engulf us as we grasp the extent and strength of the hostility, hatred, and violence towards women in the world (see Ward-Jouve, 1986; Smith, 1989; Faludi, 1992; French, 1992). Feminist academics speak of the need to knowingly and explicitly ground our theory, research and teaching in this knowledge. Young women, whose 'alarm systems are not yet developed' (Pinkola Estés, 1994: 47) may find this disturbing. Networking across differences of age and experience is therefore a vital transgressive practice for feminists in academia.[1] For feminist academics, as for women generally, speaking as girl or woman is likely to have been identified as 'talking back'.

> 'Back talk' and 'talking back' meant speaking as an equal to an authority figure. It meant daring to disagree and sometimes it just meant having an opinion. (hooks, 1989: 5)

Many of us give up talking back, faced with the demands of 'femininity' in adolescence, to defer, to avert our gaze and minds. Having done this, some women recover our voices years later. The rest of us somehow never give up talking back (see Hancock, 1990; Walsh, 1993). As feminist academics, we facilitate that talking back in our students as part of 'the process of education for critical consciousness' (hooks, 1989: 13; see Freire, 1972; hooks, 1994). Education is part of 'the struggle to end domination', 'to establish the liberatory voice — that way of speaking that is no longer determined by one's status as object — as oppressed being' (hooks, 1989: 15).

This is a collective process of developing courage, born of community. And bell hooks reminds us that 'it is silly to think that one can challenge and also have approval' (hooks, 1989: 16). This can be a predicament for women who, inculcated into normative femininity which fans women's *desire* for (male) approval, may find themselves as adults (even feminists!) struggling with their *need* for approval. As Carol Smith argues in relation to the politics of health, the whole concept of success needs to be redefined (in Lorde, 1985: ix).

Already there is evidence that feminist theory is rapidly becoming another sphere of academic élitism (linguistically convoluted and difficult to understand) (hooks, 1989: 34). Resisting this process involves seeing the academy 'as a central site for revolutionary struggle', wherein 'we make the conditions for wholeness' (hooks, 1989: 31). This shifts feminist movement towards a poetics as well as a politics of education: a double transgression, and a growing tension within academic feminism. Within African-American culture, 'Poetry was not mere recording . . . It was transcendent speech. It was meant to transform consciousness' (hooks, 1989: 11).

Our work as feminist intellectuals is beleagured not only by malestream academic values and practices (maintained by women as well as men), but also as a consequence of the stress which ensues for women from 'talking back' inside a male preserve. The costs of being a feminist in the academy are becoming evident (Davies, 1993; hooks, 1993; Brodribb, 1994; Burrage and Walsh, 1994; Morley, 1994): costs to our health and well-being, our relationships, lives and careers. In addition to the problems presented to us by male academics and their culture, feminist academics face tensions between ourselves, and ourselves and other women in our institutions. In the early days of the Women's Liberation Movement, 'we began to look at other women differently, as people we could value, and in so doing we began to value ourselves' (Orbach and Eichenbaum, 1988: 25). We acknowledged women's subjectivity as 'relational', recognizing that we live in a network of relationships and 'know ourselves through these relationships' (Orbach and Eichenbaum, 1988: 154), and that it is through this social experience that we develop the affective and interpersonal skills which have acted as a paradigm for feminist academics and researchers in the development of feminist pedagogy and methodologies (Rich, 1980a,b; Walsh, 1994c). It is also likely that we developed 'merged attachments' (Orbach and Eichenbaum, 1988: 130) with those women with whom we had campaigned, who had been personal and political allies. Now, having increased our presence and influence in academia, we face, not just expanding differences between women, but also our *fear* of difference. For example, 'presenting oneself as competent can feel too aggressive and self-serving' (Orbach and Eichenbaum, 1988: 107), and/or result in other women, including students — female as well as male — variously identifying us as, for example, 'superwoman' or 'witch'!

Pinkola Estés has highlighted the problem of women moving beyond victim status. 'Being able to say that one is a survivor is an accomplishment', but 'sometimes people are afraid to continue beyond survivor status, for it is just that — a status, a distinguishing mark', and 'once the threat is past, there is a potential trap in calling ourselves by names taken on during the most terrible time of our lives' (Pinkola Estés, 1994: 197). Although it would be hard to argue that the threat to women is past, perhaps there is now a felt and practical need for building feminist strategies and coalitions for 'the transition from surviving to thriving' (Pinkola Estés, 1994: 198), both inside and outside academia. However, if 'women have come to identify the gratifying of their needs with the meeting of needs in others' (Orbach and Eichenbaum, 1988: 90); and if 'so much of women's relating revolves around supporting one another through difficult times' (Orbach and Eichenbaum, 1988: 84), being visibly capable and confident and therefore more separate may lead women to fear envy and fear in other women (Orbach and Eichenbaum, 1988: 82).

Perhaps we need to consider whether there is 'an ethos within women's relationships . . . about staying in the same place together, or moving forward together at the same time' (Orbach and Eichenbaum, 1988: 79)? Is there a sense in which difference cannot be allowed, not just at the macro level of dominant white feminism, but at the micro level of the politics of feminisms, for example *within* different feminist groupings? Is transgression within feminist contexts and women's relationships likely to be identified as betrayal rather than innovation? Whatever the roots of these conflicts, many women are now wondering, even grieving: 'How could women, apparently with so much in common, be so destructive?' (Orbach and Eichenbaum, 1988: 4). In addition, 'those women who fought it out for years on their own in male preserves, may have become completely accustomed to competing in male terms' (Orbach and Eichenbaum, 1988: 104). What happens when these very different professional and/or academic women encounter each other inside organizations? Mistrust, conflict, pain . . . competitiveness, individualism, not networking.

Weaving Transgression and Reconciliation

Knowing that women have thrived in each other's company, believed in each other, encouraged each other — made each other possible — we now face intensified differences of power, status and opportunity, not just within the male academy but within the new female academy. Some women who identified/identify as feminists are also ambitious professional women. For some of these women, feminist knowledge may function as a commodity which enhances academic or professional visibility, improves self-confidence, and helps carve out career paths. They will be working alongside other ambitious professional women who decline to identify themselves as feminists. These non-feminist, even anti-feminist women confront us with what Delphy has called the 'self-hatred of the oppressed' (1984a: 118–119) and further contradictions for feminists:

> When we are struggling against their 'opinions', we are not struggling against anti-feminist women, but against this common enemy (false consciousness) — and thus for them, and for ourselves. (Delphy, 1984a: 119)

But these women can feel like the enemy, and when they stand alongside the men, or act destructively towards us, it seems to hurt more, not less.

> We need a mediating force that can sustain us so that we are not broken in this process, so that we do not despair . . . Not enough feminist work has focussed on documenting and sharing ways individuals confront differences constructively and successfully. Women and men need to know what is on the other side of the pain experienced in politicization. (hooks, 1989: 26)

As feminist teachers, researchers, managers and students (for we are all students), our social experience is not simply a resource: we also have to cope with it on a daily basis, inside and outside the academy. We already know that feminist Women's Studies draws from these dilemmas and contradictions, conflicts and fears, and can transform pain into material for hope. Previously, however:

> Naming the pain or uncovering the pain in a context where it is not linked to strategies for resistance and transformation created for many women the conditions for even greater estrangement, alienation, isolation, and at times grave despair. (hooks, 1989: 32)

While the development of Women's Studies has been productive in suggesting answers to the question, 'What role in the struggle can and should be played by feminists who are also intellectuals, or intellectuals who are also feminists?' (Delphy, 1984b: 147), it has also, as hooks indicates, raised additional and unforeseen problems and challenges. Ablebodiedness, heterosexuality and whiteness have hardly begun to be deconstructed and problematized in relation to their naturalization within academia (Hill Collins, 1991; Morris, 1991; Kitzinger *et al.*, 1992; Ware, 1992; Kitzinger and Wilkinson, 1993, 1994; Morrison, 1993; Matthews, 1994; Rosa, 1994), so increasing the number of white women academics may actually compound existing inequalities and exclusions. The problem of the language and culture of academia is at the core of any feminist challenge and purposes:

> Production of knowledge . . . is under present conditions, inseparable from the production of a learned discourse which is defined in opposition to 'popular' language — i.e. that of the group which is dominated. (Delphy, 1984b: 151)

More recently, black feminists and disabled feminists have expanded on the dangers of a normative or dominant *feminist* discourse (Hill Collins, 1991; Morris, 1991; Matthews, 1994; Potts and Price, chapter 7), pointing to the importance of feminist methods in relationship, research and teaching (hooks, 1993, 1994; Walsh, 1994c, 1995) which support diversity by facilitating not just access but also ownership in the learning environment. In terms of academic propriety, this too is unruly, even 'irresponsible' behaviour: academics, after all, are supposed to be 'experts' and in charge.

Neither can we idealize feminism or Women's Studies and its methods. The complex oppressions experienced by many women and feminists in their relations with feminists and 'mainstream' feminism, must be acknowledged and owned by the abusers. The painful contradictions of women's increased presence in the academy suffuse Women's Studies. The expansion of Women's Studies (see Adkins and Leonard, 1992), and the rise of Equal Opportunities as a managerial rhetoric (Humm, 1994; Walsh, 1994a), have had an impact on both institutional culture (Evans *et al.,* 1994) and women's organizational aspirations, identities and styles. Individualism and competitiveness are for some women markers of both feminist and professional assertiveness and upward mobility: 'success', undeconstructed and welcome. These developments highlight the importance of feminism as an ethic (Hill Collins, 1991; Walsh, 1994b,c, 1995) which informs and frames our methods, relations and purposes, and joins issues of justice and diversity as underpinning imperatives inside and outside academia. We must stop endangering each other.

'Not Drowning but Waving . . .'[2]

To live out the paradox and complexities of women's presence in the academy is hard, often lonely, and bad for our health. So what keeps us there? We return to the unacademic, for example our hope, imagination, love and anger: 'Our only weapon against the potential treason written into our status as intellectuals is precisely our anger . . .' (Delphy, 1984b: 153). Anger (like love) is the ultimate affront to 'objectivity', to the 'scientific', the 'academic', the 'professional' . . . But it is also painful, 'because to remain angry is to keep permanently in mind the cause of this anger; . . . which we want to forget'. On the other hand, women can take pleasure in the knowledge that working together to transform traditional ways of teaching and learning, evaluation and assessment, and knowledge production, creates an excitement which sustains hope, energy and affection even inside academia. 'Teaching for transgression' (hooks, 1994), feminists ask fundamental questions like: 'Where does knowledge come from?' (Hevey and Spence, 1992: 9) and what is it for? We explore the consequences of 'inhabiting the centre of the web, inhabiting the theories' (Hevey and Spence, 1992: 10), and demonstrate the cycle and rhythm of experience and theory, to produce something which is both: a living web of connections to sustain us. This is enthralling and empowering work, at the heart of cultural and political renewal. It is a model which provides ways forward for the whole academy, not just feminists.

Only by transgressing the limits and constraints placed upon us as women, can we survive and thrive, contributing creatively to social and ecological sustainability. Yet as transgressers we are targets for the turbulence many male academics feel towards women generally, and perhaps feminists, lesbians and 'single' women in particular. Our personal predicaments and potential are inseparable from our professional and political prospects.

A feminist Women's Studies which actively promotes multimedia and interdisciplinary methods to facilitate the liberatory voice, brings together the hitherto opposed discourses of art, therapy and politics. 'The conditions for wholeness' (hooks, 1989: 31) we seek, will be the consequence of the aesthetic, the therapeutic, the political, being redefined and realised in terms of each other (Walsh, 1994b). No longer separable, certainly not opposed, for our strategies for survival are also our search for safety and beauty. 'Social relatedness and ecological healing' (Gablik, 1991: 27) are coterminous, not optional extras, but simultaneously prerequisites and goals, for the academy no less than the world at large.

The laughter and humour of women, our poetry, dance and art, must all play a part, not as products, or commodified as material for Women's Studies, but as equal means and ends in the process of women's empowerment. No longer marginalized as objects of the female or feminist gaze, but *the gaze itself.* Despite the painful contradictions of women's position in the academy, we must persist by directing our emotional and political energies towards each other (students and tutors alike), rather than allowing them to be drained off trying to implement, for example, managerial Equal Opportunism. For: 'If we collaborate with the powerful, then our language will lose its currency as a means to tell the truth in order to change the truth' (Jordan, 1989: 131).

Feminist academics are well placed to develop transgressive performance into an art-form, thereby realizing our revolutionary potential, that is, our social use value inside as well as outside the world of academia.

Acknowledgements

This chapter is based on a paper presented in 1992 at the Women's Studies Network (UK) Annual International Conference, University of Central Lancashire, Preston. For detailed and thoughtful comments on the conference paper, and loads of encouragement, warm thanks to: Marilyn Poole (Australia), Jo Stanley, Tobe Levin (Germany), Louise Morley, Julie Matthews, Bobbie McNerney, Gerard McDermott, Katy Macleod, and Barbara Körner. Additional stimulation for this version came from talk and thought with Jacquie Swift, Sheila Freedman, Val Baxter, and Margaret Merone.

Notes

1   At a meeting convened by ANEF (Assocation Nationale des Études Feministes, the French national Feminist Studies association) during the WISE (Women's International Studies Europe) Workshop, *Travelling Through European Feminisms: Cultural and Political Practices* (8–10 October 93) Paris, Christine Delphy drew attention to the lack of intergenerational feminist continuity in France. French feminism is overwhelmingly located in and identified with the academy and urban centres; there is no movement outside university with which Women's Studies students can connect (Ezekiel, 1992, 1993). The age profile of French representatives present confirmed both the absence of younger women, and the gap that has opened up in France between longstanding feminists in their forties, fifties and sixties, and women under forty. Delphy was asking, where are the feminists to continue the struggle? — implicitly highlighting the dangers of feminism as a Women's Studies severed from its originating links to women's lives and political struggles. While the situation in the UK is not as extreme or polarized, the French example nonetheless warns of

the damage to feminist struggles of academization, and signals the 'life and death' role of intergenerational networking for women and feminists.

2 Adapted from Stevie Smith (1971) 'Not Waving But Drowning', *Two In One (Selected Poems and The Frog Prince and Other Poems)*, London: Longman.

References

ADKINS, LISA and LEONARD, DIANA (1992) 'From Academia to the Education Marketplace: United Kingdom Women's Studies in the 1990s', *Women's Studies Quarterly*, **XX**, 3 + 4, Fall/Winter, pp. 28–37.

BAGIHOLE, BARBARA (1993) 'How to Keep a Good Woman Down: An Investigation of the Institutional Factors in the Process of Discrimination against Women Academics', *British Journal of Sociology of Education*, **14**, 3, pp. 262–274.

BATTERSBY, CHRISTINE (1989) *Gender and Genius: Towards a Feminist Aesthetics*, London: The Women's Press.

BRODRIBB, SOMER (1994) 'Urgent Fax', University of Victoria, British Columbia, 6 January.

BURRAGE, HILARY and WALSH, VAL (1994) 'Equal Opportunities Work in Academia: Only Victims (or Fools) Need Apply. A Casestudy in Oppression and Empowerment', Paper at British Sociological Association Annual Conference, *Sexualities in Context*, University of Central Lancashire, Preston.

BUTLER, JUDITH (1990) *Gender Trouble (Feminism and the Subversion of Identity)*, London: Routledge.

CARTER, PAM (1994) 'Consensual Relations' workshop at National Association for Teachers in Further and Higher Education National Women's Conference, Britannia House, London.

CARTER, PAM and JEFFS, TONY (1995) 'A Very Private Affair', *Education Now*, forthcoming.

DAVIES, CELIA (1993) 'The Equality Mystique, The Difference Dilemma and the Case of Women Academics', *University of Galway Women's Studies Centre Review*, **2**, pp. 53–72.

DELPHY, CHRISTINE (1984a) 'Our friends and ourselves: the hidden foundations of various pseudo-feminist accounts', in LEONARD, DIANA (Ed.) *Close to Home*, pp. 106–137, London: Hutchinson.

DELPHY, CHRISTINE (1984b) 'Patriarchy, feminism and their intellectuals', in LEONARD, DIANA (Ed.) *Close to Home*, pp. 138–153, London: Hutchinson.

DELPHY, CHRISTINE (1984c) 'Protofeminism and antifeminism', in LEONARD, DIANA (Ed.) *Close to Home*, pp. 182–210, London: Hutchinson.

EVANS, MARY, GOSLING, JULIET and SELLER, ANNE (Eds) (1994) *Agenda for Gender*, (Discussion Papers on Gender and the Organization of Higher Education) Canterbury: University of Kent at Canterbury (Women's Studies Committee).

EZEKIEL, JUDITH (1992) 'Radical in Theory: Organized Women's Studies in France, the Women's Movement and the State', *Women's Studies Quarterly*, Special Issue: Women's Studies in Europe, Fall–Winter, pp. 75–84.

EZEKIEL, JUDITH (1993) 'What's a Nice Girl Like You . . . ? (Teaching American Women's Studies in France)', *Women's Studies Network (UK) Newsletter*, March, pp. 28–29.

FALUDI, SUSAN (1992) *Backlash (The Undeclared War on Women)*, London: Chatto & Windus.

FINEMAN, STEPHEN (Ed.) (1994) *Emotion in Organizations*, London: Sage.

FREIRE, PAULO (1972) *Pedagogy of the Oppressed*, Harmondsworth: Penguin.

FRENCH, MARILYN (1992) *The War Against Women*, London: Hamish Hamilton.

GABLIK, SUZI (1991) *The Re-Enchantment of Art*, London: Thames & Hudson.

HALLAM, JULIA and MARSHALL, ANNECKA (1993) 'Layers of Difference: The Significance of a Self-Reflexive Research Practice for a Feminist Epistemological Project', in KENNEDY, MARY, LUBELSKA, CATHY and WALSH, VAL (Eds) *Making Connections: Women's Studies, Women's Movements, Women's Lives*, pp. 64–78, London: Taylor & Francis.

HANCOCK, EMILY (1990) *The Girl Within (A Radical New Approach to Female Identity)*, London: Pandora.

HEVEY, DAVID and SPENCE, JO (1992) 'Interview: Marks of Struggle', *Women's Art*, **47**, July/August, pp. 8–11.

HILL COLLINS, PATRICIA (1991) *Black Feminist Thought (Knowledge, Consciousness and the Politics of Empowerment)*, London: Routledge.

hooks, bell (1989) *Talking Back (Thinking Feminist — Thinking Black)*, London: Sheba.

hooks, bell (1991) *Yearning (Race, Gender, and Cultural Politics)*, London: Turnaround.

hooks, bell (1993) *Sisters of the Yam (Black Women and Self-Recovery)*, London: Turnaround.

hooks, bell (1994) *Teaching to Transgress*, London: Routledge.

HUMM, MAGGIE (1994) 'Equal Opportunities and Promoting People', in EVANS, MARY, GOSLING, JULIET and SELLER, ANNE (Eds) *Agenda for Gender*, pp. 28–35, Canterbury: University of Kent at Canterbury (Women's Studies Committee).

JACKSON, DAVID (1990) *Unmasking Masculinity (A Critical Autobiography)*, London: Unwin Hyman.

JORDAN, JUNE (1989) *Moving Towards Home (Political Essays)*, London: Virago.

KITZINGER, CELIA and WILKINSON, SUE (1993) 'The Precariousness of Heterosexual Feminist Identities', in KENNEDY, MARY, LUBELSKA, CATHY and WALSH, VAL (Eds) *Making Connections: Women's Studies, Women's Movements, Women's Lives*, pp. 24–36, London: Taylor & Francis.

KITZINGER, CELIA, WILKINSON, SUE and PERKINS, RACHEL (Eds) (1992) *Feminism and Psychology*, Special Issue: Heterosexuality, **2**, 3, October.

KUHN, THOMAS (1962) *The Structure of Scientific Revolutions*, London/Chicago: The University of Chicago Press, enlarged 2nd edition 1970.

LORDE, AUDRE (1984) *Sister Outsider*, Trumansberg, NY: The Crossing Press.

LORDE, AUDRE (Ed.) (1985) *The Cancer Journals*, London: Sheba.

MARCHBANK, JENNIFER, CORRIN, CHRIS and BRODIE, SHEILA (1993) 'Inside and "Out" or Outside Academia. Lesbians Working in Scotland', in KENNEDY, MARY, LUBELSKA, CATHY and WALSH, VAL (Eds) *Making Connections: Women's Studies, Women's Movements, Women's Lives*, pp. 155–166, London: Taylor & Francis.

MARSHALL, ANNECKA (1993) 'Sensuous Sapphires: A Study of the Social Construction of Black Female Sexuality', in PURVIS, JUNE and MAYNARD, MARY (Eds) *Researching Women's Lives*, pp. 106–124, London: Taylor & Francis.

MATTHEWS, JULIE (1994) 'Empowering Disabled Women in Higher Education', in DAVIES, SUE, LUBELSKA, CATHY and QUINN, JOCEY (Eds) *Changing the Subject: Women in Higher Education*, pp. 138–145, London: Taylor & Francis.

MAY, ROLLO (1976) *The Courage to Create*, London: William Collins.

METCALF, ANDY and HUMPHRIES, MARTIN (Eds) (1985) *The Sexuality of Men*, London: Pluto.

MORGAN, DAVID (1981) 'Men, masculinity, and the process of sociological enquiry', in ROBERTS, HELEN (Ed.) *Doing Feminist Research*, pp. 83–113, London: Routledge & Kegan Paul.

MORLEY, LOUISE (1994) 'Glass Ceiling or Iron Cage: Women in UK Academia', *Gender, Work and Organization*, **1**, 4, October, pp. 194–204.

MORRIS, JENNY (1991) *Pride Against Prejudice*, London: The Women's Press.

MORRISON, TONI (1993) *Playing in the Dark*, London: Pan Books.

ORBACH, SUSIE and EICHENBAUM, LUISE (1988) *Bittersweet (Love, envy and competition in women's friendships)*, London: Arrow Books. (Reprint (1994) as *Between Women*, Colchester: Tiptree.)

PATEMAN, CAROL (1989) *The Disorder of Women*, London: Polity Press.

PINKOLA ESTÉS, CLARISSA (1994) *Women Who Run with the Wolves (Contacting the Power of the Wild Woman)*, London: Rider.

RAYMOND, JANICE (1986) *A Passion for Friends (Toward a Philosophy of Female Affection)*, London: The Women's Press.

RICH, ADRIENNE (1980a) 'Toward a Woman-Centred University', in *On Lies, Secrets, and Silence: Selected Prose 1966–1978*, pp. 125–155, London: Virago.

RICH, ADRIENNE (1980b) 'Taking Women Students Seriously', in *On Lies, Secrets, and Silence: Selected Prose 1966–1978*, pp. 237–245, London: Virago.

RICHARDS, PAMELA (1986) 'Risk', in BECKER, HOWARD (Ed.) *Writing for Social Scientists*, pp. 108–120, London: University of Chicago Press.

ROSA, BECKY (1994) 'Anti-Monogamy: A Radical Challenge to Compulsory Heterosexuality', in GRIFFIN, GABRIELE, HESTER, MARIANNE, RAI, SHIRIN and ROSENEIL, SASHA (Eds) *Stirring It: Challenges for Feminism*, pp. 107–120, London: Taylor & Francis.

SEGERMAN-PECK, LILY L. (1991) *Networking and Mentoring (A Woman's Guide)*, London: Piatkus.

SEIDLER, VICTOR J. (1991) *Recreating Sexual Politics (Men, Feminism and Politics)*, London: Routledge.

SILVERSTEIN, MICHAEL (1974) 'The history of a short, unsuccessful academic career', in PLECK, JOSEPH and SAWYER, JACK (Eds) *Men and Masculinity*, pp. 107–123, New Jersey: Prentice Hall.

SMITH, CAROL (1985) 'Forward', in LORDE, A. (Ed.) *The Cancer Journals*, pp. i–xii, London: Sheba.

SMITH, JOAN (1989) *Misogynies*, London: Faber & Faber.

STOLTENBERG, JOHN (1989) *Refusing to be a Man*, London: Fontana.

VERNON, P.E. (Ed.) (1972) *Creativity*, Harmondsworth: Penguin.

WALSH, VAL (1989) 'Purity, Binary Thought and Creativity: The Importance of Boundary Transgression', *AND (Journal of Art and Art Education)*, **18/19**, January, pp. 56–57.

WALSH, VAL (1990) '"Walking on the Ice": Women, Art Education and Art', *Journal of Art & Design Education*, **9**, 2, pp. 147–161.

WALSH, VAL (1991) 'Femininity, Fine Art and Art Education: Sexuality and Social Control', research paper; part presented as 'Women and Art: Past and Present', *A Celebration of Women and Art*, Exeter College of Art (now University of Plymouth), 9 March 1989.

WALSH, VAL (1993) 'Digging up Tangled Roots: Feminism and the Resistance to Working

Class Culture', Women's History Network Conference, London; and British Sociological Society Study Group, *Auto/Biography* 4th Annual Conference (1994) Manchester.

WALSH, VAL (1994a) 'Virility Culture: Academia and Managerialism in Higher Education', in EVANS, GOSLING and SELLER, *Agenda for Gender* (Discussion Papers on Gender and the Organization of Higher Education).

WALSH, VAL (1994b) 'Feminism and Nature: Intertwining Aesthetics, Ethics and Politics', 2nd European Feminist Research Conference, *Feminist Perspectives on Technology, Work and Ecology*, July, Graz, Austria.

WALSH, VAL (1994c) 'Not as Strangers: Women's Empowerment, Feminism and Women's Studies', WHEN? (Women in Higher Education Network) Conference papers, *Women and the Higher Education Curriculum*, University of Central Lancashire, Preston.

WALSH, VAL (1995) 'Eyewitnesses, not Spectators/ Activists, not Academics: Feminist Pedagogy and Women's Creativity', in DEEPWELL, KATY (Ed.) *New Feminist Art Criticism: Critical Strategies*, pp. 51–60, Manchester: Manchester University Press.

WARD-JOUVE, NICOLE (1986) *'The Streetcleaner' (The Yorkshire Ripper Case on Trial)*, London: Marion Boyars.

WARE, VRON (1992) *Beyond the Pale (White Women, Racism and History)*, London: Verso.

WILKINSON, SUE and KITZINGER, CELIA (1994) 'Dire Straights? Contemporary Rehabilitations of Heterosexuality', in GRIFFIN, GABRIELE, HESTER, MARIANNE, RAI, SHIRIN and ROSENEIL, SASHA (Eds) *Stirring It: Challenger for Feminism*, pp. 75–91, London: Taylor & Francis.

WILLIAMSON, JUDITH (1987) 'A Piece of the Action: Images of "Woman" in the Photography of Cindy Sherman', *Consuming Passions (The Dynamics of Popular Culture)*, London: Marion Boyars.

WILTON, TAMSIN (1993) 'Queer Subjects: Lesbians, Heterosexual Women and the Academy', in KENNEDY, MARY, LUBELSKA, CATHY & WALSH, VAL (Eds) *Making Connections: Women's Studies, Women's Movements, Women's Lives*, pp. 167–179, London: Taylor & Francis.

WOOLF, VIRGINIA (1928, reprint 1972) *A Room of One's Own*, Harmondsworth: Penguin.

Chapter 7

'Out of the Blood and Spirit of Our Lives':[1] The Place of the Body in Academic Feminism

Tracey Potts and Janet Price

This chapter is, in part, a response to an absence: my absence from this year's Women's Studies Network Conference. Along with Margrit Shildrick, Janet and I had planned to write and present a paper which, as one of its issues, discussed how the boundaries of what we call health are not as reliable as we would like them to be and how health, as a term, is achieved through the denial of its other, illness (Price and Shildrick, 1994). What I didn't know, as we sat planning our argument, was that I was to discover this for myself in no uncertain terms only a few weeks later. In early June, I had what I think was flu, which seems to have triggered the symptoms that I was convinced I'd walked away from two years previously, and as a result I have been left with the difficult task of getting used to using a wheelchair again.

The irony of all this did not escape me. Here I was, a living enactment of our paper but unable to 'speak' about it in the context of the Academy. Although too ill to write, I was not too ill to think. As I lay in my bed, I began to consider how, in order to participate in academic feminism's 'events' (conferences, publishing for example) you need a reasonably reliable body. You need to be able to take it for granted that your legs will transport your mind to the places it needs to go — to the means of academic production such as the library, photocopier, etc. The problem comes, I feel, when, in taking this 'work' for granted, it goes unnoticed and becomes a repressed at the heart of the feminist exchange of ideas.

Academic discourse in general isn't very good at acknowledging the materiality of its own production, the resources and labour that enable its existence. Usually, all traces of a text's occasion are carefully effaced from its surface and content. Only the acknowledgements page — split off from the main body of the text, either unnumbered or given Roman numerals, a euphemized recognition of hierarchized 'debts', intellectual over personal or

---

Nicola Treglown, Gerry Carlin, Kate Chedgzoy, Jay Daley, Grindl Dockery, Kevin Ennis, Mair Evans, Harjit Khaira, Gill Price, Jon Russell, Margrit Shildrick, Jane Treglown, Nicola Treglown, Gerry Carlin,

domestic — gives any clue as to the text's material origins. Our own 'debts' — Janet's and mine — cannot be accounted for in such a way, they cannot be passed off in a ritualized paragraph, summed up and dispensed with before we turn to the proper business of theorizing. But for the generosities of specific people, there would be no words here to read. And that's precisely the point. Consequently, we have attempted to inscribe our 'text' with the traces of its genesis. Running underneath our words, underpinning our theories, are the names of those who've enabled this chapter to be written. Where appropriate, we have footnoted the specific person who obtained a particular text. These names appear in brackets at the end of a reference. In doing this, however, we both recognize that this is not to say that we can fully account for the various acts of labour and love that have sustained us during the production of this piece.

This paper addresses the embodied nature of academic work, and the experience of writing *together* has been a crucial influence on what we have produced. We had to let go of any fantasies of 'writing' as an autonomous intellectual act, to relinquish any claims to a single authorized voice. But our sense of security in this joint intellectual venture was fragile, for we both knew that either one of us could fade out of the process at any time — we both have myalgic encephalomyelitis (ME) — that our reliance upon each other was purely provisional and yet entirely necessary to the process of writing. Paradoxically, our physical uncertainties became a source of strength, the basis for many of our ideas, rather than a stress, something to be fought against.

We have tried to write against the dematerialization of the embodied subject and to reflect on ways in which the creative and disruptive presence of our bodies is a necessary element in the process of theorizing, teaching, writing and learning. We recognize how the visibility of our bodies can threaten our academic authority — that you may have already decided that the personal experience of our illness fits uncomfortably with any attempt we may subsequently make to theorize the place of the body in academia. But the point of disrupting our academic arguments with a singular, though often unidentified, 'I' is not to lay claim to 'experience' as unique knowledge, an essential part of who we are, for experience is always mediated and, in particular, here, has been influenced by our discussions with each other. Rather, we use a personal voice as a way of breaking the disembodied flow, the more distanced 'we' — in this case Janet and Tracey, not a collective feminist 'we' — of other parts of the paper. It is the apparent contradiction between our experience of writing as an embodied act and the disembodied space of academia that we have tried to address in what follows.

The western Academy has been held as the site, *par excellence*, for the expression of cartesian logic. During the Enlightenment era, it was the site where the universal subject came most fully into 'his' own, the arena in which

Kate Chedgzoy, Jay Daley, Grindl Dockery, Kevin Ennis, Mair Evans, Harjit Khaira, Gill Price, Jon Russell, Margrit Shildrick, Jane Treglown, Nicola Treglown, Gerry Carlin, Kate Chedgzoy, Jay Daley, rational thought, predicated on a transcendence of the body, could be most fully sought. In this life of the mind, bodies were a constant threat, for they were held to contaminate reason, to interfere with the 'view-from-nowhere'. Women's bodies, with all their associations with childbirth, menstruation and the 'natural', unreasoning, instinctual world, were seen as particularly dangerous. Unable to ever fully transcend their ties to their bodies and nature and thus incapable of achieving pure rationality, women were both the contaminating and contaminated Other (Price and Shildrick, 1994), to be excluded not simply from the Academy but from any claim to full subjecthood. The claim here is not just that women were excluded from rationality but that rationality itself was defined 'against the feminine and traditional female roles' (Gatens, 1992: 120–121, collected from library by Grindl Dockery). In short, women were cast as 'reason's "other"' (Braidotti, 1991: 148).

Rationality, as the foundation stone for our understanding of the world, has come under sustained critique over recent decades, and feminist writers have been at the forefront of these moves. Braidotti suggests that where feminist thinking differs from other theoretical approaches to the crisis of reason, is in 'its desire to disclose not only the violent, power-centred character of rationality, but also the sexed nature of this violence' (1991: 175). In proposing new epistemological approaches, what further distinguishes feminist thinking (from other critical perspectives) is the widespread insistence on the embodiedness of theory, the materiality of discourse, 'the corporeal ground of our intelligence' (Rich, 1976: 39).

The links between the body, power and knowledge have occupied a central place in second-wave feminism — women's right to control over our bodies was one of the basic tenets of the women's liberation movement. Supporting and underlying this demand was a wide-ranging critique, which 're-conceptualized the body from a purely biological form to an historical construction and medium of social control' (Bordo, 1993: 182). The work of authors such as Andrea Dworkin, Shulamith Firestone and Germaine Greer highlighted the relationships between the female body, the demands of femininity and the maternal role, and patriarchal oppression, and mapped out the corporeal roots of patriarchal power. Susan Bordo argues that this work, written for the movement and specifically political in its intent was *'embodied* theory'. Her point here is not so much that it was theory grounded in the body (although women's bodies were a focus) but that 'their theory never drew attention to *itself*, never made an appearance except as it shaped the "matter" of the argument' (Bordo, 1993: 185).

Women, entering the academy as feminists during the 1970s and 1980s, worked to develop a distinct and explicit feminist theory. This was distinguishable from masculine theorizing, not simply by its content, but by its approach to the questions of reason, subjectivity and knowledge. There was a constant tension between the need to establish the validity of feminist knowledge production by proving that women could meet intellectual and academic criteria, and 'think like a man'; and the desire to critique the process of abstracted, disembodied theorizing which separated thought from life, the mind from the body. In the alien territory of the academy, women were constantly aware of their 'otherness' (Bordo, 1990: 148), of the ways in which their bodies were seen to compromise thought.

The rise of postmodern thinking provided a new challenge to women's embodied subjectivity. Postmodernism's displacement of the universal modern ungendered subject has been welcomed by some feminists, but there has been an anxiety about the way in which certain theoretical positions have caused the fragmentation, dispersal and dematerialization of the body, potentially rendering the basis of a feminist politics invalid. In the face of this, many feminist postmodernist writers have put out a renewed call for the embodied subject, situated in time and place and marked by (sexual) difference. And yet, feminists' ongoing engagement with the spectre of essentialism evoked the fear that this could be seen as taking recourse in a fixed anatomical body, prior to discourse, upon which meaning was then inscribed.[2] Whilst fears of essentialism could be said to have produced a defensive over-investment in the idea of a discursively constructed body in feminist postmodern theory, there remain those who are critical of anti-essentialism's neglect of 'matter'. In a critique of Monique Wittig's 'anti-essentialist materialism', for example, Diana Fuss (1989, loaned by Margrit Shildrick) argues that Wittig's insistence on a constructionist view of the body leads her to overlook the body's *materiality* which is crucial to her analysis of the oppression of women.[3]

For Fuss, the notion of the body as discursively mediated should not preclude the body's materiality, even whilst recognizing that there is no point of access to pure 'matter'. One way of negotiating the tension between matter (essence) and discourse (social construct), Fuss suggests, is through what has been termed 'The Politics of Location' (Rich, 1986). Building on Adrienne Rich's much quoted proposal for a 'moratorium on saying "the body"' (1986: 215), Fuss stresses the importance of the particular as a means of 'beginning the project of reintroducing biology, the body *as matter*, back into poststructuralist materialist discourse' (1989: 52). As a counter to the grandiose abstraction signified by the reference to the (universalized) body, the particular; one's own body, *my* body is viewed in terms of its materializing potential: 'whereas the determiner "the" essentializes its object through universalization, the possessive "my" de-essentializes its object through particularization' (Fuss, 1989: 52).

Put more simply, embodying poststructuralism in Fuss's terms entails 'recognising our location, having to name the ground we're coming from' (Rich, 1986: 219) and thus emphasizes 'the centrality of subject positions'

Mair Evans, Harjit Khaira, Gill Price, Jon Russell, Margrit Shildrick, Jane Treglown, Nicola Treglown, Gerry Carlin, Kate Chedgzoy, Jay Daley, Grindl Dockery, Kevin Ennis, Mair Evans, Harjit Khaira, Gill

(Fuss, 1989). What is more, as Elspeth Probyn points out, there are attendant dangers in privileging the local as a means of countering the global excesses of the grand narratives of the Enlightenment; 'it seems that an unspecified local becomes the site for an unnamed politics. As such, local, locale and location become abstractions, cut off from a signifying ground and serving as signposts with no indication of direction' (Probyn, 1990: 177).[4]

With her problematization of the essentialism/constructionism binary and her rigorous interrogation of the term essence, Fuss seems fully mindful of the dangers of the unspecified local, and continually states her commitment to a specific politics. She calls on the critic's responsibility to historicize and acknowledge their own particular signifying ground.[5] That Fuss intends more than a discursive intervention in the debate over essentialism is further signalled by her inclusion of a discussion of the operations of essentialism in a more 'worldly' context: the classroom. The shift of focus from text to classroom marks an important move in the essentialism debate, in that it implies a commitment to exploring the workings of ideology as it is *lived*, a means of engaging with what Edward Said has referred to as 'the very life of texts in the world' (1976: 41).

'Essentialism in the Classroom', the final chapter in Fuss's discussion, takes as its focus the issue of the 'authority of experience' i.e. 'the way in which essence circulates as a privileged signifier in the classroom' (113). Briefly, Fuss contends that experience constitutes shaky ground epistemologically speaking, in so far as it is offered as a self-evident basis for establishing authority or more simply presented as (immediate) truth itself. Fuss then goes on to outline 'some of the unwelcome effects of essentialism in the classroom, and with the pedagogy and politics of "essentially speaking"' (1989: 115). As a piece of textual analysis, it is hard to fault Fuss's exploration of the *sign* 'experience', and we certainly agree that like biology, like essence, experience is a term that we should not shy away from theorizing. Despite the repeated articulation of her commitment to specificity, to particularity and location, Fuss presents an alarmingly ungrounded and depersonalized account of her students' appeals to experiential knowledge; the particular voices of experience become transmuted into hardened essences, into authoritarian texts to be deconstructed.

In addition to allowing the term essentialism to slip back over the ground of her thesis to assume the negative critical pole to constructionism (a surprising move given the central concern of *Essentially Speaking* to problematize the essence/construction binarism) Fuss fails to honour her self-assumed 'responsibility to historicize, to examine each deployment of essence, each appeal to experience, each claim to identity in the complicated contextual frame in which it is made' (1989: 118). In the place of specific analyses of specific articulations of particular experiences between embodied agents, 'Essentialism in the Classroom' offers an overarching generalized equation of experience with

Price, Jon Russell, Margrit Shildrick, Jane Treglown, Nicola Treglown, Gerry Carlin, Kate Chedgzoy, Jay Daley, Grindl Dockery, Kevin Ennis, Mair Evans, Harjit Khaira, Gill Price, Jon Russell, Margrit essence; experience = transcendental signified = conservative, authoritarian fiction.

As bell hooks has pointed out, Fuss does not pause to consider that all of the instances of 'essentialism' that she mentions are attributed to marginalized students, which not only creates the illusion that it is only the marginalized who essentialize (hooks, 1991: 176), but also renders her own privileged position silent and invisible. Nowhere does Fuss articulate or acknowledge her own location of power, or how her location relates to those of her students. In her position as teacher at least, she will exert a hegemonic presence over her students, a presence of which she takes no account in her assessment of their 'essentialist' utterances.

Fuss proposes that one of the ways to deal with essentialism in the classroom is to foreground it, make it the explicit topic of debate. In most discussions on essentialism within pedagogic situations, the teacher operates from a context of privileged knower. Unless this authority can at least be brought into question, the debate will be *about* the deconstruction of essence, and thus take place within an abstracted sphere through the disembodied voice of authority, rather than being an example of deconstructive practice which makes evident the provisional nature of embodied subjectivity and of any claims to authority. Spivak says:

> Rather than make it a central issue, work it into the method of your teaching so that the class becomes an example of the minimalizing of essences, the impossibility of essences; rather than talk about it constantly, make the class a proof of this new position. (1993: 18, photocopied by Grindl Dockery)

This proposal of Spivak's seems to offer the possibility of different strategic approaches to teaching situations — on the part of both students and teacher. But to follow it through, to make the classroom a space in which essence, identity, experience and authority constantly come under question, in which they are not allowed to line up neatly together, is not an easy task.

In feminist and other critical pedagogies, a long adopted strategy, which attempts to challenge these hierarchies of knowledge, has been to draw on the lived experience of students. Reflection on such experience has been used as the basis both for illustrating theory (which also serves to meet the demands of the institution for academic content) and as a route to *conscientization*, to empowerment. Patti Lather suggests that these critical pedagogies require 'a subject who is an object of our emancipatory desires' (1991: 141, collected from library by Grindl Dockery), and that they draw upon Enlightenment values of a universal consciousness, transcendence — 'knowing the world to set herself free from it' (Lather, 1991: 141) — and autonomy. Never fully able

Shildrick, Jane Treglown, Nicola Treglown, Gerry Carlin, Kate Chedgzoy, Jay Daley, Grindl Dockery, Kevin Ennis, Mair Evans, Harjit Khaira, Gill Price, Jon Russell, Margrit Shildrick, Jane Treglown, to split herself off from her embodied self, never able to reach a state of complete knowledge, the subject in/of liberatory pedagogy is caught in an endless struggle where that which she desires (or we desire for her) will always be beyond her grasp.

Lather suggests that we shift our focus from the subject of pedagogy to the 'power-saturated discourses that monitor and normalize our sense of who we are and what is possible' (1991: 142), that we take these discursive constructions and normalizations as our object of study. Thus, we can provisionally identify a way in which we can both question the demands of essentialism and allow experience a place in the classroom. Our experiences, brought into teaching/learning situations, are not representative of some 'real truth', but are particular, local embodied expressions of our insertion into discourse. They offer us the chance to examine our own claims to centrality and marginality, to look at how these are shaped by dominant discourses and moments of resistance. We can recognize the provisionality of subject positions we occupy when speaking 'with a particular voice' and acknowledge the construction and destabilization of the apparently stable bodies which form the ground from which we speak.

I write here as someone who is 'in the classroom' as both teacher and student. What strikes me about the plea I have made above for a deconstructive pedagogy is how, when I teach, I have the authority to legitimate or demand this approach from students, and when I act as a student, I potentially feel myself under threat if required to 'submit' my experience to deconstruction. This authority cannot itself be done away with, but we can make it the focus of study, look at how it is constituted, trace its effects and in so doing 'foreground a relation between knower and known, teacher and taught, from an embodied perspective' (Lather, 1991: 193).

Going into a teaching situation, my body is marked. When I speak I may be read as 'speaking as' woman, as teacher, as disabled, as lesbian, as middle-class, as white, though the weight of each of these 'markings' will vary depending upon those who read me, how they interpret my authority or lack of it, how I have been constituted by and inserted into the discursive norms of academia. The identity from which I am seen to speak is 'read off' my body, my accent, my movements and gestures. It is this reading, which takes place in silence, that essentializes, if ways are not found to deconstruct it and to 'minimalize the essence'. In a recent interview Gayatri Spivak makes reference to the idea of 'essentialist readers' (1993: 17). This seems to be a useful formulation to introduce into debates over essentialism; acknowledging the role of the reader simultaneously involves the acknowledgement of essentialism as something that is attributed/conferred by specific readers/agents; it is an action and not a hardened substance that exists 'out there' or at the heart of certain discourses.

My body may also act to disrupt expectations and call my authority into

Nicola Treglown, Gerry Carlin, Kate Chedgzoy, Jay Daley, Grindl Dockery, Kevin Ennis, Mair Evans, Harjit Khaira, Gill Price, Jon Russell, Margrit Shildrick, Jane Treglown, Nicola Treglown, Gerry Carlin, question from the moment I enter a room. I am female, disabled and teaching. *The body* in academia is taken-for-granted — able and invisible, necessary only as the site for the mind. 'Indeed the queer neutrality of the phrase "the body" in its strenuous colourlessness suggests that something is up' (Riley, 1988: 104). *My body*, when I am using a wheelchair, is all too visible. My temptation is to silence this potential crack in the hegemony of the teacher, reassert my authority despite my body — 'it makes no difference'. And yet it does make a difference, not only in how I am viewed but in a very material sense — in how I can move around the classroom, in which classrooms I can actually reach, in how I deal with teaching aids, in how long I can run a session before my energy fades. And so I try to use these differences, the ways in which my self, embodied, teacher, female . . . has been constituted, as the subject of discussion. It challenges me, for I find I long to police my own boundaries — it is far safer for me, if I have used a wheelchair for my first teaching session with a group of students, to go on using a wheelchair, even if I have enough strength to walk some weeks. There is too much disruption, too much uncertainty in breaking boundaries. I find myself more concerned than ever to show that I have a 'complete' grasp of my subject — so that students shall not be able to put any limits in my knowledge down to the fact that I'm disabled (I'm a woman, I'm lesbian . . .), so that they cannot see my body as compromising authority. The way in which my body enters into and affects the teaching situation as disabled and female highlights how the disruptive materiality of any of our particular bodies becomes most marked at the points when we resist or destabilize the discursive norms of academia. These demand, for example, that we carry our gender lightly, unobtrusively — that we are feminine but not too feminine, confident but not assertive, clever but not brilliant. If we wear makeup and nail varnish, we are held to have slept our way to our degrees. If we are confident and refuse to be overawed by the authority of male colleagues, it is our 'lesbian body language' that is held against us. The position of women in academia and the failure of many to be granted promotion, despite outstanding research and publications records, should lead us to problematize not just the intellectual but the bodily. It is precisely the implication that bodies can be 'taken-for-granted' within the academy that should alert us to the often unspoken but highly disruptive role played by the presence of particular women's bodies.

I no longer have the energy for this. I'm so tired. For a start everything takes so long. There's a book I want, *Homo Academicus*, it should be in the library, they have most things by Bourdieu. But it's not just a matter of whether they have it or not. For me, getting that book involves asking someone either to get it for me or else to wheel me to it. Most of the time that's OK, but today there's no-one around to ask. I'll have to wait.

Kate Chedgzoy, Jay Daley, Grindl Dockery, Kevin Ennis, Mair Evans, Harjit Khaira, Gill Price, Jon Russell, Margrit Shildrick, Jane Treglown, Nicola Treglown, Gerry Carlin, Kate Chedgzoy, Jay Daley,

Becoming ill again has made me notice the bodily work of academic writing in that I now have to ask for things that I used to do unthinkingly. Finding books, photocopying articles, typing, for example, are all activities that I used to overlook or not notice when I had the privilege of forgetting my own body. While I have no shortage of willing volunteers, sometimes the act of translating what used to be automatic action into requests for help is too much. Making explicit and visible what previously went unnoticed is a tiring business; articulating what I need often wears me out. Other times I feel it is too much to ask, so I find myself censoring my needs and instead living with my frustrations.

Not that the effort stops when I have the books I need. Reading, thinking and writing often demand of me energy that I don't have. Consequently, I have many anxieties that I won't be able to make it theoretically, that I won't be rigorous or thorough enough. During my reading for this paper, I was struck by a comment made by feminist geographer Gillian Rose. After describing her seduction by masculinist claims to exhaustiveness and methodical precision, she outlines her response.

> The mobility that I adopt is an effort to resist by playing with the powerful, by knowing their language and juggling with its possibilities — it is a strategy enabled by intimacy with masculinist geography. (Rose, 1993: 15)

I, too, recognize that I am seduced by the orthodoxies of the discursive field in which I am engaged. I, too, privilege exhaustiveness, the need to be 'on top of' my material. I, too, have adopted strategies that involve playing the dominant at their own game, that involve outwitting and outmastering the master. This is all very well but what happens when you're too exhausted to be exhaustive, what happens when you don't have the energy or the agility to play or to juggle? 'The mobility' that I adopt is compromised by my body and can't be taken for granted. What I mean is that my access to these debates around essentialism, or perhaps even to the scene of theorizing in general, is circumscribed by my body at every turn and that this circumscription has an effect upon what Linda Kauffman has termed my 'epistemic authority' (1989: 119, collected from library by Gerry Carlin). Had I more energy, I would investigate this equation of mobility and exhaustiveness with authority and hence legitimacy, but I'm going to have to pause, for the time being at least. Even as I write about embodiment, I'm engaging in my own acts of splitting, I'm denying my body. I'm exhausted. To be honest, I want to just walk away from this but there's something else I need to say. It can wait a while though. . . .

The questions we've been trying to address throughout this chapter revolve around the relations between theory, experience and knowledge and

Grindl Dockery, Kevin Ennis, Mair Evans, Harjit Khaira, Gill Price, Jon Russell, Margrit Shildrick, Jane Treglown, Nicola Treglown, Gerry Carlin, Kate Chedgzoy, Jay Daley, Grindl Dockery, Kevin Ennis, how they are embodied. There is an implication in *Essentially Speaking* that experience as a discursive currency will only be valued when it is adequately theorized. In whose terms will this occur? What is knowledge if it is so entirely dissociated from experience? Is knowledge legitimated (theorized) experience? What is the relation between theory and practice? What assumptions underpin theory's dissociation from practice? In short, alongside Patti Lather, we want to ask:

> Given the postmodern tenet of how we are inscribed in that which we struggle against, how can I intervene in the production of knowledge at particular sites in ways that work out of the blood and spirit of our lives rather than out of the consumerism of ideas that can pass for a life of the mind in academic theory? (1991: 20)

In writing together, in acknowledging some of the material costs of theorizing and producing this paper, we have tried to show how theory can never be an abstracted term, but is always the result of specific acts of labour or production. Merleau-Ponty reminds us that 'all higher mental functions are also somatic activities' (Turner, 1992: 43). In arguing that theorizing is an embodied act, we do not wish to give the impression that we view matter, or the material, as something immediate or fixed, but alongside Judith Butler we would argue 'that there is no reference to a pure body which is not at the same time a further formation of that body' (1993: 10). Butler thus lays the ground for a material body which is not a natural body, for embodied subjectivity which is both the object and effect of discourse, and for theorizing as an embodied act.

Rather than view theory as a superior and separate activity to practice, detached from any enactment, Gayatri Spivak offers a more useful notion — strategy — which not only repudiates the split but also serves as a means of thinking theory as an embodied activity.

> Strategy works through a persistent (de)constructive critique of the theoretical. 'Strategy' is an embattled concept metaphor and unlike 'theory' its antecedents are not disinterested and universal. . . . A strategy suits a situation; a strategy is not a theory. (1993: 3–4)

Spivak's explanation of strategy seems to light a way out of the essence/construct, theory/practice impasses. We read it to entail a complex negotiation of the discursive and material forces at play between specific agents that thereby refuses the kind of abstract predictive moves that can characterize theory in as much as it is split off from practice. For example, strategy can be mindful of the persistence of Enlightenment discourses despite their repeated deconstruction in the Academy. Spivak notes 'knowing an ideology does not dissipate its

Mair Evans, Harjit Khaira, Gill Price, Jon Russell, Margrit Shildrick, Jane Treglown, Nicola Treglown, Gerry Carlin, Kate Chedgzoy, Jay Daley, Grindl Dockery, Kevin Ennis, Mair Evans, Harjit Khaira, Gill effect' (1993: 5). However far we may critique the exhaustive search that we are pulled into in our efforts to produce this paper, in order for our words to count they need to adhere to the conventions of the dominant discourse even as they bring them into question. 'To break with the convention is to risk not being heard at all' (Tompkins, 1989: 124, photocopied by Harjit Khaira).

We wish to question the violence with which the Other of legitimated knowledge, the known that 'is always in excess of knowledge' (Spivak, 1993: 8), that which exceeds its theories, gets cast out of the frame. It is fixed as essence and hence as negative, as authoritarian. As anti-essentialism's focus has widened from the metanarrative of the Enlightenment, its critique has been brought to bear upon those who not only were never admitted to the realm of the enlightenment subject, but whose exclusion provided the foundation for the grand narratives of truth and rationality. It is not that we want to argue that an anti-essentialist critique is inappropriate to marginalized groups, but that such a critique needs not only to take account of its own investment in declaring particular utterances essentialist, but also to acknowledge its own participatory role in the creation of 'essence'. In failing to acknowledge their own signifying ground, many anti-essentialist critics disqualify not only the dominant modernist discourses in play, but also silence the voices of many who have never yet been heard. Foucault suggests that these delegitimated knowledges are subjugated knowledges.

> I believe that by subjugated knowledges one should understand something else. . . . namely a whole set of knowledges that have been disqualified as inadequate to their task or insufficiently elaborated: naïve knowledges, located low down on the hierarchy, beneath the required level of cognition or scientificity. (1980: 81–82)

Writing this paper we have tried to bring to light our own subjugated knowledges, our experiences of how the process of writing, theorizing, teaching has had to change for us as a consequence of our illnesses. In doing so, we have encountered moments of great anxiety, of worry about the ways in which those reading may take a particular moment of this experience and fix it, label us essentialists. We have struggled to hold onto our personal voices which allow us to acknowledge the embodiedness of our acts and serve to situate our writing at the breakdown of the theory/practice binary, recognizing such writing as an act that seeks to have impact outside the academy. Yet we have also consciously used the privileged, disembodied voice of our academic background, not only to lift us over and beyond our moments of fear, but because, along with bell hooks, we believe that '. . . ideas and theories are important, and absolutely essential for envisioning and making a successful feminist movement, one that will mobilize groups of people to transform this society' (1984: 112). Throughout

Price, Jon Russell, Margrit Shildrick, Jane Treglown, Nicola Treglown, Gerry Carlin, Kate Chedgzoy, Jay Daley, Grindl Dockery, Kevin Ennis, Mair Evans, Harjit Khaira, Gill Price, Jon Russell, Margrit the paper we have highlighted the dilemmas that we face in trying to develop a feminist practice within academia that can incorporate our bodily knowledges into teaching, research and writing. The implications of this are encapsulated in Ellsworth's remarks on emancipatory pedagogy.

> The terms in which I can and will assert and unsettle 'difference' and unlearn my positions of privilege in future classroom practices are wholly dependent on the Others/others whose presence — with their concrete experiences of privileges and oppressions, and subjugated or oppressive knowledges — I am responding to and acting with in any given classroom. My moving about between the positions of privileged speaking subject and Inappropriate/d Other cannot be predicted, prescribed or understood beforehand by any theoretical framework or methodological practice. It is in this sense that a practice grounded in the unknowable is profoundly contextual (historical) and interdependent (social). (Ellsworth, 1989: 323)

Relinquishing an advanced theory of essences may plunge us into uncertainty but it simultaneously opens up new possibilities.

Notes

1 From Patti Lather (1991: 20).
2 Some writers have adopted a notion of embodiment that is itself disembodied, arguing that the body of which they write is not a material body, a body that bleeds, that aches, that feels, but rather is a 'decidedly literary evocation', a point underlined by a speaker on the body in Irigarayan writing who, on being asked about the status of the body of which she spoke, pinched herself and said, 'Well, I certainly don't mean *this* body' (Kirby, 1991: 91). In response to Kirby's concern as to how 'feminist practice can effectively engage the problematic of corporeality *without* meaning this body' (Kirby, 1991: 91) and without laying claim to a natural, biological body, we would argue that bodies have materiality, but that we can never have access to such bodies unmediated by discourse, to bodies that are prior to construction (Shildrick and Price, 1994).
3 Through the 'nearly imperceptible slippage from the formulation "the body *is* not matter" to the position "the body *does* not matter: it matters not . . ."' Fuss suggests that 'what is lost in her work is precisely a materialist analysis of the body *as* matter' (1989: 50).
4 Such insistence on the particular or the local is certainly not unusual; as Elspeth Probyn points out, 'Again and again we have heard (and also uttered) the need for specificity, as yet another postmodernist publication ends with a cry for the "local"' (1990: 77).
5 Fuss says, 'We need to continue to be rightly wary of such efforts by hegemonic groups to use essentialism as a political tool waged against less powerful groups. Still, it is precisely these powerless groups we need to listen to more carefully as we rethink the problem of essentialism in feminist theory, for it may well be that

Gayatri Spivak is right: in the hands of the dispossessed themselves, essentialism can be a powerful strategic weapon' (1989: 40).

References

Bourdieu. P. (1988) *Homo academicus*, Cambridge: Polity Press.

Bordo, S. (1993) 'Feminism, Foucault and the politics of the body', in Ramazanoglu, C. (Ed.) *Up against Foucault: explorations of some tensions between Foucault and feminism*, London, New York: Routledge.

Bordo, S. (1990) 'Feminism, Postmodernism, and Gender-Scepticism' in Nicholson, L. (Ed.) *Feminism/Postmodernism*, London, New York: Routledge.

Braidotti, R. (1991) *Patterns of Dissonance*, Cambridge: Polity Press.

Butler, J. (1993) *Bodies That Matter: on the discursive limits of 'sex'*, London, New York: Routledge.

Dworkin, A. (1981) *Pornography: men possessing women*, London: Women's Press.

Ellsworth, E. (1989) 'Why doesn't this feel emp[owering? Working through the repressive myths of critical pedagogy', *Harvard Educational Review*, **59**, 3, pp. 297–324.

Fuss, D. (1989) *Essentially Speaking, Feminism, Nature and Difference*, London, New York: Routledge.

Foucault, M. (1980) *Power/Knowledge: Selected Interviews and Other Writings 1972–77*. (Ed. Gordon, C.) Brighton: The Harvester Press Ltd.

Firestone, S. (1970) *The dialectic of sex: the case for feminist revolution*, New York: Morrow.

Gatens, M. (1992) 'Power, Bodies and Difference', in Barrett, M. and Phillips, A. (Eds) *Destabilizing Theory, Contemporary Feminist Debates*, Cambridge: Polity Press.

Greer, G. (1970) *The Female Eunuch*, London: MacGibbon and Kee.

Greer, G. (1984) *Sex and Destiny: the politics of human fertility*, London: Secker and Warburg.

hooks, b. (1991) 'Essentialism and Experience', *American Literary History*, **3**, 1, pp. 172–183.

hooks, b. (1984) *Feminist Theory: from margin to centre*, Boston: South End Press.

Kauffman, L. (Ed.) (1989) *Gender and Theory: dialogue in feminist criticism*, Oxford: Blackwell.

Kirby, V. (1991) 'Corpus delicti: the body at the scene of writing', in Diprose, R. and Ferrell, R. (Eds) *Cartographies: Poststructuralism and the mapping of bodies and spaces*, Sydney: Allen & Unwin Australia Pty Ltd.

Lather, P. (1991) *Getting Smart: Feminist Research and Pedagogy With/In the Postmodern*, London, New York: Routledge.

Miller, J. (1990) *Seduction: Studies in Reading and Culture*, London: Virago.

Price, J. and Shildrick, M. (1994) *Breaking the Boundaries of the Broken Body: Mastery, Materiality, and ME*, paper presented at Women's Studies Network (UK) Conference, Portsmouth, July.

Probyn, E. (1990) 'Travels in the Postmodern: Making Sense of the Local', in Nicholson, L. (Ed.) *Feminism/Postmodernism*, London, New York: Routledge.

Rich, A. (1976) *Of Woman Born*, New York: W.W. Norton.

Rich, A. (1986) *Blood, Bread and Poetry: Selected Prose 1979–85*, New York and London: W.W. Norton & Company.

RILEY, D. (1988) *'Am I That Name?' Feminism and the Category of 'Woman' in History*, London: The MacMillan Press Ltd.

ROSE, G. (1993) *Feminism and Geography. The Limits of Geographical Knowledge*, Cambridge: Polity Press.

SAID, E. (1976) 'Interview with Edward Said', *Diacritics*, **6**, 3.

SHILDRICK, M. and PRICE, J. (1994) 'Splitting the Difference: Adventures in the Anatomy and Embodiment of Women', in GRIFFIN, G., HESTER, M., RAI, S., and ROSENEIL, S. (Eds) *Stirring It: Challenges for Feminism*, London: Taylor & Francis Ltd.

SPIVAK, G.C. (1993) *Outside in the Teaching Machine*, London, New York: Routledge.

TOMPKINS, J. (1989) 'Me and My Shadow' in KAUFFMAN, L. (Ed.) *Gender and Theory: dialogues in feminist criticism*, Oxford: Blackwell.

TURNER, B. (1992) *Regulating Bodies: Essays in Medical Sociology*, London, New York: Routledge.

WITTIG, M. (1981) 'One is Not Born a Woman', *Feminist Issues*, Fall, pp. 47–54.

Chapter 8

Measuring the Muse: Feminism, Creativity and Career Development in Higher Education

Louise Morley

Scheherazade's Stories

This chapter examines the tension between writing and research as major outlets for academic women's creativity, and the role of publication as a performance indicator for purposes of academic career development. It explores how 'coercive creativity' affects the process of writing, and considers internalized narratives activated when women claim authority to write in dominant organizations of knowledge production. By gendering both the concept and the application of creativity, it problematizes the relationship between gender, knowledge and power and highlights how feminist discourses influence opportunities for inspiration and publication.

The UK academy privileges research and publication, not only for purposes of intellectual prestige, but also for reasons of economic survival. In the new enterprise culture of Higher Education, research output is used as a major performance indicator of productivity. British universities are subjected to government-led research assessment exercises, with funding consequences. The transition from welfare to market values in Higher Education means that the pressure to generate income, publish and attract research funding has become an increasingly prominent part of academic life, reinforced at appraisal interviews and promotion boards. This juxtaposition of the economic with the aesthetic, and the salience of the written word, has a clear gender dimension in the context of promotion and retention criteria. The matrix of power relations in which feminist academics are enmeshed is further compounded by the relationship between gender, language, knowledge and power. In power-laden daily social interactions, it is not just a question of what is said, but of who is entitled to speak. Women's relationship to writing has been a subject of much feminist analysis (Cixous, 1986; Gilbert and Gubar, 1989). For academic women, the web of power relations is enacted in the organizational structures of production and distribution, as well as the conventions of teaching, writing and research.

This coercive creativity in a gendered context lends itself to a multiplicity of images from popular culture. Like Scheherazade in the Arabian Nights, life in the academy is prolonged with the production of words that please predominantly male assessors, confusing whether women academics write from anxiety or from desire. In her feminist critique of the effects of patriarchal science on women, Donna Haraway (1991) produced the image of the Cyborg. This is a machine/organic hybrid, caught between the discourses of modernism and postmodernism, visually represented on the book cover as a semi-human woman with her fingers welded to a word processor. Increased productivity has been an objective behind the New Right's policy reforms, reinforced in management dictates and strategies. The end goal of this productivity, in relation to research, is unclear, and there are fears of surplus resulting in 'knowledge mountains' and 'thought lakes' (Fisher, 1994: 81).

Women's access to intellectual production is problematic (Lewis, 1994). Universities are sites of cultural production, and the absence of women in positions of seniority has intellectual and political repercussions (Hansard Society, 1990; Morley, 1994). Male domination of academic journals and publishing and androcentric research methods have also been explored in relation to their gate-keeping role and ensuing silencing of women (Roberts, 1981; Stanley and Wise, 1983; Eichler, 1988; Fonow and Cook, 1991; Stanley and Wise, 1993). Studies on the sociology of knowledge outline the gendered roots of scholarship and demonstrate how the powerful have traditionally assessed the quality of ideas (Fuchs Epstein, 1988). In the academy, there is an ongoing tension between the success ethic and creativity, with quality of work inevitably evaluated by situated interpretations. The addition of market forces and the resulting commodification of Higher Education introduces further stakeholders. The new commercialism requires academics to define and competitively market their products to potential purchasers in industry, commerce and the overseas market. One example is the academic conference, as it transforms into a trade fair, with participants paying large registration fees for the privilege of displaying their intellectual products. The more one writes/speaks, the more successful one is deemed to be, with silence or non-writing deplored and seen as a signifier of passivity, inertia, dullness and powerlessness.

Several questions can be explored in relation to the interconnection between gender, creativity and career development. In the UK, only four per cent of professors are women. If research is a central criterion in promotion, is the under-representation of women in positions of seniority a result of lower research and publication output? Are women academics less productive, or less likely to get published, or less likely to have their publications recognized for promotion purposes? Is the notion of academic excellence dependent on the denial of difference based on gender, social class, 'race', sexuality, age? Do power relations in the academy stifle or inspire creativity? Is creativity itself a gendered term? (Carroll, 1992). To answer these questions, it is important to examine the preconditions that enhance or interrupt the creative process for academic women.

The publish or perish cliché oversimplifies the conditions under which women academics labour. Lionel Lewis exposed this myth in 1975 when he described it as a 'protective device to conceal the true reasons why someone is forced to leave a department'. It suggests a meritocracy and 'promotes the idea that an objective standard is utilized in arriving at decisions which are made subjectively' (Lewis, 1975). Simeone claims that women perish more due to lack of publications, while men gain more from productivity (Simeone, 1987). This is particularly relevant to recession-torn Britain, where public sector under-funding has reduced the number of employment opportunities and created a highly competitive intellectual atmosphere of negative equity and educational inflation.

In 1994 in the UK, women were disproportionately represented in the lower grades and on fixed-term contracts in the academy (Morley, 1994). As a consequence, women are often in teaching-led situations. In her UK-based research, Barbara Bagihole noted that women were 'good campus citizens', and likely to take on more pastoral care and teaching than their male colleagues. One of her interviewees commented, 'at the expense of my research, my door is always open' (Bagihole, 1993). The imbalance between demand and capacity can result in poor psychological health. Fisher (1994) maintains that creative processes are stress-sensitive, and that stress can be both environmental and cognitive.

Research undertaken in the USA during the 1970s highlighted the fact that out of 10 000 faculty members, more than one-third of men, but fewer than one-fifth of women, spent more than eight hours a week in scholarly research, with the result that over a third of the men had published at least five articles and seven per cent at least one book (Astin and Bayer, 1979). In 1980, these publication proportions remained the same (Astin and Snyder, 1982). North American researchers also found that when productivity is equal, rewards for women are smaller (Cole, 1979). Simeone (1987) attempts to explain this by suggesting that women's work is judged less favourably than men's, particularly if it is from a feminist perspective, as this is dismissed as minor or self-serving by mainstream academics. Carroll cites a sex discrimination case in the USA in which tenure was refused to Katherine Gutzwiller on the basis of her work being 'competent' but neither 'creative nor original' (Carroll, 1992: 354). Carroll maintains that terms such as 'creative' and 'original' are insubstantial, used with a political rather than intellectual purpose. She argues that the concept of creativity is used to maintain a class system of the intellect, and the term is used to devalue women's work (Carroll, 1992: 353).

Feminism as Creativity

Feminisms have challenged the class system of the intellect, by exposing the gendered basis of knowledge and by providing intellectual space for women's ideas (Morley, 1995). The decade 1985–1995 has witnessed a proliferation of feminist publications in both fiction and non-fiction. Britain has at least five feminist publishing houses, and leading publishers have sizeable sections on Women's Studies. Zmroczek and Duchen's survey (1991) indicated the existence of an impressive range of feminist research in the UK, with sociology leading the way. To suggest that women are operating sub-optimally could be erroneous, if women's creativity is synonymous with publication output. In the context of the academy, where women's contributions to policy, management and organizational development are limited by their under-representation in positions of seniority, writing remains a powerful contradiction to the silencing of women's ideas. The combination of a feminist consciousness with daily experiences of sexist oppression, both without and within dominant organizations of knowledge production mean that many academic women are 'bursting' with data. The academy, like other organizations, provides unlimited opportunities for the observation of complex power relations. Academic feminism can serve to both articulate and challenge dominant ideologies. But there is always the threat of dismissal of this knowledge and its relegation to the status of maverick research, on the basis that emotions and personal involvement subvert knowledge. Stanley and Wise (1993: 126) suggest that 'sexist males are a good source of information about their sexism'. It could be argued that the experience of sexist oppression is a valuable source of data for theorizing gender, exemplifying a postmodernist concept that power can be productively linked to knowledge (Giroux, 1993). This raises questions as to whether oppression generates or stifles creativity, or a complex combination of both. Val Walsh (1993) argues that 'oppression and accompanying fear and sense of powerlessness reduces our energy . . . rendering us less alive, more inert, more dead'. Kristeva (1980) celebrates the poetic and subversive power of marginality. In Foucauldian tradition, power is both repressive and productive. For academic feminists, oppression can be a source of creativity, with writing a major form of resistance and revenge.

The psychology of creativity has been theorized for several decades. Kelly's Construct Theory maintains that people under threat are likely to behave rigidly and unquestioningly, and if a person feels at ease, the constructs are more permeable (Kelly, 1955). This notion is colloquially exemplified in the saying 'when you are up to your ass in alligators you won't think of draining the swamp' (Holly, 1993: 162). In his study of creativity, Koestler argued that by 'setting up conditions of psychological safety and freedom, we maximize the likelihood of an emergence of constructive creativity' (Koestler, 1964: 146). Yet there is evidence that writing provides a cathartic/healing/liberatory function for those suffering materially and psychologically oppressive, or life-threatening conditions. Literal confinement such as imprisonment or hiding has produced some very powerful literature (Frank, 1960; Jackson, 1971). Threats to one's physical existence, such as coming to terms with terminal illness, can also provide the material of reflexive creativity (Lorde, 1985). As a political act, writing can give a voice to subordinate groups, and create a sense of community and solidarity. Munt (1992: xi) theorizes this notion in relation to lesbian oppression and believes that 'books have functioned as rites of passage, and signs of kinship for lesbians'. Zimmerman (1992: 4) argues that by writing 'the lesbian creates a narrative or textual space in which she interrogates accepted norms of textuality and sexuality, and constitutes herself as subject'. Brossard (1988: 134) goes further to claim that 'a lesbian who does not reinvent the word/world is a lesbian in the process of disappearing'.

Exploring the conjunction of gender, creativity and academic writing raises many crucial questions. At what stage does sexist oppression interact with academic women's writing? Is this a creative, destructive, disempowering tension, or a combination? Is it a question of the gendered psyche, with women's potential to write being diminished because their creative confidence is undermined by oppressive conditions and work practices and the gendering of knowledge? Is it also an act of resistance, allowing expression of an oppositional consciousness, with writing a liberatory exercise providing opportunity for catharsis, consciousness-raising and communication with other women? What relationship does writing have to wider social and political changes for women? Or does the problematic reside in the publication, rather than in the creative process, with knowledge of reader reaction a dominant internalized narrative for women academics? The 'writing for whom' discourse is a constant pressure for members of subordinate groups.

Stanley and Wise believe that 'all feminists who are involved in writing and research should be more adventurous, more daring, and less concerned with being respectable and publishable' (Stanley and Wise, 1993: 137). This view exemplifies the debate about incorporation or marginalization of feminist knowledge in the academy, countered by mainstream fears as to how a political movement such as feminism could contribute to the growth of scientific knowledge. Stanley and Wise (1993: 169) claim that professions make a fetish out of ignorance and that membership of groups is in itself taken as proof of 'subjective involvement' and thus of disqualification from research competence. Whereas Anglo-American feminist critics have highlighted the role of language in women's oppression, stressing the power of 'naming', many French feminists believe that it is in what language does not say that the feminist revolution must find a base (Sellers, 1991). If this is applied to academic life, it becomes increasingly relevant to examine what is *not* being researched, expressed and taught.

In the current economically-driven climate in the academy, it is debatable as to whether the practice of writing from a counter-hegemonic position is still undesirable. Paradoxically, whilst there has been a closure of academic space for women, there is also an urgency to generate publications. A cynical view would be that so long as it contributes towards the research ratings, the ideological underpinning of the work is irrelevant. Indeed, a defence for academic feminism is the high productivity rate. A report on Women's Studies courses in Higher Education (1993) undertaken by Her Majesty's Inspectorate, highlighted quality and quantity of research and publications in the area. Women academics' relationship to writing and research in hostile organizations could be viewed as the feminist equivalent of holding up a crucifix to Dracula! But

Rosemary Hennessy warns that feminists need to forestall efforts to absorb and domesticate feminism and that it must maintain its potential as an oppositional discourse in the university (Hennessy, 1993).

Internalized Narratives Meet External Obstacles

In 1929, Virginia Woolf argued that women's opportunities to write were severely restricted by lack of material independence and intellectual and literal space (Woolf, 1929). In the 1990s, while some academic women may have economic and spatial freedom, writing and publishing remain problematic. Alice Walker (1984) criticized Woolf for failing to consider women bound to silence by slavery and racial, as well as economic, oppression. Trinh T. Minh-ha draws attention to the internalized narratives of distress and guilt which interrupt many women's belief in themselves as writers. She particularly considers the position of black women writers and defines 'writing' as, 'not letting it merely haunt you and die over and over in you until you no longer know how to speak'. Similarly, she sees getting published as 'not loathing yourself, not burning it, not giving up' (Minh-ha, 1989: 9). She emphasizes how 'every women who writes and wishes to become established as a writer has known the taste of *rejection*'. Sylvia Plath (1971: 211) exemplified how rejection led to self-loathing, when she exclaimed, 'Nothing stinks like a pile of unpublished writing'. Rejection and depreciation are particularly difficult for members of subordinate groups. It is confirmation of worthlessness for those who have been led to believe they should not attempt to enter the privileged world of creativity.

Conversely, Peggy McIntosh (1985) has suggested that praise, recognition and acknowledgement are difficult for women to accept and can lead to them feeling like 'frauds'. She argues the complexity of this position by stating that when we experience the feeling of fraudulence, or the 'impostor syndrome', this is evidence of the extent to which we have internalized hierarchical value systems. Feeling fraudulent can also be a 'deeply wise refusal to carry on the pretence of deserving and feeling good about roles in conventional and oppressive hierarchies' (McIntosh, 1985: 2).

Pretence in the academy is endemic, with academics pressurized to present themselves as authoritative and objective. This could be viewed as a legacy from cartesian dualistic thinking which effectively banished emotions from the domain of scientific inquiry. Stanley and Wise (1991: 266) observe how the 'research process appears a very orderly and coherent process'. They term this absence of personal statements 'hygienic research', or research as described rather than experienced. The academic imperative to live in the mind constructs a powerful organizational culture, evocative of Jung's concept of individuation, by which we develop those aspects of ourselves which appear to be most adaptive to our survival and growth and we neglect other aspects. 'It is not merely the "shadow" side of our personalities that we overlook, disregard and repress. We may also do the same with our positive qualities' (Jung, 1968: 51).

French feminism's focus on the relationship between language and power repeatedly returns to the question of what it means, given that language shapes our knowledge of the world, to speak as a woman (Sellers, 1991). French feminism's concern with psychoanalysis, and the privileging of the unconscious, serve to highlight collisions between definitions of academic excellence and the gendered psychology of creativity. A psychoanalytical view is that creativity originates in the subconscious and the task of the artist is to bring ideas across the threshold into consciousness. When asked about her creative process, Helene Cixous said 'I write in the morning. In fact what this means is that I begin writing at night, in my dreams.' (Sellers, 1989: 18). Luce Irigaray asks if the unconscious is also marked by sexual divisions, with a feminine — as opposed to a masculine — unconscious. For Irigaray, woman's unconscious has been repressed by a phallocentric order to the extent that it can only exist in the 'silences' that inform the gaps and borders of a male-oriented world (Irigaray, 1985). So, if the unconscious feeds creativity, but is repressed in the case of women, what is/is not being expressed in women's creative endeavours?

Marie Louise Von Franz, a Jungian analyst, is clear that the artist's emotional life *feeds* creativity.

> To be cut off from one's emotional basis always means complete sterilisation. Whoever cannot connect with his (*sic*) emotions feels, and is, sterile. (Von Franz, 1972: 138)

This idea contravenes academic training which mistrusts the intrusion of emotionality in the realm of rationality. Traditional positivistic research training teaches the academic to be ever vigilant for bias and subjectivity. One fear is that the researcher will simply find voices elsewhere to say what she really wants to say for and on behalf of herself. The issue of autobiography as research remains heavily contested (see Stanley, Chapter 12). Recently, many feminist academics have openly disclosed personal investment in their writing and research. For example, Stanley and Wise (1991) were able to translate their experience of receiving obscene phonecalls into a valuable research project. Rosalind Coward states, in the Introduction to her book, that it arose out of her confused feelings following the birth of her child (Coward, 1992). These examples challenge the polarization between validity and autobiography. Myers contests that in the absence of knowledge on women, women have to sift through their own lives for explanation and understanding (Myers, 1988: 143).

But Cixous warns that the autobiographical can dominate.

> 'I' the author have to disappear so that you, so other, can appear . . . The author's 'I' should be the lightest, the most transparent possible . . . (Sellers, 1989: 153)

The use of the first person 'I' calls into question some of the principles defining the characteristics of academic writing and research. Celia Lury suggests that the validity of autobiographical writing is dependent on the success with which the use of 'I' transforms the issue into one of theory through a transcendence of the personal (Lury, 1991). In traditional academic writing the third person 'he' represents the 'pure' sign, upheld by power relations who construct it as masculine. The use of 'I' has particular gender connotations, as when women use the term it can signal the claiming of a newfound authority, with women speaking as full subjects. However, 'I' can be intellectually discredited, if linked to the voice of subordinate groups. In the case of academic writing, it can represent an abuse of the researcher's power as she appropriates and competes for space with the researched, thereby implying that she is carrying a mass of unfinished personal business into research situations which minimizes her ability to listen to others.

If women occupy uneasy positions in intellectual traditions in the academy, they are also ambiguously placed in relation to role expectations. In addition to claiming authority, the practicalities of writing necessitate becoming independent and agentic and saying no to the demands of others. This contradicts the cultural prescription for women's accessibility and availability. Moments of creative self-absorption disrupt the academic woman's socially constructed nurturing role both within and without the workplace. Conflict arises between achievement and care as women make themselves less available to meet demands from students and colleagues (Morley, 1992, 1993). In the academy, collaborative/collective writing is penalized, as it reduces the research ratings. Writing demands temporary withdrawal from interaction with others. Thus 'selfishness' with all its negative connotations is an essential prerequisite for women's writing. Trinh T. Minh-ha (1989: 7) identifies guilt as a major obstacle for women writers to overcome. hattie gossett relates this to black women writers who claim authority to write. Her internalized narrative runs as follows:

> Who do you think you are (to be writing a book)? and who cares what you think about anything enough to pay money for it . . . (gossett, 1981: 175)

Gloria Anzaldua (1981: 166) expresses similar doubt when she says,

> How hard it is for us to think we can *choose* to become writers, much less *feel* and *believe* that we can.

The process of writing can be simultaneously exhilarating and stressful. Von Franz (1972: 15) believes:

> the creative personality (*sic*), when weighed down and depressed by a creative task, does very often behave like an awful neurotic, in a maladjusted and impossible way.

The stress can be related to a variety of reasons: difficulties in bringing unconscious ideas to consciousness; crises of self-belief, practical struggles to secure prolonged periods of uninterrupted time. Rosalind Brackenbury, writer and teacher of creative writing, describes how she learned to realize that 'Real writing flourishes with space around it' (Sellers, 1989: 44). Whereas in the academy, creativity invariably takes place amidst a series of psychological and material interruptions, causing additional tension.

Von Franz described how self-isolation is essential in creative work to allow the unconscious to 'dam up'. By being alone, the energy 'normally used up in relating to other things ... "the social energy", is suddenly dammed up and has no outlet and therefore flows back into and constellates the unconscious' (Von Franz, 1972: 119). Tillie Olsen observed that 'When the claims of creation cannot be primary, the results are atrophy; unfinished work; minor effort and accomplishment; silences.' (Olsen, 1978: 13). The image of the solitary intellectual worker has become a stereotype of creative endeavour. Lewis (1994: ix) believes that this representation contradicts collectivity and the social interaction required to spark creative work. She writes: 'forefronting the solitary work of writing and the singularity of authorship ... belie the many hours of discussion, shared disclosure, critique and debate'.

Whilst it would appear that artistic production is only possible for the leisured classes, another perspective is that every oppressive action experienced by the writer becomes further data. Paritcularly in dominant organizations, where it is unsafe to retaliate or express anger, for fear of being positioned as 'unprofessional', the anger generated by sexist oppression can be recycled into pure creative energy. When analysing the relation between her writing and her feminism, Marcella Evaristi said 'Good art gives people back their dignity' (Sellers, 1989: 180). Paradoxically, the vulnerability of women academics can be the foundation for empowerment.

Claiming Authority

Mixed messages about the value of writing in the academy abound. On the one hand, publication output is constantly evaluated and non-performers treated like pariahs. On the other hand, in organizations with high student numbers, heavy teaching loads, new course developments and the ensuing bureaucratic requirements, it is perceived as the avoidance of 'real work'. This is reminiscent of Toni Cade Bambara's observations about her early attitude to writing:

> I always thought writing was rather frivolous, that it was something you did because you didn't feel like doing any work. (Cade Bambara, 1979: 232)

Trinh T. Minh-ha (1989: 10) comments on this view, stating that the concept of writing here seems to be incompatible with the concept of 'work'. If women academics enter in deficit, by virtue of their gender, they have to publish feverishly in order to justify their existence. To draw attention to the emotional and practical difficulties involved in writing is to attract further attention to the negativity associated with one's gender. Childbirth is often a metaphor for the pain and pleasure of the creative process (Stanford Friedman, 1987). But the academy's insistence on the hygienic and the banishment of emotions, imply that writing and research in the academy occupy the same position as pregnancy in Victorian novels. Children and babies feature, but the production process/gestation period must remain invisible.

Dissatisfaction with the product of the creative process is also a well-worn cliché.

> The mountains have labour pains and a ridiculous little mouse is brought forth. (Von Franz, 1972: 85)

Continuing the metaphor, Von Franz explains how:

> the birth is a deflation, because while you are carrying the new creative idea it is still connected with the wholeness of the unconscious, and therefore you feel so full of ideas. (Von Franz, 1972: 85)

If self-doubt and disappointment are an intrinsic part of creativity, these feelings may be magnified if internalized narratives are confirmed by external critical appraisal. The political implications of the term 'creativity' are not included for discussion in traditional academic disciplines. How we think is regulated by dominant discourses and open to allegations of bias and incompleteness. This is exacerbated by the academic practice of dividing the world into disciplines and licensing individuals only to speak about specific areas. Feminism has long regarded these barriers as false as national boundaries. Discipline means closure, rigidity, control. The process is similar to heterosexual marriage vows. You make a commitment, usually at a young age and are expected to stay faithful. A transdisciplinary or interdisciplinary approach is transgressive, akin to promiscuity, and is seen as evidence of instability. As the sociologist, Znaniecki recognized,

> scholarly discipline hampers originality . . . There is a mistrust of new ideas, unless they come from men (*sic*) whose reputation for scholarliness is well assured. (Znaniecki, 1968: 135)

Feminist theory and practice are strong challenges to academic disciplines. But claiming authority to write from a holistic point of view can leave feminist academics open to charges of superficiality. Equally, if feminist academics stay firmly within their disciplines, their feminism can serve to undermine their disciplinary authority.

The modernist discourse of patriarchy parading as universal reason is highly visible in the publishing world. The notion that gender is an unmarked category for men is prominent in Dale Spender's research on sex bias in publishing. She records how male referees disputed allegations of bias against women writers in mainstream and academic publishing houses. When the same men were asked if they would submit their work to feminist publishers:

> They were exceedingly scornful and actually declared that it was obvious that as they were men, their work would never be given a fair hearing. When it was explained that this was how women felt about submitting their work to men's presses and male literary editors, the men remained dismissive and claimed that whilst men in reputable publishing houses would remain objective, women in (disreputable) publishing houses i.e. feminist, would be subjective and biased. (Spender, 1989: 49)

The antipathy towards women's writing can be experienced as a form of violence against women, with publishers' rejections being particularly brutalizing. The anonymous referencing system in academic journals and publishing houses privileges the silent reader who exerts power over the one who speaks. The writer is seen, but cannot see and there is a one-way gaze reminiscent of pornography.

In the academy, there is a declared value base which privileges publication. But there is a gendered subtext which positions women writers as 'language stealers' (Minh-ha, 1989: 19). Margaret Duras outlines the resentment many men can feel when women appropriate the right to write: 'Men are the ones who started to speak, to speak alone and for everyone else, on behalf of everyone else' (Duras, 1980: 111). A woman member of the Association of University Teachers reports how her creativity was described as publishing 'excessively' by her male interviewer in a formal appraisal situation. She was also told that she should wait for promotion and 'allow her male colleagues to catch up', i.e. 'to stop doing research and publishing' (AUT, 1991). It would appear that in women's hands, research and writing are often constructed as forms of arrogance, exhibitionism and self-aggrandisement.

Young-Eisendrath and Wiedemann, two Jungian analysts, highlight the difficulties many women have in ceasing to judge themselves by masculine standards.

> Because her self-esteem is directly connected to male evaluations, a woman constantly monitors her legitimate value in terms of internalised male judgements . . . she always falls short of the standards she applies because she is not a member of the privileged group; she is not a man. (Young-Eisendrath and Wiedemann, 1987: 88)

Feminist academics, aware of male domination of knowledge production, are also susceptible to allegations of privilege when claiming authority to speak and write on behalf of all women. Recent feminist concern with difference and diversity recognizes that thoughts and ideas are situated, partial, incomplete and potentially oppressive to other women. The practice of white, middle class, heterosexual, able-bodied women retaining hegemonic control of the *feminist* knowledge producing process has been challenged (Hill Collins, 1990). Discontinuity and the absence of a universal identity for women has often resulted in women's writing becoming a site where women can actively structure the meaning of sexual difference, especially as it applies to differences between women.

Write, or be written off

Feminist academics are frequently caught in the interstices between contradictory discourses. Feminist analysis and postmodernism have problematized subjectivity and objectivity in relation to power and knowledge production. French feminism's contribution to the debate between language, gender and power problematizes the gendering of the unconscious and, in some cases, contends that women have no position from which to speak. Anglo-American feminists have continued to expose patriarchal domination of organizations and structures of knowledge production and have highlighted how women's under-representation in the academy denies difference, diversity and pluralism.

In the midst of these varying discourses resides the unreconstructed notion of success in the academy linked to the imperative to write and publish. Women academics, privileged in relation to many other women, and yet disempowered in relation to male academics, have to find an intellectual and psychological space from which to speak. From this marginalized and disempowered position women have to claim authority to write, whilst wading through layers of internalized narratives of self-doubt, feelings of fraudulence and guilt. To exclude one's emotional life and gendered experiences can result in sterile, mechanistic tracts and incorporation and subjugation. But to include them opens up possibilities of allegations of bias and unreflexive, non-academic, maverick research. The postmodernist view that all desire is socially constructed means that it is an oversimplification to invite women to write what they want, because all wants and thoughts are mediated by a discourse. It is only left for feminist academics to continue to make a commitment to use the creative process to challenge the validity of external discourses of domination, and work towards social and organizational change. Paying attention to the creative process also necessitates working collectively to support one another to notice and discharge destructive patterns of internalized oppression.

References

ANZALDUA, G. (1981) 'Speaking in Tongues: A Letter to Third World Women Writers', in MORAGA, C. and ANZALDUA, G. (Eds) *This Bridge called My Back*, pp. 165–175, New York: Kitchen Table Press.

Association of University Teachers (AUT) (1991) *AUT Woman*, 23 Summer, unpaginated.

Astin, H. and Bayer, A. (1979) 'Pervasive Sex Differences in the Academic Reward System: Scholarship, Marriage and What Else?', in Lewis, D. and Becker, W. (Eds) *Academic Rewards in Higher Education*, pp. 211–229, Cambridge, MA: Ballinger.

Astin, H. and Snyder, M. (1982) 'A Decade of Response', *Change*, **14**, pp. 26–31.

Bagihole, B. (1993) 'How to Keep a Good Woman Down: an Investigation of the role of institutional factors in the process of discrimination against women academics', *British Journal of Sociology of Education*, **14**, 3, pp. 262–274.

Brossard, N. (1988) *The Aerial Letter*, translated by Marlene Wildeman, Toronto: The Women's Press.

Cade Bambara, T. (1979) 'Commitment: Toni Cade Bambara speaks, interview with Guy-Sheftall, B.', in Bell, R.P., Guy-Sheftell, B. and Parker, B. *Sturdy Black Bridges: Visions of Black Women in Literature*, pp. 230–250, New York: Anchor/Doubleday.

Carroll, B. (1992) 'Originality and Creativity', in Kramerae, C. and Spender, D. (Eds) *The Knowledge Explosion*, pp. 353–361, New York: Teachers College Press.

Cixous, H. (1986) *The Newly-Born Woman*, Minneapolis: University of Minnesota Press.

Cole, J. (1979) *Fair Science: Women in the Scientific Community*, New York: The Free Press.

Coward, R. (1992) *Our Treacherous Hearts: Why Women let Men Get their Own Way*, London: Faber and Faber.

Duras, M. (1980) 'Smothered Creativity', in Marks, E. and De Courtivron, I. (Eds) *New French Feminisms*, pp. 111–113, Amherst: University of Massachussets Press.

Eichler, M. (1988) *Non-sexist Research Methods*, London: Allen and Unwin.

Fisher, S. (1994) *Stress in Academic Life: The Mental Assembly Line*, Milton Keynes: Open University Press/Society for Research in Higher Education.

Fonow, M.M. and Cook, J. (Eds) (1991) *Beyond Methodology: Feminist Scholarship as Lived Research*, Bloomington: Indiana University Press.

Frank, A. (1960) *The Diary of Anne Frank*, London: Hutchinson.

Fuchs Epstein, C. (1988) *Deceptive Distinctions: Sex, Gender and the Social Order*, New Haven, CN, London: Yale University Press.

Gilbert, S. and Gubar, S. (1989) *No Man's Land: The Place of the Woman Writer in the 20th Century*, New Haven, CT: Yale University Press.

Giroux, H. (Ed.) (1993) *Postmodernism, Feminism, and Cultural Politics*, Albany: State University of New York Press.

Gossett, H. (1981) 'Who Told You Anybody Wants to Hear From You?' in Moraga, C. and Anzaldua, G. (Eds) *This Bridge Called My Back*, pp. 175–176, New York: Kitchen Table Press.

Hansard Society for Parliamentary Government (1990) *Pay at the Top*, London: Hansard Society.

Haraway, D. (1991) *Simians, Cyborgs and Women: The Reinvention of Nature*, London: Free Association Books.

Hennessy, R. (1993) *Materialist Feminism and the Politics of Discourse*, London: Routledge.

Her Majesty's Inspectorate (1993) *Aspects of Women's Studies Courses in Higher Education*, 371/92/NS.

Hill Collins, P. (1990) *Black Feminist Thought: Knowledge, Consciousness and the Politics of Empowerment*, New York: Routledge.

HOLLY, M.L. (1993) 'Educational Research and Professional Development: On Minds that Watch Themselves', in BURGESS, R. (Ed.) *Educational Research and Evaluation*, pp. 157–179, London: Falmer.

IRIGARAY, L. (1985) *The Sex Which Is Not One*, New York: Cornell University Press.

JACKSON, G. (1971) *Soledad Brother: The Prison Letters of George Jackson*, Harmondsworth: Penguin.

JUNG, C. (1968) *Man and His Symbols*, New York: Dell.

KELLY, G. (1955) *The Psychology of Personal Constructs*, New York: Norton.

KOESTLER, A. (1964) *The Act of Creation*, London: Hutchinson.

KRISTEVA, J. (1980) *Desire in Language*, New York: Columbia University Press.

LEWIS, L. (1975) *Scaling The Ivory Tower: Merit and its Limits in Academic Careers*, Baltimore: The Johns Hopkins University Press.

LEWIS, M. (1994) *Without a Word: Teaching Beyond Women's Silence*, London: Routledge.

LORDE, A. (1985) *The Cancer Journals*, London: Sheba Press.

LURY, C. (1991) 'Reading the Self: autobiography, gender and the institution of the literary', in FRANKLIN, S., LURY, C., and STACEY, J. (Eds) *Off-Centre: Feminism and Cultural Studies*, pp. 97–108, London: HarperCollins.

MCINTOSH, P. (1985) *Feeling Like a Fraud*. Work in Progress No. 18 The Stone Center, Wellesley College, MA 02181.

MINH-HA, T.T. (1989) *Woman, Native, Other: Writing Postcoloniality and Feminism*, Bloomington: Indiana University Press.

MORLEY, L. (1992) 'Women's Studies, Difference and Internalised Oppression', *Women's Studies International Forum*, **15**, 4, pp. 517–525.

MORLEY, L. (1993) 'Women's Studies as Empowerment of "Non-Traditional" Learners in Community and Youth Work Training: A Case Study', in KENNEDY, M., LUBELSKA, C. and WALSH, V. (Eds) *Making Connections*, pp. 118–129, London: Taylor & Francis.

MORLEY, L. (1994) 'Glass Ceiling or Iron Cage: Women in UK Academia', *Gender, Work and Organization*, **1**, 4, pp. 194–204.

MORLEY, L. (1995) 'The Micropolitics of Women's Studies', in MAYNARD, M. and PURVIS, J. (Eds) *(Hetero) Sexual Politics*, London: Taylor & Francis.

MUNT, S. (Ed.) (1992) *New Lesbian Criticism: Literary and Cultural Readings*, London: Harvester Wheatsheaf.

MYERS, M. (1988) 'Pedagogy as Self-Expression in Mary Wollstonecraft', in BENSTOCK, S. (Ed.) *The Private Self*, London: Routledge.

OLSEN, T. (1978) *Silences*, New York: Delta.

PLATH, S. (1971) *The Bell Jar*, London: Faber and Faber.

ROBERTS, H. (1981) *Doing Feminist Research*, London: Routledge and Kegan Paul.

SELLERS, S. (Ed.) (1989) *Delighting The Heart: A Notebook by Women Writers*, London: The Women's Press.

SELLERS, S. (1991) *Language and Sexual Difference*, London: Macmillan.

SIMEONE, A. (1987) *Academic Women: Working Towards Equality*, South Hadley, MA: Bergin and Garvey.

SPENDER, D. (1989) *The Writing or the Sex*, New York: Pergamon Press.

STANFORD FRIEDMAN, S. (1987) 'Creativity and the Childbirth Metaphor: Gender Difference in Literary Discourse', *Feminist Studies*, **13**, 1, pp. 49–81.

STANLEY, L. and WISE, S. (1983) *Breaking Out*, London: Routledge.

STANLEY, L. and WISE, S. (1991) 'Feminist Research, Feminist Consciousness and

Experiences of Sexism', in FONOW, M. and COOK, J. (Eds) *Beyond Methodology: Feminist Scholarship as Lived Research*, pp. 265–283, Bloomington: Indiana University Press.

STANLEY, L. and WISE, S. (1993) *Breaking Out Again*, London: Routledge.

VON FRANZ, M.L. (1972) *Creation Myths*, Dallas, TX: Spring Publications.

WALKER, A. (1984) *In Search of Our Mothers' Gardens*, London: The Woman's Press.

WALSH, V.A. (1993) 'Unbounded Women? Feminism, Creativity and Embodiment', paper presented at WISE (Women's International Studies Europe) Conference, Paris, October 1993.

WOOLF, V. (1929) *A Room of One's Own*, New York: Harcourt Brace Jovanovich.

YOUNG-EISENDRATH, P. and WIEDEMANN, F. (1987) *Female Authority*, London: The Guilford Press.

ZIMMERMAN, B. (1992) 'Lesbians like this and that', in MUNT, S. (Ed.) *New Lesbian Criticism: Literary and Cultural Readings*, pp. 1–15, London: Harvester Wheatsheaf.

ZMROCZEK, C. and DUCHEN, C. (1991) 'Women's Studies and Feminist Research in the European Community', in AARON, J. and WALBY, S. (Eds) *Out of the Margins*, London: The Falmer Press.

ZNANIECKI, F. (1968) *The Social Role of the Man of Knowledge*, New York: Harper Row.

Chapter 9

The Good Witch: 'Advice to Women in Management'

Lesley Kerman

In the summer of 1939 my Uncle, Leslie Kerman, went on holiday to Germany. It was his first and only trip abroad and his command of the language was confined to the ability to order eggs and chips. We possess a 16 mm film of this adventure. The flickering, scratched, black and white image shows my Uncle with a glass of beer, my Uncle with wet hair, wearing a one-piece bathing costume laughing by the pool, my Uncle up a mountain grinning. In the background of this film, there is a continuous frieze of passing swastikas, emblazoned on flying flags, buildings and the arm bands of young men who are also holding glasses of beer and grinning at the camera. This film was a source of great amusement to us as children, how could he have been so optimistically oblivious to the menacing surroundings?

When I reflect on the 30 years I have spent working in Higher Education, I see myself in this smiling image of my Uncle's blinkered optimism. An innocent player in a drama, the dimensions of which I am only now beginning to grasp.

'Do not appear if you do not want to disappear' (Michel Foucault, 1976: 8)

I read *Witchcraft: Confessions and Accusations* a collection of conference papers edited and introduced by Mary Douglas (Douglas, 1970).

> Witch craft has no fixed dogma, no single logic; it is utilised in many different kinds of situation as a means of explaining misfortune and expressing social tension. (Brain, 1970: 177)

Academic Institutions in the early 1990s were certainly burdened with social tensions, generated by cuts in unit funding, changes in roles and responsibilities and the pressure to expand. One institution was being absorbed into another. There was bad feeling around and as Douglas points out, 'Bad Feeling is charged with mystical Danger' (Gluckman, 1955: 94).

There is an increase in witch phenomena in communities undergoing social breakdown. Douglas's thesis, drawing on the methodology of Evans Pritchard (1937) and the insights of structuralism, is that there are 'quiescent beliefs' within a culture, mechanisms that can be activated should the need arise (Douglas, 1970: xxiv). 'People can do without explanations of misfortune . . . The precondition is that they should be free to move away from each other whenever strains appear.' It is when they are locked into a relatively closed system that the trouble arises.

> Witchcraft beliefs are essentially a means of clarifying and affirming social definitions . . . People are trying to control one another albeit with small success. The idea of the witch is used to whip their own consciences or those of their friends . . . The witch is a dangerous deviant. (Too powerful or rich, dangerously demanding.) The function of the accusation is to control deviants in the name of community values . . . The witch is an internal enemy with outside liaisons. The function of an accusation is to promote factional rivalry to split the community and to redefine hierarchy. (Douglas, 1970: xxv–xvii)

Lewis (1970: 306) proposes that instead of 'witchcraft' and 'spirit possession' we substitute 'oblique' and 'direct mystical attack'.

> It is the accuser and not the accused who sets the whole process in motion, and it is certainly the 'witch' against whom public opinion is mobilised and who is ultimately the victim of social action. (Lewis, 1970: 307)

If the presence of 'eyebiting' witches in Academic Board meetings strikes you as far-fetched, consider that Freud makes a parallel between what he reads in the *Malleus Maleficorum* (1496), and what he sees in the women he is treating: 'the medieval theory of possession, upheld by the ecclesiastical tribunals was identical to the theory of the foreign body and the splitting of consciousness . . . The parallel with witchcraft is taking place and I believe it is conclusive. Details have started crowding in . . .' (Freud, 1954: 187–188). Kramer (1994: 49–50) cites Freud's psychoanalysis as the connecting medium in the 'synthesis of ethnography and classical education' that enables the 'Educated European' to 'grasp remote cultural beliefs and drives'. (The example that he examines is the Tallensi belief in destiny.) Through the analogies between psychoanalysis and world picture (Horton, 1983), Kramer's synthesis allows us to include mythical narratives and 'primitive' social constructs to gain particular insights into beliefs which are deeply embedded in the fabric of our own social organization and relationships. There are illuminating resonances in the anthropology of witchcraft for the observer of academia.

Amongst the Damba, for example, the means of choosing the chief is by dancing. A decision to dance for the chiefship is daring, as to do so is to declare oneself a witch and therefore to challenge other witches. Esther Goody (1970:

226–227) describes a successful dance made by a man who kept his left hand in his pocket throughout, a clue to the fact that he might have powerful 'medicine' in his pocket. He wore a found pair of glasses. This was taken as an indication of his vision. An important feature of the dance was that it should be restrained, not too good so as to attract divine jealousy or the implication of evil sorcery. The importance of mediocrity posing as restraint in the presentation of the dance invokes an image of the dance as proceeding along the management spine of academia.

Amongst the Mcapi, witch finders can be hired to identify the witch. The witch finder, with his four assistants, arrives at the village to carry out

> the Smelling out process — for this he employs an ordinary looking glass, and standing with his back to the people, looks in the glass over his left shoulder and points out such and such a person as having a bad medicine in his house. (Willis, 1970: 134)

The accusation when it comes is arbitrary and oblique. 'The descriptions suggest that accusations are often pre-arranged' (Willis, 1970: 130). Goody writes of the Gonja in modern Ghana:

> Women even when they hold political or ritual roles are above all women. And as such they cannot be permitted to act aggressively without endangering the dominance of men, and throwing into doubt the affective relationships on which the domestic group depends. It is because aggression is not permissible in women that Gonja women who are thought to have witchcraft powers are always condemned as evil. (Goody, 1970: 242)

Women accused of witchcraft can be put to death, sold into slavery, or taken under the direct protection of the chief, who according to the Gonja must have more powerful magic than the witch and is therefore in a position to control her (Goody, 1970: 229). The battlefield within the institution is a battle for power. Strangely, the expulsion from the institution (death or being sold into slavery in the Damba system) is a confirmation of power. No chief could be found of sufficient powers to contain the disruptive force and neutralize the power of the offending witch. Expulsion from academia reveals the reputation of power and as Pitt-Rivers (1970: 203) reminds us, 'Reputation of Power **is** power, because it draweth with it the adherence of those that need protection' (Hobbes, 1979: 150). The outcast is therefore not a victim but a threat.

'To think is to speculate with images' (Aristotle; Yates, 1964: 335[1])

In 1976, I read *Natural Symbols* (Douglas, 1973). This book had an important influence on my teaching style. As an anthropologist, Douglas had succeeded in gaining sufficient distance from our culture to be able to propose a matrix of cultural bias and its influence on an individual's relationship with the world. I learned to alter my teaching style to accommodate the individual learning styles of others. Douglas's work made me conscious of the depths of the engendered conditioning of my male colleagues in academia. I was aware that they were projecting stereotypic images onto me. These were images generated by cultural conditioning and they restricted my ability to do my job in Higher Education. Accommodating these projected stereotypes was not compatible with being effective within the institution, which meant initiating developments, defending academic areas, obtaining resources. It was necessary, therefore, to counter each projected identity with an alternative one. By continually posing in either a knowing or a contradictory way, I was able to function effectively — until the moment when it seemed to me that a powerful fiction was attached to me, one that summed up elements contained in all those images that I had so far managed to avoid.

Janice Raymond (1986: 233) has defined the position of women working in the male ordered world as being an 'inside outsider'. She describes 'women who see the man made world for what it is and exist within it with worldly integrity, while at the same time seeing beyond it to something different'. This situation demands its own set of compromises if you are to function effectively. As an 'inside outsider' I was acutely conscious of the wisdom of Virginia Woolf's advice

> It is fatal for a woman to lay the least stress on any grievance; to plead even with justice any cause; in any way to speak consciously as a woman. (Woolf, 1928: 99)

As an outsider I can identify with Irigaray's (1985) frustration.

> How can we speak so as to escape from their compartments, their schemes, their distinctions and oppositions, how can we shake off the chains of their terms, free ourselves of their categories, rid ourselves of their names, disengage ourselves alive from their concepts? (Irigaray, 1985: 212)

Irigaray 'had a University post and was relieved of it' (Irigaray, 1993: 52). Her 'relief' came about as a result of the publication of *Speculum of the Other Woman* in 1974.

> Being denied the right to speak can have several meanings and take several forms. It can be a conscious effort to ban someone from institutions . . . Such an action can mean, if only in part: I don't understand what you're doing so I reject it, we reject it. (Irigaray, 1993: 52)

As Linda Nochlin (1989: 2) says, 'Ideology manifests itself as much by what is unspoken, unthinkable, as by what is represented in a work of art'. How is the unthinkable to be thought? Elleyn Kaschak (1992: 6) describes being a woman in a male world. In writing *Engendered Lives*, she says that she has become aware of:

> the limits of language to express new perspectives. That of women is often invisible not simply because it is unrepresented but because it is unrepresentable in our current language. Once one is aware of the biases of language itself, everything from the use of the pronoun I, which can seem overly personal and intrusive, or we, which may be too general and presumptuous or even the presumably neutral one, which cloaks value and opinion in the garb of neutrality and objectivity, becomes problematic. (Kaschak, 1992: 6)

It is the inadequacy of language that has led me to work with images. They seem less fixed, more speculative, more instrumental for furthering the state of the critical argument. I made a set of six etchings called 'Advice to Women in Management'. The title was ironic. It implied a scenario that was contradicted by the imagery which was associated with witchcraft. Through the allusions and contradictions in the etchings, I intended to make a field for thought which reveals the complexity of gender relations in an institutional context. I subsequently discovered that in Manchester Metropolitan University Library, the *Malleus Maleficorum* (1496), the Hammer of Witches, Kramer and Sprenger's handbook for the European Witch trials, was filed under 'Business Management'. My representation of the relation between the parallel worlds of management training and witch finding were confirmed by the librarian's classification. The academy began to appear in retrospect as pregnant with 'quiescent beliefs' (Douglas, 1970: xxiv).

'It's a Man's Life in the Regular Art School'[2]

The subject hierarchy within the Art School mirrored that within the cultural institution of Fine Art.[3] It was arranged with painting at the top, and in descending order, sculpture, printmaking, photography, design and at the bottom, if not underground, art history or 'art hysteria' as it revealingly became known. The argument between Leonardo and Michaelangelo regarding the superior status of either painting or sculpture had evidently been won by painting.[4] Printmaking and photography appear in the sequence of their invention as technical processes, design was tainted with commerce.[5]

Many of my colleagues believed that women were not capable of being artists or poets. The highest levels of creative achievement, those involving inspiration, were reserved for men. This idea was closely tied up with their sexual identity. The potential for reproduction was thought to be inconsistent with the act of poetic creation. The two capabilities were seen as mutually exclusive, a theory benignly explained to me by one of my senior colleagues as a compensation for his inability to give birth. There is a perpetuation of

Aristotle's idea in this observation. 'The universe was composed of form and matter', with reference to procreation 'women constituted matter chaotic and formless, while men provided the life giving principle of form' (Pfeffer, 1989: 58). I recently heard a Gallery Director, speaking of a woman artist, 'Imagine, the artist stops work to have a baby!' as if there were a conflict here. This was intended generously. Having a baby can also be read as evidence of a lack of commitment to art. Stevie Smith confided in 1968 that she had refused to allocate a poetry award to a promising young poet who had just become a father for this was an indication of his lack of true commitment.[6] Iris Murdoch (1978) accounts for Plato's contribution to this idea:

> There is a limited amount of soul energy (Republic 458 d) so, for better or worse, one desire will weaken another. Eros is a form of desire for immortality, for perpetual possession of the good, whatever we may take the good to be . . . This desire takes the form of yearning to create in and through beauty (Symposium 206 b) which may appear as sexual love (Laws 7216) or love of fame (the poets have immortal children) or love of wisdom. (Murdoch, 1978: 34)

Continuous studio practice, much like daily prayer, was preached as essential for the serious artist. This is not a practical option for many women, or men come to that. It can become a damaging idea when the continuous practice is disrupted by life responsibilities, leading to a sense of failure and causing many women to stop making work altogether.

From a woman student's point of view, the entire range of the fine art subject hierarchy was open for access. This can be accounted for by the very high value placed on beauty, eroticism, and 'talent', as characteristics of the fine art subject definition.[7] So long as they were students, that is, and thus in a position to be controlled. The outstanding result of a woman student could be celebrated as a confirmation of her teacher's ability. It was very difficult for women to obtain establishment posts in painting and sculpture. The great weight of history and mythology was held as a kind of sacred trust.[8] It was dangerous to admit a woman to the level at which the subject was defined by its embodiment in the teacher. Her inclusion might well change the character of the subject. Women 'Fellows' were appointed in painting and sculpture, but they were not taken onto the establishment as sometimes were male 'Fellows'. One particularly effective woman 'Fellow' was rejected in favour of an adequate male one on the grounds that her effectiveness was the result of 'pastoral care' as opposed to 'good teaching'. Further questioning revealed that the accusation of 'pastoral care' meant an inclination towards student-centred learning.

This diagnosis revealed the cartesian divide that underpinned thinking within the Painting School. This binary model: subject/object, figure/ground, form/content, man/woman, was very unhelpful to the students being taught within it, as it appeared to provide a clear pathway, but for many, women in particular, in fact it acted as a trap. The woman fellow's enthusiasm in setting up seminars on her own initiative was also a problem, as it contradicted the unspoken agreed level of commitment to teaching negotiated between the existing full-time male staff. She might have been entitled to assume that she was fulfilling her brief to the best of her ability, but by exceeding it she was in fact posing a threat. Her excellence implied mystical power, though it never reached the level of an accusation, her rejection was predictable, as it would serve to affirm social definitions.

Goody (1970) identifies three levels in a believed witchcraft attack. These are:

1   Gossip — an attack believed to be witchcraft but not named as such. This is an attack that comes from outside the group. Gossip distances the attack and formulates norms.
2   Allegations — victim and witch are named, there is 'an imputation of mystical power'; this can be advantageous or not advantageous.
3   Accusations and counteraction — power, but illegitimate, beyond the bounds of tolerance. Through accusation, private grievances receive public validation (Goody, 1970: 229).

These three levels appear to be connected to the distinction made in the *Malleus Maleficorum* between 'three degrees of suspicion, the first light, the second great and the third very great' (Kramer and Sprenger, 1928: 237).

I am reflecting on the past from the 'outside' now. As an 'inside outsider' I believed that in spite of difficulties, things would improve, were improving. I was working my way through a little regional difficulty. My optimism was first seriously dented when as part of 'The Sixty Percent Event — A Week of Work with and about Women Artists' I asked the deputy librarian to bring all the books in our library on Women Artists to the foyer. At the Exhibition opening, there were so few books on the table that, in order to cover its surface, it had been necessary for her to lay them out flat. There were, perhaps, 15 books from our library section of 20 000 books. I was overwhelmed with sadness as I was forced to recognize the extent to which I had deluded myself. My teaching was contributing to a culture from which I and 60 per cent of my students were all but excluded. From then on, I believed that only by participating in the management of the Institution could I hope to contribute to making effective changes in that culture. I agreed with Coyle (1989: 23) that 'Women need to change hierarchical structures, relationships and ways of working'. I would have been reassured by her observation that 'There is evidence that women managers can and do use the scope of their power to create change' (Coyle, 1989: 23).

Above the Glass Ceiling

At the present time, there aren't many women working in institutions. Those that do are often restricted in how far they can go in their career.

> Very few women reach the highest posts and they pay very dearly for it one way or another. (Irigaray, 1993: 53)

Coyle points out that:

> Most women have real difficulties in reconciling their values with the values they perceive as management values and as a result often consciously opt out or hold back from making any progressive step into the management hierarchy. (Coyle, 1989: 22)

An established male management team may have difficulty in accepting a woman as a colleague. Many women find themselves fulfilling the function without the status. The appointment may be conceded as 'acting', the salary may be slow in forthcoming. How many women have seen a role relinquished to a male colleague upgraded and rewarded with a title and a raise in salary? In the United Kingdom, crossing the divide between Senior Lecturer and Principal Lecturer is in fact crossing the Rubicon.[9] This is where the 'glass ceiling' is situated. The difference is that the Principal Lecturer has a budget, and money is power in Academia. A woman entering an all-male management team is likely to need a powerful male colleague to support her if she is to make the crossing. This colleague must often carry the burden of a suspected sexual liaison, the only logical means of accounting for his behaviour in some people's eyes. Promotion to Head of Department is much more straightforward.

As Head of Department it was not possible to be half-hearted about the battle for power, as the way in which you were regarded reflected on the staff in your department. Power was measured in terms of the status of the courses for which you were responsible and their place in the hierarchy. Equipment was an outward sign of the Department's rank within the academy, like pigs to New Guinea tribesmen. Douglas enjoys juxtaposing figures from different worlds engaged in parallel activities; 'It is pleasing to think of Lord Thomson in the guise of a New Guinea Hero; the feasts, the balance sheets, the dynamism, it all makes the same sense, whether newspapers are bought with money or pigs with shells' (Douglas, 1973: 134). The parallel could be extended to academia.

As a newly-appointed manager you must make your own way. Your immediate colleagues in the management team may be inclined to see themselves as being in competition with you and will be alert to capitalize on your mistakes. Management training is desirable: 'Research on women managers indicates that they experience far more stress than their male counterparts and this stress is caused by the specific pressure women managers face as a minority — of high visibility, isolation and little or no support' (Coyle, 1989: 22).

Just as it can be a 'problem finding enough female role models in top management' (Straw, 1989: 175), it is a problem for the woman manager to develop a support, advisory and opportunity-providing network, from amongst the very few managers in a similar position who are women. If she is working in a culture that is not comfortable with women as managers, it is only from women colleagues scattered in other institutions that such opportunities and advice will be forthcoming.

The most useful text on management for me was Machiavelli's *The Prince* (1513), because it provided an insight into a calculating way of operating. I recognized that my male colleagues, who had aspired to management, had grown up with access to training in the strategic, and even the 'dirty tricks' element of management, from playground gangs to competitive sports. In academia, wandering or missing memos, misinformation and stirring up student unrest, were all part of the game. As a counterweight to Machiavelli, before each important meeting I read one of Francis Bacon's *Essays* (1597): 'Of Negotiating', 'Of Discourse', 'Of Cunning', 'Of Seeming Wise', in an attempt to remain conscious of the benign intentions of patriarchy.

There was an unnerving sense that hidden networks and relationships could be running through and behind the visible ones in the institution. Was this the camaraderie of patriarchy within which they had not yet found a way to include me, or was it something more formal such as a Masonic connection? *World Freemasonry* (Hamill, 1991) represents a recent and possibly authoritative view on the subject of women and Freemasonry:

> Regular Masonry does not recognise mixed orders or those that admit women . . . Most masons would probably not wish for any change and would echo the sentiments of John Coustos who in 1743 told the Portuguese Inquisition: that the reason why women were excluded from the society was to take away all occasion of calumny and reproach, which would have been unavoidable, had they been admitted to it. Further, that since women had in general, been always considered as not very well qualified to keep a secret; the founders of the society of Freemasons, by their exclusion of the other sex, thereby gave a proof of their prudence and wisdom (Hamill, 1991: 187).

'We won't play nature to your culture' (Barbara Kruger, 1983: 28)

As the only woman member of Academic board meetings, Governor's meetings, Finance Committee meetings, interview panels for students, interview panels for staff, Departmental Board meetings, Management Group Meetings, I was accustomed to being made to feel out of place. I recognized as exclusion devices, the opening lewd joke, made with an eye cast in my direction, the detailed discussion of football tactics before we got down to business, the chairman (*sic*) who began with his feet on the table. They were tiresome, but they did not really bother me as they appeared to confirm that the meeting was changed because of my presence. Certain things could not be said because of my being there, certain other things could be said. Janice Raymond (1986: 233) points out that 'Women's appearance in the world is staged only on men's terms'. Every woman working in academia has tales to tell on dress. For example, 'Please don't have one of your extreme hair do's before the interview!' And:

> Certain members of staff have commented that you look more like a student than a member of staff. I have decided to give you a petunia coat and dress set that belonged to my daughter, you can collect it from the porter's Lodge at lunchtime. (I see now that an act of kindness was intended.)

Dressing up, now according to Vogue, now according to the topic of the lecture, took on a strategic significance as I endeavoured to contradict the stereotypic expectations of my colleagues.

> When the women represent figures from society they are not bowing to the power of the society; on the contrary they are acting in contradiction to this power when they present themselves as changed or as others, or putting it another way, when they present the social world as it appears to them not as it pretends or wishes to be. (Kramer, 1994: 116)

Kramer is speaking of the women in the 'zar' cult in Northern Sudan. They live in harems, and their masquerade is a product of their exclusion from the world of social action. Should I wear the Armani suit to the Academic board meeting? Might the Armani be received like the women in the zar cult masquerade as parodying the convention established by the men? A woman Head of Department complained at an academic conference in the early 1980s that she felt that she could not wear a bracelet to a meeting. At the time, I was surprised at her concern over what seemed a trivial matter. Later I came to recognize that she had identified how a 'mistake', wearing a bracelet (did not Salome wear bracelets?), could mark her out as an enemy within.

> A polluting person is always in the wrong. He (*sic*) has developed some wrong condition or simply crossed some line which should not have been crossed and this displacement unleashes danger for someone. (Douglas, 1966: 113)

By wearing my bracelet I am defiling the boardroom table. In terms of its perceived effect, I have put a gun on the table.

I was once the lone woman member of an interview panel for a very senior post in academia. The men on the panel competed to ask the male candidates the most interesting and authoritative question. The only woman candidate was met by a complete lack of interest. One after another the panel said 'No question'. It fell to me to ask her something. With escalating panic, I recognized that whatever we found to discuss could only be used in confirmation of this serial group rejection. She had not been present in the other interviews and had no means of reading how her interview had been managed.

The Rejection

I dreamed I was walking down a path through a dark wood. I was walking with a young member of staff in my department, she was holding a sheet of paper. On the sheet of paper was written a poem. Ahead of us a car was parked on the side of the path. Under the car a Wolf was hiding. I was very frightened. Then I realised that the wolf was frightened of the gleaming sheet of white paper. We were fighting a wolf with a poem.

I was accused of laughing in an Academic Board meeting. I was not laughing, the matter in hand was not amusing, my accuser had imagined it. A colleague drew my attention to a passage in Cixous and Clement (1987: 32–33):

> She laughs and it's frightening — like Medusa's laugh — petrifying and shattering constraint. There she is facing us. Women witches often laugh . . . It is the moment at which the woman crosses a dangerous line, the cultural demarcation beyond which she will find herself excluded.

It was through Cixous and Clement that I discovered the *Malleus Maleficorum* This text reveals the depths of misogyny. With a sick heart, I recognized that profound fears had been projected onto my body.

> Hear what Valerius said to Rufinus: You do not know that woman is the Chimera but it is good that you should know it; for that monster was of three forms; its face was that of a radiant noble lion, it had the filthy belly of a goat and it was armed as the virulent tail of a viper. And he means that a woman is beautiful to look upon, contaminating to touch and deadly to keep . . . I have found a woman more bitter than death, who is the hunter's snare and her heart is a net and her hands are bands. (Kramer and Sprenger, 1928: 46)

I made an etching which placed the image of woman the Chimera amongst fashion models. The juxtaposition of these two conflicting representations of women opened the way for the 'Advice to Women in Management' series.

'Those who know have wings' (*Pancavimsa Brahmana*; Eliade, 1989: 479)

It is clear to me now that women in academia have no idea how threatening they appear to be. It seems that to take her place in that world, a woman must have abilities which then become the seeds of her rejection. As Angela Coyle (1989: 22) observes: 'The more effective women are, the more they are experienced as a threat, and the more men try to block their initiatives'. J.S. Mill (1994: 162) warns that 'Mediocrity is the ascendant power among mankind'. He feared that through the 'tyranny of the majority', we could arrive at the point where we 'endeavour to make everyone conform to the approved standard. And that standard, express or tacit, is to desire nothing strongly. Its ideal of character is to be without any marked character; to maim by compression, like a Chinese lady's foot' (Mill, 1994: 138). Mill observed that, 'Originality is the one thing which unoriginal minds cannot feel the use of' (Mill, 1994: 133).

A strategy for coping with men's fears has been to accommodate them. To be generously persuasive in the interests of being effective. You remain silent because what is being proposed is almost right and you can manage to make it work, you give the credit for an idea or an initiative to a male member of staff because there is more likelihood of a successful outcome if he steers it through the committee, you ignore some things in order to achieve others. Small adjustments, and no doubt men who manage could claim the use of all these devices. But the sum total of this strategy has cost women their identity and ultimately their self respect, as the lack of recognition leads to lost opportunities and leaves a rancid taste in the mouth. 'How long do you want to remain at the first step?' (Beuys, 1979: 1). Will my three granddaughters be treading along the same path? It is time to represent ourselves effectively, to recognize that we too are in a position to impress and influence. If I am going to be a witch then let me be a powerful one. St Paul advised the Corinthians (C.7 v 9)[10] to marry if they must. For the Good Witch 'it is better to manage than to burn'.

Notes

1 Yates here quotes *De Imaginum Compositione* Giordano Bruno, who quotes Aristotle *Synesius De Somnis*, translated by Ficino.
2 Catch Phrase repeatedly used by a Head of Painting, who was making a pun on the 1970s slogan 'It's a Man's Life in the Regular Army'. The joke was in the substitution of 'Art School' for 'Army', the 'Man's Life' was at that time seen as an unquestionable element of the phrase.
3 I am using the term 'institution' in the anthropological sense here. As in Douglas's text 'How Institutions think'.
4 Leonardo da Vinci 'That sculpture is less intellectual than painting, and lacks many characteristics of Nature'. From Notebook 'On Painting' (655) p. 178 Michelagniolo Buonarroti Letter to Benedetto Varchi 1549: 193, for an account of this debate see Holt, Elizabeth, G. (1947) 'Literary Sources of Art History', Princeton University Press.
5 A lecturer in photography disagrees with the order set out here. She places photography at the bottom of the hierarchy now, but she may be describing her experience as a woman teaching photography.

6   Conversation with the author, Lambton House Gosforth where Smith stayed while reading at the Morden Tower, Newcastle.
7   See Greer, Germaine (1980) *Slade Women*, Concord films.
8   See Kris, E. and Kurz, O. (1979) *Legend Myth and Magic in the Image of the Artist*, Yale University Press 1979. I am currently working on a series of 31 paintings based on this text.
9   Rubicon is the 'ancient name of a small stream which formed part of the boundary between Italy and Cisalpine Gaul; the crossing of it by Caesar marked the beginning of the war with Pompey thus to cross or pass the Rubicon, to take a decisive or final step, esp. at the outset of some enterprise or undertaking' (*Oxford English Dictionary*).
10 St Paul's Letter to the Corinthians Chapter 7 v 9 'It is better to marry than to burn'.

References

BACON, FRANCIS (1985) *The Essays* (1597), London: Penguin Books.
BEUYS, JOSEPH (1979) 'Foreword', in ADRIANI, G., KONNERTZ, W. and THOMAS, K. *Joseph Beuys Life and Works*, translated by Lech, New York: Barron's Educational Series.
BRAIN, ROBERT (1970) 'Child Witches' in DOUGLAS, MARY (Ed.) *Witchcraft: Confessions and Accusations*, pp. 161–182, London: Tavistock.
CIXOUS, HELENE and CLEMENT, CATHERINE (1987) *The Newly born Woman* (1975), Manchester: Manchester University Press.
COYLE, ANGELA (1989) 'Women and Management; Fit Work for Women?', in COLE, S. and COYLE, A. (Eds) *Women Educating Women — Exploring the Potential of Open Learning*, pp. 21–24, The Open University and The City University London.
DOUGLAS, MARY (1966) *Purity and Danger*, London: Routledge and Kegan Paul.
DOUGLAS, MARY (1970) 'Witchcraft: Confessions and Accusations', in DOUGLAS, MARY (Ed.) *Witchcraft: Confessions and Accusations*, pp. xii–xxxvii, London: Tavistock.
DOUGLAS, MARY (1973) *Natural Symbols. Explorations in Cosmology*, London: Barrie and Jenkins.
ELIADE, MERCIA (1989) *Pancavimsa Brahmana* X1V, 1, 13 (translated by W. Calland), quoted in *Shamanism*, London: Arkana.
EVANS PRITCHARD, E.E. (1937) *Witchcraft Oracles and Magic among the Azande*, Oxford: Clarendon Press.
FOUCAULT, MICHEL (1976) *The History of Sexuality*, London: Penguin Books.
FREUD, SIGMUND (1954) *The Origins of Psychoanalysis — Letters to Wilhelm Fliess Drafts and Notes 1887–1902*, Freud, Ernst, L. (Ed.) London: Imago.
GOODY, ESTHER (1970) 'Legitimate and Illegitimate Agression', in DOUGLAS, MARY (Ed.) *Witchcraft: Confessions and Accusations*, pp. 207–244, London: Tavistock.
GLUCKMAN, M. (1955) *Custom and Conflict in Africa*, Oxford: Blackwell.
HAMILL, JOHN GILBERT, R.A. (1991) *World Freemasonry*, London: The Aquarian Press.
HOBBES, T. (1979) *Leviathan* (1651), Great Britain: Pelican.
HORTON, ROBIN (1983) 'Social Psychologies: African and Western', in FORTES, M. and GOODY, J. (Eds) *Oedipus and Job in West African Religion* (Cambridge Studies in Social Anthropology 48), Cambridge: Cambridge University Press.
IRIGARAY, LUCE (1979) *Speculum of the Other Woman*, translated by Gill, C., New York: Cornell University Press.

IRIGARAY, LUCE (1985) *This sex which is not one*, translated by Catherine Porter with Carolyn Burke, Ithaca, NY: Cornell University Press.

IRIGARAY, LUCE (1993) *je, tu, nous*, translated by Martin, Alison, London: Routledge.

KASCHAK, ELLYN (1992) *Engendered Lives*, New York: HarperCollins.

KRAMER, FRITZ (1994) *The Red Fez*, translated by Green, Malcolm R., London/New York: Verso.

KRAMER, H. and SPRENGER, J. (1928) *Malleus Maleficorum* (1496), Suffolk: John Rodker.

KRUGER, BARBARA (1983) *Texts*, Owens, Craig and Weinstock, Jane (Eds) London: The Institute of Contemporary Arts, and Basle: Kunsthalle.

LEWIS, M. (1970) 'A structural approach to Witchcraft and Spirit Possession', in DOUGLAS, MARY (Ed.) *Witchcraft: Confessions and Accusations*, pp. 293–310, London: Tavistock.

MACHIAVELLI (1988) *The Prince* (1513), Skinner and Price (Eds) Cambridge: Cambridge University Press.

MILL, J.S. (1994) *On Liberty* (1859), G. Williams (Ed.) London: Everyman.

MURDOCH, IRIS (1978) *The Fire and the Sun: Why Plato Banished the Artists*, based upon the Romanes Lectures 1976, Oxford: Oxford University Press.

NOCHLIN, LINDA (1989) *Women, Art and Power*, London: Thames and Hudson.

PFEFFER, W. (1989) 'The Historical Context', in FIERO, G.K., PFEFFER, W. and ALLAIN, M. (Eds) *Three Medieval Views of Women*, pp. 28–83, Michigan: Yale University.

PITT-RIVERS, JULIAN (1970) 'Spiritual Power in Central America', in DOUGLAS, MARY (Ed.) *Witchcraft: Confessions and Accusations*, pp. 183–206, London: Tavistock.

RAYMOND, JANICE (1986) *A Passion for Friends*, London: The Women's Press.

STRAW, JANE (1989) *Equal Opportunities, The Way Ahead*, London: Institute of Personnel Management.

WOOLF, VIRGINIA (1990) *A Room of One's Own* (1928) London: Grafton Books.

WILLIS, R.G. (1970) 'Identifying Witches — Instant Millenium', in DOUGLAS, MARY (Ed.) *Witchcraft: Confessions and Accusations*, pp. 129–140, London: Tavistock.

YATES, FRANCES (1964) *Giordano Bruno and the Hermetic Tradition*, London: Routledge and Kegan Paul.

Chapter 10

Black Women in Higher Education: Defining a Space/Finding a Place[1]

Heidi Safia Mirza

Introduction

As the title of this chapter suggests, the issue I want to address is 'how do we as black women, carve out our space and find our place in Higher Education?' I want to suggest we do it in small ways, over the years: we subvert, rationalize and calculate until the cumulative effect of being there begins to show. I want to suggest that the driving force behind women being there comes from the bottom up, not from the top down. It is not simply the pathbreakers, role models or women leaders that make the difference in Higher Education. That is a masculine cultural deficit model we should resist (Mirza, 1993, 1995). This model emphasizes our internal lacking and highlights our negative self esteem.[2] It suggests that we need to look up to others, deflecting attention away from the real cause of our marginal position in academia: racism and discrimination. Such a model holds up symbols of great women achievers at the expense of the 'everywoman'. But it is the consistent tireless efforts of women everywhere that make the difference. If there was no role model they would still persist. My black students do not come to university because of Zenab Badawe, Tessa Sanderson or Diane Abbott, they come because of themselves, and the difference it makes to their lives. I know I did not end up in university because of role models. There were precious few when I was at school during the 1970s. Our female icons were Cleopatra Jones, the karate heroine of the blaxploitation movies; Lieutenant Uhura of Star Trek; and the singer, Diana Ross. No, my motivation lay in my determination to reveal the myths about black women's underachievement. From where I was standing there was no such thing; there was, however, discrimination and prejudice.

Prejudice and discrimination was something about which I learnt when I came to school here in England in the 1970s. I was 16 years old when my family left Trinidad and settled in London. Working on the assumption that all people from the Caribbean are backward and have learning problems, my new school in Brixton was visibly shocked when I passed the entrance test with ease. In fact they made me sit the test twice to make sure I was not cheating. They clearly did not want me at the school, I upset their world, and had the potential to be a trouble-maker. But they had no choice, there was no objective reason to bar my entry. The Head took my mother aside and told her that I could only enter the school if I learned to speak English properly, and insisted that I be put down a year to catch up. But I was determined to show them and by the sixth form my peers voted me in as Head Girl. I had to give speeches or presentations in 'proper' English. I learnt their lingo and this made them mad. The teachers attempted to sabotage my desire to go to university by various means, such as preventing me from sitting entry exams. It culminated in the tactics of one teacher who took me aside and told me that I was far too cocky for my own good and that, if I tried to go too far, one day I would fall flat on my face.

But I did not and lived to tell the tale. I returned to that school several years later to research and write my book *Young, Female and Black* (1992). In my years there I had witnessed the strategic ways young black women employ to negotiate the system so they can succeed in spite of the odds. It is to an investigation of these strategies of mass educational mobility that I want now to turn.

Understanding Black Women's Educational Motivation

During my research on two innercity secondary schools, I looked at the background factors that lead up to young black British women taking the route into post-compulsory schooling. Drawing on research data on over 200 students, I asked the question, 'what factors influence young black women's decision to enter Further and Higher Education?' My research revealed three influences on educational motivation.

The first influence on educational motivation was the notable drive for qualifications. Second-generation Caribbean women, like their migrant parents, showed a strong commitment to education, and in particular identified with the meritocratic ideal as a means of 'getting on'. They shared the fundamental belief that no matter who you are, if you work hard and do well at school you shall be rewarded in the world of work. The goal of 'equality of opportunity' that this meritocratic ideology encompasses, suggests that regardless of gender, race and class, the jobs they get should be a reflection of their educational achievements. The irony is that this ideology persists among the young women and their parents in spite of the reality of their schooling, which denies them this opportunity. It is also ironic that such an outwardly individualistic ideology (expressed in the desire for personal academic qualifications) should also be a central ideology of a radical, black, female educational movement: a movement whose motivation appears to be a strategic rationalization of the very system that oppresses them.

The second influence on educational motivation was the unique outlook on work among the young black women. In interviews, the young women showed that they expected to work just as their sisters, mothers, aunts and grandmothers had done for generations before them. They (and this is the important point) expected to do so without the obstacle of male disapproval. Explanations as to why this may be so point again to the central concept of the ideology of meritocracy in West Indian working-class life. There was a particular definition of masculinity and femininity in which few distinctions were made between male and female abilities and attributes with regard to work. This meant the young women did not regard their male relationships, whether within the institution of marriage, or not, as inhibiting their right to work in any way. It was these values, and not the positive role model of the strong black mother, that resulted in the positive black female outlook on work and education.

The third influence on educational motivation was the strategic rationalization of post-16 education and careers by young black women. Young black women appeared to be primarily motivated in their career aspirations by the prospect of upward mobility. A job was an expression of their desire to move ahead within the educational process. The belief in the promise of a meritocracy and the rewards of credentialism spur black women on to take up whatever opportunities become available and accessible to them, especially opportunities that entail a chance to increase their further educational qualifications. The young black women chose realistic careers, those that they knew to be accessible and (historically) available to them. For example, social work and other caring jobs such as nursing or office work. The occupations they chose always required a course, or several courses, of rigorous professional training. Thus, while it may appear they were reproducing stereotypes of black women's work, the young women were in effect expressing their meritocratic values within the limits of opportunity allowed in a racially and sexually divisive educational and economic system. They were in effect operating a back door entry to Further and Higher Education.

From 'Just Being There' to a Mass Movement

These findings are fascinating for they reveal an ingenious strategy that these young women have developed over time to enable them to overcome the disadvantages of racism in their schooling experience. Young black women who identify with the notion of credentialism, meritocracy, and female autonomy, strategically used every means at their disposal in the educational system and classroom to achieve some measure of mobility in their world of limited opportunities.

Recently, I have followed on this research with a new project looking at the experience of black students in university (Mirza, 1994). This is still in progress, but what is beginning to emerge is a confirmation of the continued instrumental nature of black women's achievement strategy. When I asked more than 100 students at South Bank University what is the most important thing about university most replied: 'just having a degree to advance my career'. Furthermore, 90 per cent are mature women who have come via caring or administrative career backgrounds, verifying my thesis that the black female strategy to overcome racism is to take the long (back door) route into Further and Higher Education.

There is a mass movement from the bottom up that promises to change the face of Further and Higher Education in years to come. Significant numbers of black women are already in universities, colleges and other educational institutions. The 1993 Labour Force survey shows 61 per cent of all black women (aged 16–59) to have higher and other qualifications (*Employment Gazette*, 1993). Of these 37 per cent were 'mature' (aged 25–44). Moreover, 77 per cent of all black women gained their highest qualification in UK institutions (Jones, 1993). A recent study for the PSI (Policy Studies Institute) shows that in relation to their respective population sizes, ethnic minority groups, overall, are over represented in Higher Education (Modood and Shiner, 1994). This over-representation was especially apparent in the new universities. Here people of Caribbean origin were over-represented by 43 per cent, Asians by 162 per cent and Africans by 223 per cent! This was compared with the white population which was under-represented by 7 per cent. Modood and Shiner remark that in spite of this evidence, many, and this includes the quality press, still continue to speak of 'black' or ethnic under-representation in Higher Education.[3]

Explaining the Absence of Black Lecturers and Staff

It is no myth, however, to talk about under-representation of minorities as academic staff in Higher Education in the UK. The mass movement of black students from the bottom up, is not matched by an increase in black lecturers and staff, let alone black female lecturers and staff. It is almost impossible to know the numbers of female black lecturers in Higher Education. As we all tend to know each other, we know the numbers are small. In senior positions we could probably count the numbers on one hand. That we are forced into this anecdotal position with regard to quantifying our numbers in Higher Education, has much to do with our lack of importance in the discourse of equality in Higher Education, as I found out when I attempted to do research on the matter.

In researching for this chapter I looked up the UFC (University Funding Council) statistics, (now the HEFCE, Higher Education Funding Council for England). When I found no recorded figures on minority status I rang them up. I was told what the university staff record contains in detail. It documents 18 areas of our employment profile; everything from gender, pay, academic interest, previous employment, superannuation, to the cost centre where we are paid; everything, short of our shoe size, but not ethnic origin. I enquired if this was a progressive policy taking on the contentious nature of ethnic monitoring. The woman on the other end of the phone was baffled, 'No dear,' she replied, 'ethnic origin has never been considered necessary for looking at staff recruitment patterns.' Exasperated, I turned to the DFE (Department for Education), there the results were similar, no statistics on black women, though the story was different. A very keen researcher explained the numbers of black women in Higher Education in the UK would be too small to show up in a statistical cell. Collecting this data, he said, would therefore be pointless.

Finally, I found something. Not very reliable by their own admission but something. The lecturers' union, NATFHE (National Union of Teachers in Further and Higher Education) collects ethnic data on their membership form. Their February 1994 statistics showed that 2.27 per cent of their 75 000 membership was black. Though their data were not broken down into male and female categories, they were divided into Higher Education and Further Education institutions. From this analysis it is clear that the actual numbers of black lecturers, never mind numbers of black women, are appallingly low; in the Higher Education sector there were just 11 Caribbean lecturers, 52 Asian and 7 African lecturers, with 19 categorized as 'other' black.

Though the scale of the matter is significantly different, the issue of low black representation among academic staff is similar to the gender experience, where equal access to Higher Education in the UK has not been matched by equal participation and promotion in teaching and management (Aziz, 1990; Evans, 1994). The 1990 Hansard Report, *Women at the Top*, shows that while there has been an increase of 43 per cent of women students, there has only been an increase of 8 per cent of women lecturers (Parkin, 1994). Now in the UK, women make up 14 per cent (2481) of all lecturers in Higher Education, only 6 per cent (449) of senior lecturers, and just 3 per cent (95) of professors (Morley, 1994). From figures like this, which illustrate the disproportionate numbers of women and black academic staff, we can ask if the increase in women students and black students has ever truly been about equality? It seems that the whole process of access has been a rather cynical exercise in accounting and funding, drawing on a 'reserve army of students', rather than a bid for equality in Higher Education (Humm, 1994).

Black Versus Female Priorities in Higher Education

In spite of this evidence, in the 20 years since women began their struggle for access to Higher Education in earnest, it appears that white women academics have drifted from issues of access and the curriculum, to issues of culture and management (e.g. Evans, 1994; Humm, 1994). However, access and the curriculum still remain the priority for black women academics (McKeller, 1989; Brewer, 1993; Guy-Sheftall, 1993; Bhopal, 1994; Henry, 1994; hooks, 1994; Moghissi, 1994). Nearly all the papers collected from a recent conference on 'Gender and the Organisation of Higher Education' (Evans *et al.*, 1994), told of the struggle not to replicate male thinking and perceptions now that women are in Higher Education. This collection, entitled *Agenda for Gender*, was the outcome of a meeting of over 80 (mainly white) women in Higher Education. They talked of how not to take on male careers and values, male behaviour and management strategies. They talked of the dangers and ease with which women can become seduced and absorbed into the malestream; and they called for a gendered approach to management (Humm, 1994). No mention was made of the struggle for access by black female academics.

There is a long history of ethnocentrism in white feminist discourse, and it lives on in the changing discourse on gender in Higher Education, where black women remain invisible (Acker, 1993). However, rather than engaging in a contentious and self-defeating debate on black female marginalization from the white academic discourse on women in Higher Education, I want to bring you back to the theme of this chapter: the black female strategic negotiation of the system.

bell hooks reminds us that, as black women, to be part of academia does not mean we have to lose sight of our place on the margins, our strategic site of resistance (hooks, 1990, 1994). She tells us about her struggle of 'becoming successful':

> When I left that concrete space on the margins, I kept alive in my heart ways of knowing reality . . . (I was) sustained by remembrance of the past, which includes recollections of broken tongues that decolonize our minds, our very beings.

She tells us:

> Separate useful knowledge (you may get) from the dominating group, from participation in ways of knowing that would lead to estrange-ment, alienation, and worse — assimilation and co-optation. (hooks, 1990: 150)

Her message is one of refusal, 'know who we are and be who we want to be' — carve out a space of resistance — be brave. I believe as black women, sharing our lived experience on the margins is what we have to offer our white sisters, many of whom are moving toward or have arrived at the centre. But separating 'useful knowledge' and avoiding assimilation, as hooks suggests, is not always easy when you are embedded in the powerful patriarchal discourse. For black women it is the patriarchal discourse of racism with its seductive use of equal opportunities and antiracism that we must resist.

The Strategic Rationalization of Equal Opportunities and Antiracism

Equal opportunities and antiracism has been traditionally presented as playing an important role in explaining the presence of black women in institutions of Further and Higher Education. However, it is my position that their presence is in spite of equal opportunities and antiracist practice, not because of it. The motivation to 'go on' comes from the women themselves, an issue long ignored in the many studies that focus on 'race', equal opportunities and access (Lyon,

1988; CRE, 1989; Brennan and McGeevor, 1990; Bird *et al.*, 1992b). The black female presence cannot simply be explained in terms of institutional access and changing white attitudes. This is only a partial and a liberal explanation. We should be clear, equal opportunities, antiracism and access programmes have not been about developing a political strategy for black people in the workplace or in universities and colleges.

In the current discourse on 'race', as black people we are expected to work within 'race', talk about race, study 'race', be experts on 'race', feel oppressed and be disadvantaged because of our 'race'. I am always asked to talk about 'black women resisting racism'. But if that were the sum total of my reality I would be seriously unhappy. Black people in Britain do not live a one-dimensional existence defined by the racism of others. Nevertheless, the current discourse on race reduces black life to little more than a response to racism. Paul Gilroy (1990: 71) responds to this construction of our identity. He remarks: 'There is more to the emancipation of blacks than opposition to racism'. I think the type of identity politics that has been fostered by the discourse on racism has been regressive, divisive, and harmful. It threatens to undermine the position of black people studying and working within educational institutions. I have seen people hurt, even destroyed in subtle ways, by the type of identity politics this notion fosters. I shall illustrate what I mean.

The other day a black student came to me and said he was leaving his course. 'Why?' I asked, 'why when you are so near the end?' He explained that he was leaving because he failed the year. He failed, he said, because of racism on the course and in particular racism of his placement officer. 'I want to be like you', he proclaimed, 'resist racism, fight as a black person. Take up a position.' Clearly he felt empowered by his action. I was impressed but not convinced. I rang a colleague, one of the few black lecturers at South Bank University, who was also his tutor. He told me another side to the story. He explained Henry had failed because he never did any work, not because of racism. He was always resisting racism in the classroom, on his placement, among his friends. Arguing with the white students who encouraged him and listened to him. 'I told him not to do it', my colleague told me, 'resisting racism is for the white students, not you, go and work; look at them, they are in the library working'. But Henry never did work, he just got angrier and angrier. He was so caught up in the discourse on racism that he had become a victim of its success. The struggle against racism gave him his identity, defined his blackness, and gave him a voice. Only now he has no qualifications, no job, and few prospects. My black colleague rationalized his predicament. He told me:

> Black people can't afford to resist racism in the way we are expected to. If we did we would be mad or dead. Our jobs are not about resisting racism but about finding a space for ourselves. I just want to be a black man that is good at my job and can make a difference. Resisting is what whites do, they can talk about it think about it, and then go away and do their work, they feel better, it's their luxury, one I can't afford.

It is an irony that antiracism can stop people in many ways from going forward and being productive; and productivity is important, because in Higher Education productivity is the yardstick for success. Finishing courses, publishing books — that is how success is measured. As black lecturers, we have to be critical and selective about our involvement in equal opportunities and antiracism. For while these are often the only forums that our white colleagues give us; our only legitimate institutional 'space'; for while we are encouraged to sit in tribunals, take colleagues to task, and sit on committees and expend all our emotional and personal energies, our (white) colleagues get on with publishing and promotion and climbing up the career ladder.

However, there are strategic aspects of the discourse on 'race' that are important. Those that can make a difference, for example, are some equal opportunity policies. Those that help break down institutional barriers; those that challenge gate keeping, and subjective decision making. In my case, in defining my strategic place in the discourse, I have chosen admissions. Along with academic tasks I process and interview over 800 applications each year. I do this so that I can forget about the porters who shut me out; the insulting way I am asked to leave a room as though I do not exist; when I am told to get off the photocopier because I am taken for a student; or when I am dismissed by colleagues as a token; or told my courses are not 'proper' or are 'disturbing'. You choose your battles and mine is to get good black students on our courses. After working for three years on social science admissions, this year (1994) we have 65 per cent black and ethnic students, 75 per cent women students, and 70 per cent mature students.

Surviving in Higher Education: Having Your Own Agenda

Thus, while equal opportunities and antiracism remains a paramount discourse for white lecturers and students, black students are preoccupied by their single-minded drive for 'success' through credentials. Like the young black women in my book, on the courses I teach, black students also have a strategy. They keep their heads down and do the course. That is their agenda: a strategy for survival and a way to progress in their university careers. Their aim is to use things to their advantage and not be side-tracked by discourses on racism. In my research study on South Bank University students, when given the opportunity to report openly on their experience, racism was not top of their list, learning and knowledge were. This did not mean that racism was not important to them — just that what we have come to call racism has many other forms. Social and economic conditions that affect all students' lives are equally influenced by racism. Finance, child care, time management, health, all preoccupied the black students at South Bank.

Like these university students, and the young black women in my book, I have also used the strategic lessons I learnt along the way to find a space for myself within Higher Education. I have learnt to make choices; who to ask for help and who not to, but most of all to turn anger into positive outcome. It is not easy, probably the hardest route to take. In fact, my book *Young, Female and Black* is the outcome of a racist comment that my PhD supervisor made. He suggested I would never complete my work as I was no different than all the single-parent black women who scrounge on the dole. Hurt, angry and with no words to respond, I vowed there and then to go away and find the answers. I knew black women were being stereotyped as failures and underachievers. I wanted to prove him wrong. I turned my PhD from a thesis on multi-cultural education to an investigation of the social, economic and educational conditions of black women. Instead of allowing his racism to destroy me, and it nearly did, I used his racism as positively as I could, as a challenge; as a means to carve out a small space and to find my place in Higher Education.

Notes

1 This chapter is based on the keynote address given by Heidi Safia Mirza at the WHEN (Women in Higher Education Network) Conference, *Women Breaking Boundaries in Higher Education: Struggles and Successes*, held at the University of Central Lancashire in November 1994.

2 Many studies on black women in academia call for more black women in visible, key positions (Moses, 1989; Reid, 1990). This demand for social justice in education is not to be confused with the commonsense preoccupation for role models that informs many initiatives that purport to address inequality by combating negative self esteem through positive images. For example, the *Images Project* Lancashire County Council, May 1994. The rationale of this project was '. . . to provide role models for young women to aspire to: encouraging them to challenge limited and conditioned roles'.

3 For example, the *Times Higher Education Supplement* editorial, 5 July 1991, reported black minority under-representation. This is not surprising as University admissions statistics are traditionally interpreted to show minority disadvantage (e.g. Bird *et al.*, 1992a; Taylor, 1993). See Connolly (1994) for a discussion of the complex nature of university entry data.

References

ACKER, S. (1993) 'Contradictions in Terms: Women Academics in British Universities', in ARNOT, M. and WEILER, K. (Eds) *Feminism and Social Justice in Education*, pp. 146–166, London: Falmer Press.

AZIZ, A. (1990) 'Women in UK Universities: The Road to Casualization?' in STIVER LIE, S. and O'LEARY, V. (Eds) *Storming the Tower: Women in the Academic World*, pp. 33–46, London: Kogan Page.

BIRD, J., SHEIBANI, A. and FRANCOMBE, D. (1992a) *Ethnic Monitoring and Admissions to Higher Education*, Employment Department, London, HMSO, Bristol Polytechnic (New University of West of England) (Co-publication).

BIRD, J., YEE, W. and MYLER, A. (1992b) *Widening Access to Higher Education for*

Black People, Employment Department, London, HMSO, Bristol Polytechnic (New University of the West of England) (Co-publication).

BHOPAL, K. (1994) 'The Influence of Feminism on Black Women in the Higher Education Curriculum', in DAVIES, S., LUBELSKA, C. and QUINN, J. (Eds) *Changing the Subject: Women in Higher Education*, pp. 124–137, London: Taylor & Francis.

BRENNAN, J. and McGEEVOR, P. (1990) *Ethnic Minorities and the Graduate Labour Market*, London: Commission for Racial Equality.

BREWER, R.M. (1993) 'Theorizing Race, Class and Gender: The New Scholarship of Black Feminist Intellectuals and Black Women's Labor', in JAMES, S.M. and BUSIA, A.P.A. (Eds) *Theorizing Black Feminisms: The Visionary Pragmatism of Black Women*, pp. 13–30, London: Routledge.

CONNOLLY, C. (1994) 'Shades of Discrimination: University Entry Data 1990–92', in HASELGROVE, S. (Ed.) *The Student Experience*, pp. 20–34, London: SRHE and OU.

CRE (1989) *Words or Deeds? A Review of Equal Opportunity Policies in Higher Education*, London: Commission for Racial Equality.

Employment Gazette (1993) 'Ethnic Origins and the Labour Market', London: Employment Department, London: HMSO, Harrington Kilbride plc. pp. 25–43.

EVANS, M. (1994) 'Introduction', in EVANS, M., GOSLING, J. and SELLER, A. (Eds) *Agenda for Gender*, Canterbury: University of Kent at Canterbury.

EVANS, M., GOSLING, J. and SELLER, A. (Eds) (1994) *Agenda for Gender*, pp. 1–49, Canterbury: University of Kent at Canterbury.

GILROY, P. (1990) 'The End of Anti-Racism', *New Community*, **17**, 1, pp. 71–83.

GUY-SHEFTALL, B. (1993) 'A Black Feminist perspective on Transforming the Academy: The Case of Spelman College', in JAMES, S.M. and BUSIA, A.P.A. (Eds) *Theorizing Black Feminisms: The Visionary Pragmatism of Black Women*, pp. 77–89, London: Routledge.

HENRY, M. (1994) 'Ivory Towers and Ebony Women: The Experiences of Black Women in Higher Education', in DAVIES, S., LUBELSKA, C. and QUINN, J. (Eds) *Changing the Subject: Women in Higher Education*, pp. 42–57, London: Taylor & Francis.

hooks, b. (1990) *Yearning: Race, Gender and Cultural Politics*, London: Turnaround.

hooks, b. (1994) *Teaching to Transgress: Education as the Practice of Freedom*, New York: Routledge.

HUMM, M. (1994) 'Equal Opportunities and Promoting People', in EVANS, M., GOSLING, J. and SELLER, A. (Eds) *Agenda for Gender*, pp. 28–35, Canterbury: University of Kent at Canterbury.

JONES, T. (1993) *Britain's Ethnic Minorities*, London: PSI.

LYON, S. (1988) 'Unequal Opportunities: Black Minorities and Access to Higher Education', *JFHE*, **12**, (3), pp. 20–36.

McKELLER, B. (1989) 'Only the Fittest of the Fittest Will Survive: Black Women and Education', in ACKER, S. (Ed.) *Teachers, Genders and Careers*, pp. 69–85, Lewes: Falmer Press.

MIRZA, H.S. (1992) *Young, Female and Black*, London: Routledge.

MIRZA, H.S. (1993) 'The Social Construction of Black Womanhood in British Educational Research: Towards a New Understanding', in ARNOT, M. and WEILER, K. (Eds) *Feminism and Social Justice in Education*, pp. 32–57, London: Falmer Press.

MIRZA, H.S. (1994) 'Black Students in Higher Education: a Movement for Change', paper presented at SRHE (Society for Research in Higher Education) 1994 Annual Conference, 'The Student Experience', University of York, December.

MIRZA, H.S. (1995) 'The Schooling of Young Black Women', in TOMLINSON, S. and CRAFT,

M. (Eds) *Ethnic Relations and Schooling: Policy and Practice in the 1990s*, pp. 77–96, London: Athlone Press.

MODOOD, T. and SHINER, M. (1994) *Ethnic Minorities and Higher Education: Why are there Differential rates of Entry?*, London: PSI.

MOGHISSI, H. (1994) 'Racism and Sexism in Academic Practice; A Case Study', in AFSHAR, H. and MAYNARD, M. (Eds) *The Dynamics of Race and Gender: Some Feminist Interventions*, London: Taylor & Francis.

MORLEY, L. (1994) 'Women's Studies and Feminist Transformations: Problematising Empowerment in the Academy', in EVANS, M., GOSLING, J. and SELLER, A. (Eds) *Agenda for Gender*, pp. 222–234, Canterbury: University of Kent at Canterbury.

MOSES, Y. (1989) *Black Women in the Academe: Issues and Strategies*, Project on the Status and Education of Women, Washington DC: Association of American Colleges.

PARKIN, D. (1994) 'The Woman Dominating Culture of Academia', in EVANS, M., GOSLING, J. and SELLER, A. (Eds) *Agenda for Gender*, pp. 21–27, Canterbury: University of Kent at Canterbury.

REID, P.T. (1990) 'African-American Women in Academia: Paradoxes and Barriers', in LIE, S. and O'LEARY, V. (Eds) *Storming The Tower: Women in the Academic World*, pp. 147–162, London: Kogan Page.

TAYLOR, P. (1993) 'Minority Ethnic Groups and Gender Access to Higher Education', *New Community*, **19**, pp. 425–440.

Chapter 11

Taking Offence: Research as Resistance to Sexual Harassment in Academia

Avril Butler and Mel Landells

Introduction

This chapter is based on a pilot study we carried out into the incidence and context of sexual harassment at an English university. In it we seek to raise some of the issues of doing such research, in a way which we hope will stimulate and encourage other women in academia as part of a larger process of creative change.

The university where our research took place welcomed our interest and offered a good level of cooperation. Significantly, it was a time when the university was about to launch a new sexual and racial harassment policy and we saw this as an opportunity to bring a feminist perspective to policy making. We also wanted to challenge attempts to treat sexual harassment as an occasional, isolated phenomenon. From the beginning of the work we were confronted with difficulties and dilemmas. Although we had stated clearly that we were feminists, our approach did not easily fit into the institution's expectations or assumptions. In describing what we did, we explore some of these concerns and how we dealt with them. We do not intend to debate, here, the relative merits of qualitative and quantitative methods in feminist research, but we explain our choice of methods and some of the results.

Since the 1970s, sexual harassment has developed as an area which is researched and theorized and the term has been integrated into common usage. Our research highlighted the positive and negative features of this and the way in which these interact with other theories of women's oppression. We began the research with an analysis of sexual harassment as being part of a continuum of sexual violence (Kelly, 1987) within the context of gendered organizational culture. In the section 'Developing analysis through the research process', we reflect on the way in which that analysis affected us as researchers in this area.

In the final section, before we summarize the particular ways in which we think the research was an act of resistance, we acknowledge the importance of women having the right to be silent. We have tried throughout the work to balance a need for visibility in this area and to recognize the associated vulnerability it brings. We hope that we have managed this with sensitivity and care and end the chapter with some reflections on what we have learned.

Concerns and Considerations in Setting Up the Research

Resources required us to limit our sample, so we chose to focus on the harassment, by men, of women teaching staff. We sent questionnaires to all the women teaching staff, full and part time, at all levels of the university, rather than try to take a small representative sample from all women at the university.

Personnel staff were concerned that students and non-teaching staff may have felt excluded and we shared this concern. We offered to explain our decision to anyone who asked and to place a short piece about the research in the in-house magazine. Some members of the university's Equality Network were very supportive of our research and intended to press for further funds to become available to extend the research to other groups of women.

We attempted to balance anonymity, sensitivity and self-protection throughout the research process. For example, as the institution employs very few black women, women from minority ethnic groups, or disabled women, to have asked for this information would have made them easily identifiable. Instead, the openness of the questionnaire invited women to put in as much, or as little, information as they chose. This issue of visibility and associated vulnerability is one which haunted us throughout the work. We found that we had to make judgements constantly about what information we could present and to whom, without exposing either the women, or ourselves, to retribution. We were cautious not to produce a situation in which we might be pressurized to identify a particular woman or harasser. In terms of self-protection we became increasingly conscious, as our work progressed, of the risks involved in this area of research. Elizabeth Stanko quotes The Alliance Against Sexual Coercion:

> sexual harassment in the workplace is an issue of power . . . complaining is stepping out of line, and stepping out of line brings on a display of power and control in our society. (AASC, 1981: 19, in Stanko, 1988: 93)

Fear of retribution is not a paranoid fantasy; during the research we became aware of the experiences of other women who had spoken out about harassment. In Canada, for example, at the University of Victoria in 1993, the university president overturned the Equity Office judgement of harassment, in spite of a wealth of evidence and support for the women speaking out. This exposed the women who had brought the complaint, particularly Somer Brodribb, to public vilification and defamation (Brodribb, 1994). Closer to home, we have been told of women who carried out similar research to ours who found themselves reorganized out of a job. It was made very clear to us that, had we wanted to do the research in our own institution and publish the results in a way which identified it, we would have been in breach of contract for 'unauthorised disclosure of ... [information] which would embarrass, harm or prejudice [the institution]'.

We sent out 178 questionnaires, received 65 responses and had in-depth interviews with three of the women who had experienced sexual harassment. We were unprepared for the detailed descriptions, particularly on the questionnaires, which some women gave of the way some men had abused their positions of power. We had to deal with our wish to expose the behaviour and our responsibility to ensure anonymity for our respondents, so we were constantly balancing a need to speak out with the feeling of being silenced. One of the ways in which we resolved this problem was to exclude specific descriptions of women's harassment from the written report for the university's senior management. This was to prevent the potential for women's experiences to be viewed out of context and individually pathologized and dismissed. We did, however, feel a responsibility to the women, and to ourselves, to express our offence at this catalogue of experience. We searched for a way to give voice to these experiences alongside a strong critique of the culture which disregarded them. At the formal presentation of the report, attended by senior management, harassment advisors and Equality Network members, we played a tape recording of some of the women's words, read by us. This powerfully conveyed their experiences in a way which allowed us to keep some control of the information and which made the most of that opportunity to offer resistance to the minimizing and silencing of women's experience. A number of women who attended the presentation said to us how much the tape had validated their experiences.

What is the Point of Statistics?

Part of our questionnaire was designed to gain statistical information about the incidence of legally actionable sexual harassment. We thought that statistics would be taken more seriously than qualitative data by management and would also encourage women to see their individual experience as widely shared. For the purpose of our research we used definitions of sexual harassment identified by the Industrial Relations Services survey of 1992.

In our survey, 55.4 per cent of respondents had experienced sexual harassment which fell under this definition (IRS, 1992) and our results were similar to many other research surveys in the same area. For example, a survey conducted by NALGO in 1981 and reported by Tess Gill and Larry Whitty (1983) found that:

> 52 per cent of the women said they had experienced unwanted sexual attention which had caused them discomfort in their workplace. (Gill and Whitty, 1983: 269)

A BBC/MORI poll (July 1993) reported in the *Guardian* (24 July 1993) revealed that 33 per cent of women are currently suffering sexual harassment at work.

The most commonly experienced form of harassment in our survey was in the form of suggestive remarks, innuendoes and lewd comments and jokes (41.5 per cent). Approximately a quarter of respondents had also experienced being leered at, or eyed up and had experienced unwanted physical contact (26.2 per cent and 21.5 per cent). We found that 15.4 per cent of respondents had experienced unwanted sexual advances and 12.3 per cent had experienced offensive flirtations and the display of sexually suggestive pin-ups or calendars. One respondent reported continued suggestions for dates outside the university which were clearly unwelcome.

Our care in collecting these statistics was to gain the attention of senior management, to demonstrate that sexual harassment existed as much in this workplace as in any other. This paved the way for our qualitative data and the connections we made with other behaviour at work. Although statistics are useful in this way, they do little to raise awareness of women's experiences of harassment. It is not possible to convey the offensiveness of the incidents with numbers (Pugh, 1990), as the following quote shows:

> The sorts of situation I would find myself in were . . . him turning up at the station when I returned from a conference. He'd given approval for the travel arrangements. He would then offer me a lift home . . . Then there was also casual touching, suggestive remarks etc. His seniority made it very hard to deal with.

Harassment: Definitions, Language and Experience

In order to explore the connections between definitions, language and experience, we chose not to confine our interest to sexual harassment, but to extend it to other forms of gender-related harassment and offensive behaviour. Sue Lees refers to the difficulty of communicating experience in a way which does not simply reinforce power relationships (Lees, 1993). The availability of the term 'sexual harassment' has worked both for and against women. Positively, it has allowed women to name distress and discomfort as something that is publicly acknowledged as offensive, and against which policy and procedures exist. It has, in some situations, contributed to cultural change because men have felt vulnerable to being accused of sexual harassment. Negatively, it delineates extreme behaviour, creating a category against which many women judge their experience and question the appropriateness of the definition (Kitzinger, 1994). Creating a dichotomy that separates gender harassment and *sexual* harassment can be unhelpful, as women do not necessarily experience 'sexual harassment' as *sexual* (Watson, 1994). Even when they do define it as such, the difficulty remains for women to prove that it was sexual harassment:

> I suppose what it seems to me like, some of the other women I've talked to who have been sexually harassed, have more evidence than I did in that instance . . . so they might be in more of a position to do something and make it stick. So I suppose it almost feels to me like it has to be something that's fairly big, or consistently going on for there to be any point in trying to do anything about it.

Indeed, it is advantageous to a man accused of sexual harassment to attribute his behaviour to sexual misunderstanding, relying on stereotypes of masculinity and 'normal' gender relations. Many respondents in our survey wrote about harassment in a general way and did not specify that it was sexual in nature. All the women we interviewed were hesitant in identifying their experience as sexual harassment and were tentative about the validity of their experiences for this research.

It was clear to us that the very process of defining sexual harassment can create a separation from our experience by forcing us to decide whether something does, or does not, fit the definition. The way in which we approached this was to attempt to bring sexual harassment back into our consciousness of daily experience by exploring the connections with other forms of gender-related behaviour. We tried to encourage women to review their experience of harassment, both gender-related and sexual, and to validate both through that connection. The difficulty of defining sexual harassment was illustrated in the interviews where there seemed to be a significant gap between what the women experienced as sexual harassment, or behaviour which made them feel the same degree of discomfort, and what they felt they could complain about.

When asked what behaviour would be serious enough to report, women gave examples of explicit, violent sexual behaviour: 'If they actually attacked me or something. If it was a rape or to suggest they want to, then yes.' This indicated to us that although the policy and procedures prohibit sexual harassment in its extreme forms and issue a warning to men about the limits of their behaviour, they do little to protect women in the majority of cases (Purkiss, 1994). Indeed, the women we heard from clearly felt tentative about naming 'normal' interaction between women and men as offensive. Unless we can make it safe enough for each other to complain about *all* offensive behaviour, we are unlikely to be able to complain about less easily categorized forms of harassment, even to one another (Lees, 1993).

Developing Analysis Through the Research Process

The interest in our research from the institution we researched was clearly focused on the extreme forms of sexual harassment which would be actionable under their new policy. Our interest in exploring the relationship between gendered organizational culture, male sexual violence and sexual harassment was somewhat at odds with this. However, the personal impact of our political analysis became clearer as the work progressed and served to raise our anxiety.

We intended the research to raise awareness, not only about the extent of sexual harassment, but also about the context in which it occurs. To do this we chose to include questions about women's experience of other offensive behaviour from men. For example, sexist or patronizing remarks, offensive comments about appearance or dress, and being interrupted or talked over in meetings or seminars. There were nine offensive behaviours altogether. This placed sexual harassment on a continuum of male sexual violence (Kelly, 1987; Ramazanoglu, 1987; Burrell and Hearn, 1989), and recognized that sexual harassment is a power resource used by men to control women in organizations:

> Organisations . . . [are] sites of sexual harassment in which patriarchy and the control it gives over women is reflected in, and enhanced by, sexual harassment. (Burrell, 1984: 104)

We do not intend by this to imply a mono-causal explanation of the power relations within organizations, but in the context of sexual harassment we considered patriarchal relations to be the most significant factor.

In seeking to make sense of the very high reporting of offensive behaviour (83.1 per cent), mostly at the hands of senior male colleagues, we referred to other research on gendered organizational culture. In particular, Cynthia Cockburn mentions tactics which men use to impede women's advancement at work (Cockburn, 1991). It is in these more covert practices that the embedded cultural values of the institution lie (Mills, 1988). A classic example of underlying assumptions was given by one woman:

> I've been expected to act in a secretarial capacity to a senior colleague . . . This happened on a visit to another site and I was annoyed not to be introduced to colleagues there as an equal colleague and had I not explained who I was I think they'd have assumed I was his secretary.

The difficulties of challenging the underlying assumptions in an organization have been highlighted by Eileen Green and Cathy Cassell:

> An organisation may . . . have a number of visible pro-women artifacts such as an equal opportunities policy . . . whilst still having a set of underlying patriarchal assumptions which reflect male interests. As they are 'invisible' and unsaid, they are very difficult to challenge. (Green and Cassell, 1993: 14)

We wanted our research to make these 'patriarchal assumptions' visible, stated and, therefore, challenged.

An example of the dual standards which apply to women in the workplace (further developed in Butler and Landells, 1994) is the way in which we are expected to behave in a professional way, but in a 'feminine' manner with stereotypical female traits of caring, submissiveness and emotionality (Cockburn, 1991; Gutek, 1985, 1989). This kind of delicate juggling of roles can often lead to women being negatively labelled by men at work (Sheppard, 1989: 148; Gutek, 1989). One woman replying to the questionnaire said:

> I have tried to say that what they are doing is sexist. They just carry on as before and put it down to me (and other female colleagues) as being too sensitive or 'the lesbian feminist Mafia'.

The (hetero)sexualization of women is compounded both by the constant cultural reinforcement of heterosexuality (Kitzinger, 1994) and by the threat of verbal abuse. The use of 'lesbian' as a term of abuse is developed by Marny Hall (1992) in her article about the position of lesbians in organizations. She describes the way in which compulsory heterosexuality is both exploited and perpetuated by the demand that women occupy the role of 'other':

> Although women, to varying degrees, collude in, or refrain from, this male narrational process, they are forbidden to contradict it by citing an opposing reality . . . The penalty for . . . mutiny is, within the organisation, at the very least, a forfeiture of goodwill; at the most retaliation, harassment and the loss of one's job. (Hall, 1992: 178)

This highlights what we saw, for us, as the risks of 'citing an alternative reality' and thereby causing offence within a relatively small academic community.

The effect of these covert practices on many women in our study was for them to distance themselves from the centre of power in the university. They did this in a variety of ways, such as avoiding meetings, avoiding working with certain men and concentrating more on work with students. In some cases, women found themselves excluded from meetings, or discovered that they had taken place informally without their knowledge or at out-of work hours when they were unable to attend. Others reported a more general feeling of exclusion:

> The hierarchical nature of this institution and the misuse of power to get decisions made . . . have involved myself and female colleagues being left unconsulted and patronised.

Additionally, when women did attend meetings, nearly half found themselves talked over or not listened to, which they experienced as frustrating and exhausting and which sometimes led to withdrawal from those occasions. Being interrupted or talked over in meetings or seminars was one of the most frequently experienced offensive behaviours in our survey, which supports the findings of Dale Spender (1980). The potential for men to describe this behaviour as 'normal' undermines and invalidates women's reasonable complaints. One woman who complained about this behaviour was told: 'I'd misread their talking me down, just the normal cut and thrust of debate'.

We found that being given more than an equal share of administration or pastoral work, having ideas recycled as someone else's, or feeling bullied or coerced, were common types of behaviour experienced by women from men. Clearly, an unreasonable amount of administration work or pastoral care allows far less time for women to pursue their own research interests and publishing opportunities. Women are, therefore, caught in a paradox which reproduces discrimination, because without attending meetings and taking part in the power structures they are viewed as less capable and have less influence in policy decisions (Morley, 1994).

It is not surprising, given the male-centred criteria for achievement at work generally, and in the academy in particular, that women choose not to draw attention to their femaleness (Ramazanoglu, 1987; McAuley, 1987; Morley, 1994). Feminist criticisms of the male-dominated nature of the academy are widespread (Ramazanoglu, 1987). For example, several writers have examined the gate-keeping role of men in academia. They often keep out women who may want to change the *status quo* (Kitzinger, 1990) or are responsible for deciding what will be published (Spender, 1981) and how that will be written (Smith, 1979; Itzen, 1984). Recent political developments in Higher Education are putting pressure on all teaching staff to publish and this has served to reinforce the power of some male gate-keepers. We became increasingly aware of the likely unpopularity of our work within this climate.

Keeping Quiet: Sexual Violence and Resistance

As we balanced how much we could, or should, expose the data and the risks of retribution to us and to them, we were conscious of the experience of those women in our study who had publicly objected. Of the 85 incidents of harassment reported in the questionnaires, women said they had confronted the harasser in 38 cases. Of these the harassment had stopped in only 10 cases and in the others, responses had ranged from surprise that the behaviour should be offensive, to laughter, derision or further harassment:

> Once I informed him that his behaviour could look like bully-boy tactics. After that his behaviour became more subtle and difficult to handle.

This indicated to us that for many women, failure to confront the harasser was based, not on internalized oppression, but rather on a realistic assessment of the risks. When asked about how they felt about confronting a harasser, women answered:

> In theory I feel we should be able to do this, in practice I find it very hard.

> It would have to be pretty serious harassment before I would think it was worth declaring open warfare.

The most common reason given was that they felt it would make things worse. We respected the decision of these women to protect themselves by keeping quiet:

> In an environment where I feel dismissed and belittled already, to ask people to stop behaving in an offensive way, particularly if they're in senior positions, would make me feel even more vulnerable. I don't expect to be listened to or taken seriously.

We hoped our research would contribute to their confidence in naming their experience and its broader context, believing that validation is one of the aspects of empowerment. In considering the difference between reported incidents of sexual harassment and our findings, we drew on the feminist literature which points to the failure of legislation to protect women from, for example, pornography, rape and other forms of sexual violence (Chester and Dickey, 1988; Kelly, 1988; Smart, 1989). The self-protective mechanisms of minimizing or forgetting incidents of sexual violence are well documented, for example rape (Resick and Schnicke, 1993), and child sexual abuse, (Kelly, 1988; La Fontaine, 1990; Mayes *et al.*, 1992). However, it is also clear that this can leave individuals exposed and isolated. A survivor of child sexual abuse wrote:

> But — this whole sexualized world of men, in which the women were colluding, mendaciously and hypocritically, was not named by anybody . . . I was wrong and twisted. Something wasn't right with me . . . A child cannot go for help when nothing recognised as bad — officially and concretely — is done to her . . . When they, the mother, the teacher, don't see it, don't see this glance, they who are grown up after all, knowing and superior, then nothing bad, threatening can be in it. Thus the child, the girl, thus I remained both vigilant and unable to react. (Gerber, 1993: 144–145)

The silencing and disempowerment through abuse was echoed by a woman in our research who described the same difficulty of objecting to behaviour because it was in public:

> I just backed away from him . . . it almost felt like I couldn't do anything because it was in a public place. Because it must have been alright if he did it in a public place.

In the interviews, two women described how the fact that the harassment occurred in front of other staff, who said nothing and accepted the behaviour, prevented them from objecting to it. We are not implying that the experience of sexually abused children is the same as that of sexually harassed women, but we wish to point to a common feature of abusive power relationships.

Women are seen as bringing sexuality into an otherwise neutral, working environment. In many cases women are specifically employed for this purpose, for example in sales and customer service (Hearn *et al.*, 1989; Cockburn, 1991). Joan Acker (1991) describes the way in which organizations present themselves as gender neutral and through this very process create conditions which automatically devalue women:

> When it is acknowledged that women and men are affected differently by organisations, it is argued that gendered attitudes and behaviour are brought into (and contaminate) essentially gender-neutral structures. (Acker, 1991: 163)

The negative reaction to women's complaints, the sexualizing and general devaluing of women would begin to offer some explanation for the very low reporting of sexual harassment and the ineffectiveness of the law in this respect. At the university we researched, there had been only two formal complaints of sexual harassment and these had been of a very serious nature. We were, therefore, not surprised to find that at another English university, which had launched a sexual and racial harassment policy and procedure the previous year, there were fewer than ten formal complaints from all staff and students. This was in spite of a network of trained and named personnel throughout the university who were available to offer support and advice to people who had been harassed.

Thus, it would seem to follow logically that an organization wishing to have an effective sexual harassment policy would need to take steps to change the organizational culture, which appears to condone sexual harassment and allied offensive behaviour, by silencing women and disregarding their experiences (Green and Cassell, 1993; Morley, 1994). It is possible for organizations to pay lip-service to equal opportunities, in order to protect themselves from liability (Walsh, 1994). Significantly, an employer must take steps to prevent sexual harassment from occurring as it is not sufficient to show that the discrimination has been properly remedied (Industrial Tribunal, Exeter, Case No. 31165/910). In the wider context of a policy of equality of opportunity, a more proactive approach will be needed to enable the policy to be effective and not simply a way of fitting women in to an organization in which they are disadvantaged (Aitkenhead and Liff, 1991).

Research as Resistance

Doing feminist research into sexual harassment is beset by dangers and difficulties, as we have indicated throughout this chapter. Now we focus on the ways in which we think it can contribute to resistance and raise some issues, questions and suggestions which may be of help to others researching in this area.

Most obviously, through our survey, we were able to produce statistics which showed a nationally consistent level of harassment for this group and to make recommendations to the policy-makers about action that could change the culture in which these women worked. These recommendations included extending the research to all staff and students, both to establish the level of harassment and to act as a way of communicating serious concern about sexual harassment and the culture in which it thrives. We recommended that the university demonstrate a commitment to a proactive approach through the resourcing of personnel responsible for training and induction, ensuring that all staff and students know what sexual harassment is and what are the policy and procedures for dealing with it. The integration into staff appraisal of a requirement to demonstrate anti-sexist and anti-oppressive practice would go some way to reinforce the pressure for cultural change.

Beyond this formal channel for communicating our analysis and recommendations, we consider that our research contributed to resistance in a number of other ways. First, the questionnaire placed sexual harassment on the agenda for a whole group of academic staff who were able to articulate their experience and express, possibly for the first time, their distress and outrage at their treatment at work, without being exposed to retribution. All the women who had been harassed, and were willing to be interviewed, were offered the possibility of meeting as a group to encourage collective resistance. Second, our identification as having an interest in sexual harassment led to us being approached, both by individuals in the university we researched and in our own university, for advice about specific instances. Third, the presentation of the research and subsequent publication of the working paper (Butler and Landells, 1994) was made widely available to women in Higher Education. It contained both the quantitative and qualitative experience of one group of women academics, which we hope will add to the debate about sexual harassment and culture. The descriptions of harassment we have recounted will, we hope, contribute to the growing body of women's voices speaking out about harassment (Sumrall and Taylor, 1992) and encourage us to be brave enough to take offence. As our research has been supported by our employing institution, the process of producing both the report and the working paper has meant that a range of senior men, and some women, have read our work prior to publication, thus placing the issues on the agenda in our own institution.

Reflecting on our experience, we would recommend both courage and caution. There is no doubt that sexual harassment is a sensitive, political issue. However, with courage we can make the most of the current organizational sensitivity about Equal Opportunities to develop discussion about sexual harassment and its connection to patriarchal oppression. With caution, we can question the possibility of doing and publishing research in our own institutions. We can ensure that we have considered whose permission we need, and for what, and to have that explicit and written before we start. We can investigate who our powerful allies might be and enlist them to support and defend our work through the gate-keeping process. Most of all we can keep saying, individually and collectively, in our interactions, our choice of research and our writing, that we are offended.

References

ACKER, JOAN (1991) 'Hierarchies, Jobs, Bodies: A Theory Of Gendered Organizations', in LORBER, JUDITH and FARRELL, SUSAN (Eds) *The Social Construction of Gender*, London: Sage.

AITKENHEAD, MARILYN and LIFF, SONIA (1991) 'The Effectiveness of Equal Opportunities Policies', in FIRTH-COZENS, JENNY and WEST, MICHAEL (Eds) *Women at Work: Psychological and Organisational Perspectives*, Milton Keynes: Open University Press.

BRODRIBB, SOMER (1994) Urgent fax, 6 January, University of Victoria, Canada.

BURRELL, GIBSON (1984) 'Sex and Organisational Analysis', *Organisation Studies*, 5, pp. 97–118.

BURRELL, GIBSON and HEARN, JEFF (1989) 'The Sexuality of Organisation', in HEARN, JEFF, SHEPPARD, DEBORAH, TANCRED-SHERRIFF, PETA and BURRELL, GIBSON (Eds) *The Sexuality of Organisation*, London: Sage.

BUTLER, AVRIL and LANDELLS, MEL (1994) *Telling Tales Out of School: Research into Sexual Harassment of Women Academics.* Plymouth: Plymouth University.

CHESTER, GAIL and DICKEY, JULIENNE (Eds) (1988) *Feminism and Censorship: The Current Debate*, Bridport: Prism Press.

COCKBURN, CYNTHIA (1991) *In the Way of Women: men's resistance to sex equality in organisations*, London: Macmillan.

GERBER, CHARLOTTE (1993) *Lugen Leben: Porträt einer Berner Beamtenfamilie*, Zurich: Biograph-Verlag. (Excerpt translated by Barbara Körner.)

GILL, TESS and WHITTY, LARRY (1983) *Women's Rights in the Workplace*, Harmondsworth: Penguin.

GREEN, EILEEN and CASSEL, CATHY (1993) *Women Managing as Women Managers*, paper presented at the Women's Studies Network (UK) Conference, Northampton.

GUTEK, BARBARA (1985) *Sex and the Workplace: Impact of Sexual Behaviour and Harassment on Women, Men and Organisations*, San Fransisco: Jossey-Bass.

GUTEK, BARBARA (1989) 'Sexuality in the Workplace: Key Issues in Social Research and Organisational Practice', in HEARN, JEFF, SHEPPARD, DEBORAH, L., TANCRED-SHERRIFF, PETA and BURRELL, GIBSON (Eds) *The Sexuality of Organisation*, London: Sage.

HALL, MARNY (1992) 'Private Experiences In The Public Domain: Lesbians In Organisations', in MCDOWELL, LINDA and PRINGLE, ROSEMARY (Eds) *Defining Women: Social Institutions and Gender Divisions*, Oxford: Polity Press.

HEARN, JEFF, SHEPARD, DEBORAH, L., TANCRED-SHERRIFF, PETA and BURRELL, GIBSON (Eds) (1989) *The Sexuality of Organizations*. London: Sage.

INDUSTRIAL RELATIONS SERVICES (1992) 'Sexual Harassment at the Workplace: IRS Employment Trends 513', *Equal Opportunities Review*, June.

ITZEN, CATHERINE (1984) '"You Can't Do It Like That": The Conflict between Feminist Methodology and Academic Criteria in Research on Women and Ageing', in BUTLER, OLIVE (Ed.) *Feminist Experience in Feminist Research*, Manchester: Department of Sociology, Manchester University.

KELLY, LIZ (1987) 'The Continuum of Sexual Violence' in HANMER, JALNA and MAYNARD MARY (Eds) *Women, Violence and Social Control*, Basingstoke: Macmillan.

KELLY, LIZ (1988) *Surviving Sexual Violence*, Cambridge: Polity Press.

KITZINGER, CELIA (1990) 'Resisting the Discipline', in BURMAN, E. (Ed.) *Feminists and Psychological Practice*, London: Sage.

KITZINGER, CELIA (1994) 'Anti-Lesbian Harassment', in BRANT, CLARE and TOO, YUN LEE (Eds) *Rethinking Sexual Harassment*, London: Pluto.

LA FONTAINE, JEAN (1990) *Child Sexual Abuse*, Oxford: Polity Press.

LEES, SUE (1993) *Sugar and Spice: Sexuality and Adolescent Girls*, London: Penguin.

MAYES, GILLIAN M., CURRIE, ELLEN F., MACLEOD, LINDSEY, GILLIES, JOHN B. and WARDEN, DAVID A. (1992) *Child Sexual Abuse: A Review of The Literature And Educational Materials*, Edinburgh: Scottish Academic Press.

MCAULEY, JOHN (1987) 'Women Academics: A Case Study in Inequality', in SPENCER, ANNE and PODMORE, DAVID (Eds) *In A Man's World: Essays on Women in Male-Dominated Professions*, London: Tavistock.

MILLS, ALBERT (1988) 'Organisation, Gender and Culture', *Organisation Studies*, **9**, 3, pp. 351–370.

MORLEY, LOUISE (1994) 'Glass Ceiling or Iron Cage: Women in UK Academia', *Gender, Work and Organisation*, **1**, 4, pp. 194–204.

PUGH, ANNE (1990) 'My Statistics and Feminism: A True Story', in STANLEY, LIZ (Ed.) *Feminist Praxis: Research, Theory and Epistemology in Feminist Sociology*, London: Routledge.

PURKISS, DIANE (1994) 'The Lecherous Professor Revisited: Plato, Pedagogy and the Scene of Harassment', in BRANT, CLARE and TOO, YUN LEE (Eds) *Rethinking Sexual Harassment*, London: Pluto.

RAMAZANOGLU, CAROLINE (1987) 'Sex and Violence in Academic Life or You Can Keep a Good Woman Down', in HANMER, JALNA and MAYNARD, MARY (Eds) *Women, Violence and Social Control*, Basingstoke: Macmillan.

RESICK, PATRICIA A. and SCHNICKE, MONICA K. (1993) *Cognitive Processing Therapy for Rape Victims: A Treatment Manual*, London: Sage.

SHEPPARD, DEBORAH (1989) 'Organisations, Power and Sexuality: The image and Self-Image of Women Managers', in HEARN, JEFF, SHEPPARD, DEBORAH, TANCRED-SHERRIFF, PETA and BURRELL, GIBSON (Eds) *The Sexuality of Organisation*, London: Sage.

SMART, CAROL (1989) *Feminism and the Power of Law*, London: Routledge.

SMITH, DOROTHY (1979) *The Everyday World as Problematic: a feminist sociology*, Milton Keynes: Open University Press.

SPENDER, DALE (1980) *Man Made Language*, London: Routledge and Kegan Paul.

SPENDER, D. (1981) 'The gatekeepers: a feminist critique of academic publishing', in ROBERTS, HELEN (Ed.) *Doing Feminist Research*, London: Routledge.

STANKO, ELIZABETH, A. (1988) 'Keeping Women in and out of line: Sexual Harassment and occupational segregation', in WALBY, SYLVIA (Ed.) *Gender Segregation at Work*, pp. 91–99. Milton Keynes: Open University Press.

SUMRALL, AMBER COVERDALE and TAYLOR, DENA (1992) *Sexual Harassment: Women Speak Out*, Freedom, CA: The Crossing Press.

WALSH, VAL (1994) 'Virility Culture: Academia and Managerialism in Higher Education', in EVANS, MARY, GOSLING, JULIET and SELLER, ANNE (Eds) (1994) *Agenda for Gender*, Canterbury: University of Kent at Canterbury.

WATSON, HELEN, (1994) 'Red Herrings and Mystifications: Conflicting Perceptions of Sexual Harassment', in BRANT, CLARE and TOO, YUN LEE (Eds) *Rethinking Sexual Harassment*, London: Pluto.

Chapter 12

Pain(t) for Healing:
The Academic Conference and the
Classed/Embodied Self

Jo Stanley

A pain(t)ed picture

I offer you a verbal snapshot from my album. Sunshine. I am lying on the grass with Astra Blaug, the poet and photographer, outside Camden Girls' School in London. Shared drinks at lunchtime. She says 'But I've been in the women's liberation movement for 20 years and I can hardly understand a thing here. What about these young women students who are just starting? The ones I've talked to are absolutely thrown!' And I say 'Look, I got my MA last week. I thought it would mean there was nothing I couldn't understand now. But this — this isn't what I thought feminism was supposed to be about.'

The place was the Women's Studies Network (UK) Conference, 1991. I went expecting to metaphorically dance and sing and explore in a gang, to celebrate how much we knew, as women, and to learn, share and understand more. I hoped to get what I daily need: inclusive, lively and deeply challenging and creative situations. One of the very foundation stones of the movement, to which I too have belonged for 20 years, is access to power/knowledge. Such access would surely exist at what might loosely be seen as a successor to the annual national women's liberation movement conferences, if women's *studies* were to be linked with women's *activism* as they logically — to me — must be. With that connection, the conference could be a site of potential empowerment — defined as (knowing our) ability to understand the processes that affect us and to deal with them appropriately, confidently, constructively, (collectively or singly). Instead I felt marginalized and disempowered, as part of a dynamic in which some professional academic speakers refused — however unconsciously — to acknowledge that their knowledge and language were privileged, and that therefore introductions and translations might be required.

While any academic conference deals with a mixture of abilities, those organized by and for groups excluded from power/knowledge might be expected to deal sensitively with issues of exclusion. To avoid doing so means that working-class and non-academic women stop learning, let alone enjoying learning, quite quickly. A central tenet of the best adult education over the last two decades has been to recognize the impediments to learning caused by marginalization and its impact on individuals' expectations of our abilities (Hughes and Kennedy, 1985; Coats, 1994). However, that recognition has not been put into practice throughout Higher Education, including the area into which those with perhaps the highest personal stakes go: women's studies.

This chapter describes an action that I — as a woman who worked in these fields, who is out about her working-class roots, who was in training to become a Pellin counsellor[1] and who was no longer economically dependent on the academy — took to deal with a situation that I felt was damaging. I ran a workshop entitled 'Feeling like a working-class thicko at academic conferences' at the 1992 Women's Studies Network (UK) conference in Preston.

My intention, first, was to face the political outrageousness of inequality's very existence — of privilege, exclusion and the denigration of the unprivileged. Second, I wanted to deal with the subsequent disaster of their impact on individuals — disempowerment, internalized shame, emotional wreckage. I sought to expose some of the ways internal negative narratives are sparked off and reinforced by external treatment. Third, my challenge was to the collusive but uneasy silence around the problems' continued existence within the academy, and hence their further embedding within structures which rely on their existence and naturalization.

The Construction of 'Thicko' Feelings

The forthright workshop title shocks me now as it did then; it was a rock-bottom, even exaggerated statement, of what might be being felt — by myself and others. I do not actually call myself a thicko, ever. I do call myself working class in origin and do so in the Marxist sense that I am not in a position of ownership to society's productive resources. Also, as such, I belong or belonged to a class with a distinctive social existence, aspects of whose culture I value and to which I feel unevenly bonded (Ryan and Sackney, 1984: 107).

My own knowledge and the self-destructive ideas about the exclusion had three sources: I am a woman; I am working-class in a society that oppresses such people; and, failing the 11-plus examination and being sent to a despised secondary modern school, despite being top of my class, compounded the idea that I was fundamentally not good enough for the Real Arbiters who could see through all the 'pretence at cleverness'. So I do readily experience a dreadful shuddering in some competitive privileged situations. However, the problem is not only the internalized oppression, the *feeling like* but also the actual objectively-existing practice: *being treated as* a working-class thicko.

Working-class women and girls, throughout the education system, face profoundly disenabling difficulties (Walkerdine and Lucey, 1989; Walkerdine, 1990). While acknowledging the creative coping strategies adopted in the face of obstacles and pathologizing practices, the effects Lucey and Walkerdine explore include internalized lack of self-worth; distressing but seemingly necessary alienation from home; splitting, or passing as middle-class; the creation of the self as Other. Feelings include loneliness, despair and rage, the desire to murder, and psychic or actual suicide. Ryan and Sackney (1984) have described the self-loathing, alcohol abuse, tensions round ambiguous roles, and self-disrespecting strategies adopted by working-class people trying to be upwardly mobile in the US academy and hence forced into unconscious collaboration with values, narratives and definitions destructive to their class. In the UK, Jo Spence and Rosy Martin have applied John Bradshaw's US work on generalized shame to their experiences of class shame within and outside the academy and the Culture Industry (Bradshaw, 1988; Spence, 1995) through photo-therapy and writing.

The knowledge/power structures that impact at an individual level are the product of social and economic systems that have for centuries excluded people of my gender, my class and those marginalized by 'race', age and bodily disabilities. Language is used to signify and reinforce class oppression; formal education institutions are just examples of the places where systematic shaming and undermining, posited on notions of superiority and inferiority, are reinforced. That eroding phrase 'working-class thicko' no longer even needs to be spoken, so well is it internalized. It is a conditioned response, quite fixed before adolescence (transmitted through advertising and the media as well as through school and social interactions), and one which is useful to a society which wants working-class women to take a usefully low and unchallenging position within it.

But it does not quite work. If I can see/say the phrase then I have challenged its seeming naturalization. On another level, the self-definition 'working-class thicko' is a defensive and unreal one for me. I sort-of choose it. It speaks of the kind of covert self-regulation whereby, for girls schooled to avoid confrontation, 'conflict is displaced on to personal feeling and rational argument' (Walkerdine, 1990: 49). I split and name myself as this lone fearful Other. Why? In order to ward off what I imagine — as victim but not coping aware adult — would be a terminal collision between systems of values. What I forget to be aware of, at that point, is that I know I am able to state firmly that I am angry, have a right to operate with my own values and even that the frightening authority is wrong (as I am implicitly doing in writing this now). Those of us working on the issues of educated working-class women (for instance Trevithick, 1988: 73 and see Appendix) have found an over-propensity to blame ourselves for not understanding, rather than to challenge the situations that bar immediate comprehension; to fall back into the schooled view that we do not know, we do not have the ability to know, and we do not have the right to know. By making myself so minimal and so abject that I am not a thing worth a middle-class academic arguing with, I thereby avoid the public pain of being individually pathologized as disruptive. In practice, as Sennet and Cobb (1977: 304–305) found in looking at male manual workers who gained administrative jobs, there are practical gains for those of us who name ourselves as this shameful but classed Other — not least a sense of solidarity: 'I am part of a group which is so named'. There is something enjoyably retaliatory about 'us working-class thickos', as with earlier feminist rehabilitation of negative language: Virago publishers, Stroppy Cow Records and Shrew magazine. And it takes the power to wound away — somewhat and for a time.

What Happens at Conferences?

These temporary events offer an enticingly open invitation: Just pay your money and enter for a feast of six or seven women simultaneously talking about issues that will interest you. In reality, especially in Higher Education, the event is one in which speakers can feel on trial, their whole career and identity at stake. Necessarily, if someone is demonstrating her superiority then there have to be people positioned as recipients, audience or fans.

The sense of being a 'thicko' is something many women experience much of the time — as the gender positioned as irrational, feeling and therefore stupid — but it can become particularly stark at academic conferences. Tensions about visible ability intensify at the display of how much there is to know, how hard it is to 'get it right' — and how many important things Others know. Some of us cope creatively and well with our working-class legacies, particularly if a good support network exists, but we do not necessarily go to conferences with that backing from our daily lives. Conference anxiety has many causes, for people of all backgrounds: re-activated early childhood fears of groups which can exclude and humiliate; a sense of desperate competitiveness caused by the employment practice of academic institutions (I have got to be seen to be doing brilliantly or I will not get tenure/promotion). Without evidence of participants being whole human beings — with bodies that can play tennis, make love, nurture ageing parents; lives that include children, bank managers and housework, for example — there flourishes an impression that this is a climate where only rarefied intellectual aspects of the disembodied self can be brought.

For people multiply marginalized — for example by 'race', age disability — the anxieties are cumulative and focus on social behaviour as well as on the session content. Like the daily academy, this temporarily relocated academy is a site where illusions of social mobility are tested out intensively and repeatedly. For women of a working-class background with unhappy experiences of early formal education and of later alienation from middle-class circles, an academic conference of seemingly middle-class authority figures can trigger a range of overwhelmingly difficult reactions. And such can be the force of these emotions — coupled with the learned habits of docile acceptance of the implicit values (Sennet and Cobb, 1977) — that they immediately, but temporarily, cancel out any abilities to cope, or at least seem to, that we may have picked up from assertiveness training, life, or good role models. It activates the feeling of being the dunce forever sentenced to the 'proles' corner, or the paranoid infant who was always relegated and who justifiably fears annihilation (Walkerdine, 1990). When such early feelings re-emerge with all their force, some women may turn to angry retaliation at that point; to disruption, drugs, self-mutilation; others hide or go home. A daunting conference can require us to take a creative approach with great rapidity, if we are to enjoy it.

Towards a Pellin view of class conflict in these situations

Some of the feelings that may face other educated working-class women at academic conferences are listed below. They were identified from discussion with the Educated Working Class Women's Group and expanded using ideas that come from my training as a Pellin counsellor. The training uses notions of Gestalt, of split-off parts of the self coming together, and old hurts making positive contributions to new growth. Pellin, a Canadian-originated and behavioural branch of Gestalt therapy, uses techniques to encourage warring aspects of ourself into dialogue and then towards an adult and calm approach to solutions: a dialectic which moves towards synthesis. One of its 'tools' is the notion that we can benefit by learning how to control our emotional pendulum swings and find a calm place between extreme binary oppositions (Fleming, 1982: 11–30).

In Pellin terms, working-class women's distress might be seen as one set of people suffering as a result of the dominating group's calloused desire to accumulate proofs of superiority, their anxieties about being treated as persons of worth and respect, and their lack of perspective about their underlying and enduring life purposes (as opposed to their superficial purpose) (Fleming, 1982: 84).

Pellin theory argues that the members of the oppressed group could be particularly prone to swinging fast to a dangerous low on their pendulum, not because of any pathology but simply because of the effect of constant negative (and structural) drips, of propaganda about unworth. The greater our history of 'referrals' or negative experiences (the longer our 'referral chain') (Fleming, 1982: 49), the harder it is to respond in creative ways with our pendulum in a sane place. The brain's mechanism chooses the course it knows: relating the current event to old memories of how bad it was last time, for example. Or else we imagine that, as it has happened so often, it must be true, that we have somehow done something to deserve it. We do not have the freedom, at that moment of 'toxic shame' (Bradshaw, 1988: 10), to say 'Hey, it never was true, it never is true. Class proves nothing about intrinsic worth or cleverness. I am just the current target of this person/agent. We can all usefully challenge this.' Instead, in Anne Dixon's terms, it is 'crumple button' time: the Other has pressed the button that will make us fall apart until we finally confront the loaded message.[2]

The anger/despair — and silence

Using these understandings about class politics and their impact on individuals, it is possible to understand how feelings at conferences and in the daily academy can include angry ones that turn other people into enemies rather than into allies, such as 'I want to kill the uppity bitches (because they are murdering me)'. There can be a sense of being collectively betrayed: 'Feminists should not behave like this', which also may have much earlier connections with disappointment in being mothered. Some women can feel self-defeating misery: 'I am not good enough' therefore 'I am nothing at all, therefore I am less than nothing, therefore I may as well die/am already dead'. Others may experience awareness of lost social and familial links coupled with a kind of displaced sympathy with the self: 'I have sold out all my old roots — and for this . . . just more isolation? / My (m)other would die of this kind of treatment'.

Pre-paring to Challenge that Situation

The process of pre-paring to propose that workshop was almost as important to me as the running of it. I assumed that the situation which had activated my feelings would recur at the next Women's Studies Network (UK) Conference and even if more accessibility was somehow created, those of us predisposed to distressed reactions at academic conferences might not be able to recognize that that usual response was inappropriate this time.

I discussed my idea of proposing to the next conference, not a well-referenced impressive paper, but a practical workshop that could attempt to tackle some of the feelings that might be being experienced, with women who largely shared my background — particularly Jo Spence and the Educated Working-Class Women's Group. I showed them what seemed like an outrageously transgressive draft proposal. I felt trepidation at the plan. Can I really say 'thicko' at a conference where everyone else will be using 20-syllable words? Can I really say 'wanting to kill lecturers'? There were a surprising number of shy and angry smiles of recognition as I asked this and the response was: 'Yes, oh yes. You can. You *should*'. Because of belonging to this group and having helped organize other conferences, I felt in a position to propose and deliver the workshop. But I experienced it somewhat as coming from the position of 'narky victim'; I feared I would be attacked in turn.

I knew that my unease about having such a workshop at academic conferences might also be shared by those agreeing to run it, and those who came to it. First, it talked about feeling, and feeling bad.

> Both feeling and healing (being perceived as discourses of the body and of the maternal) lack status in our society. Therapy in the West is not academic, and is difficult to accommodate within masculinist notions of efficacy and power. (Walsh, 1993: 22)

To recognize and to give an hour's space to emotional needs in the conference setting required courage — and possibly acknowledgement of a buried need. Second, to go to such a workshop would mean owning up to being working class in a place where women might prefer to disregard that identity. Third, given academic exclusion of art practice, to do something so embodied, unruly, colourful and experiential as painting, was to deny the academy's mores. Conferences are places for notetaking, for the cerebral, surely? (Walsh, 1993)

A comforting physical resource for the whole self

As 'changing class' can cause such a sense of dislocation and homelessness, and in recognition of how much more effective we can be when our whole selves, including our bodies, are brought to a situation, I envisioned the workshop as an almost physical resource with at least some home comforts. Amenities such as the warmth and comfort of canteen, the direct hit of chocolate, the strokes of friends, the safe closet of a dark and distant lavatory for when misery struck, are heartening. These resources recognize the self that feels, the body that has transported itself all those miles and years; the person who cannot just be a machine for impressively processing certain kinds of high-status information.

But what methodology was needed? Individual therapy was not viable, not least because my interest was collective engagement with the problem rather than individuals hiving themselves off from the main body of the conference and individualizing, or indeed pathologizing, an objective structural problem.

Art as the method

I can recover from almost any situation if helped to face difficulties creatively as a whole person and not a disablist diagnosed type (schizoid, for example). This is taught by taking part in a variety of therapies for over 15 years, as analysed and as practitioner. Art therapy, the Jungian-based technique for accessing the unconscious by illustrating feelings then speaking about them, has proved an effective way to arrive quickly at the places that words do not always reach. Painting or drawing feelings, then discussing them in a group, is one way in which strangers can work together usefully. Art is a means of communication that does not require sophisticated speech (Case and Dalley, 1990: 2), which means that we could bring our distressed or inarticulate child-selves to the session if we wanted. It can be useful where there is little time and no opportunity to develop trusting relationships, such as at conferences.

Above all, an art-based approach is a particularly effective way of achieving left and right brain integration. This was important to me, given that one of the difficulties of most academic approaches is that they encourage the use of the left (logical reasoning) brain and not the right brain also, which requires objects and behaviour to be assessed holistically (Shone, 1986: 9). We are composed of many 'I's and are at our most creative when more than one of them is permitted to operate — in harmony. A both-hemispheres approach might overcome the frozen restrictions of the intellectually performing 'I' who operates in pressurized academic situations. Working with images brings not only an opening up and a laying-to-rest of deep-rooted pain; it usually suggests ideas for ways forward.

Personal effectiveness trainer Dorothy Badrick teaches a useful excercise for understanding our attitudes to institutional situations. It involves acknow-ledging split experiences (feeling OK and not OK, in transactional analysis terms) (Harris, 1969) and then finding a way to evolve a synthesis, and viable means of feeling OK in not-OK situations. Confident because I had first painted this exercise within the academy, on an academy-funded course, I adapted it for this workshop. It had to be followed by a shared discussion to deal with the feelings that being a working-class woman at academic conferences can bring up. By painting, then airing, those images collectively and the issues/feelings the process exposed, we could gain the liberating opportunity of discovering both commonality and difference in emotional response, and the practical ben-efits of hearing about others' strategies that we too might adopt.

At the Workshop

About 25 women attended the workshop. We sat round one huge table, the brushes, felt pens, paint, glitter, glue, scissors and paper in front of us. During the initial round of brief self-introductions it became clear that about half the women were lecturers, and one-third were students. All were white, as most of the conference participants were. The age range was from early 20s to one woman in her 70s, although most seemed to be in late 20s to early 40s.

Most had had problems with the definition working-class, which did not feel so applicable since they had started Higher Education. I knew from being in the Educated Working-Class Women's Group and in a women writers' group within the Federation of Worker Writers and Community Publishers how fraught the self-labelling issue is, how much women differ about what it means and whether they 'still qualify' for membership (Stanley *et al.*, 1987). Naming could be a workshop in itself. To deal briefly with this I suggested at the start that if women defined *themselves* as working-class, that was all that mattered — how ever problematized that definition was for them. Two women quickly left, one silently and the other with the distressed assumption that 'we' would not 'let' her stay.

After the introductions, we painted, drew, glued, snipped or tore. Many were alarmed at having to use art as a method: because of notions that there was a correct and trained way to do it; because it was an unexpected activity at an academic conference; and because their products might be overlooked/discussed/implicitly held up to ridicule. Within élite culture 'art is associated with connoisseurship . . . as part of culture it positions women as onlookers, gate-crashers and material' (Walsh, 1993: 12), which meant women had to ignore such notions in order to proceed. Conversely, because formal education uses verbal language as a medium, paint was a frighteningly unfamiliar — even a 'babyish' — medium that some women thought they had forgotten how to use or could not use. Such feelings were addressed as thoroughly as possible by reassurances that women did not have to be good at art; that here there was no such word as 'failing', and that women did not have to show anyone what they had done. And all the women did actually take up a pen, brush or scissors.

The first five minutes of drawing were on the topic 'When I feel OK about being working-class'. The second five-minute period was illustrating 'When I don't feel OK about being working-class in academic situations'. The final ten minutes involved the difficult feat of putting the two together, creating an amalgamation or synthesis of the dialectic: in Gestalt terms, 'a whole'. It was a way of recognizing what made us feel damaged in academic situations and then working actively on ways to make ourselves feel better in them. We could take the richness and ease from our well-being, recognize the material situation that militated against its expression, and then deliberately take the holistic and embodied self that can cope with (and even enjoy) its working-class identity out into troubling academy and this conference.

Dis-covering ourselves and each other

The final fifteen minutes of the workshop were used for discussing the feelings that the painting process had brought up. Disclosure, by showing the pictures and/or by talking about them, was self-determined. About half the women held up their pictures, sometimes despite some fear and distress. Building on experiences of other members of the Educated Working-Class Women's Group, I knew that people might be expressing feelings they had suppressed for 20 or more years.

Presumably reflecting the level of safety they felt and their prior experience of such sharing, women spoke at a length they determined, within the severe time constraints, about what their image had shown them, where it had come from within them and — in some cases — where it led them. Afterwards some women did talk to each other informally about their pictures, acknowledging common experience.

While respecting the privacy of what each woman said in this situation, it is possible to say that several main areas emerged as important. These images represented, as such imagery does, 'an overlap of the inner and outer worlds, a mixture of reality and fantasy' (Case and Dally, 1990: 3); for example the nightmare staffroom and the real canteen.

Feeling OK

'Feeling OK about being working class' was represented in a number of ways that spoke of warmth and attention: they were very physical. Symbols of this included sources of heat and comfort: a cosy rocking chair by fire, mugs of steaming coffee; and sources of attention: a bank of listening ears. Women pictured themselves as energetic, seen and heard and respected, sometimes painting. Their bodies looked comfortable. One woman drew a picture of herself as smiling, with powerful wings and good lungs and a steady foothold.

Feeling not OK

'Feeling not OK about being working-class in academic situations' was frequently most agonizing in staffrooms, rather than at conferences. Images focused on the experience (and/or expectation) of being put down for our ways of expressing ourselves, especially with inept use of language. One picture portrayed the woman as a bloody blot being squashed by an elegant thumb for saying 'bath', with a flat a rather than 'barrth,' or for describing her mother as 'me mum'. The other images indicating these feelings included being caged off in corners and not given the room (physical and metaphorical) and resources to express ideas and work properly. There was isolation; one woman painted herself shrinking with meek body language on the far edge of a group. Another showed herself being talked down to by massed authority figures (male or thin or tall). Speech bubbles from such figures included not only 'difficult' words, e.g. acronym, but also 'Blah!' indicating that the recipient knew that rubbish was being talked; she could dismiss it on one level. Symbols included barred doors, a sad sun and dog faeces. Classically, art therapy holds that in many cultures people purify themselves and dispose of their unwanted or evil aspects by transference to objects and people. Painting mess or faeces is one method that sexually abused children use to express the sense of being messed up, full of someone else's bad stuff (Schaverien, 1987: 75; see also Milner, 1957). When women talked about these 'not OK' pictures, they described the pain of academic exclusion, of being treated like dog faeces, as being the greater because it affronted their expectations of justice and empowerment within Women's Studies. Some saw this discipline within which they studied and taught as becoming an élitist stronghold which was not only having an excluding and destructive effect on women whom they saw as being like themselves, but also impoverishing education and new knowledge production. Their pain was not only personal, but that of advocates and educators.

Putting It All Together

The synthesis pictures, 'Feeling OK about being working-class in academic situations', in many cases involved much reflection and/or conscious effort to change the behaviour that we visualized ourselves doing. In moving deliberately into 'survivor' position (away from 'victim' status) women necessarily had to feel and show fantasies legitimated, anger validated and creative competence welcomed. All the images that I saw showed women in good company, not at all as lonely successes on high thrones. One picture showed a woman smiling, coping, well able to hold off the oppressive thumb (which was still hanging above her, though). She was using her wings, and her good lungs. She could easily handle the bulky swagbag full of words including 'intimidate, semiotic, nightmare and phallogocentric'. Another woman drew a picture where women had enough space to work. Lorry loads of books were arriving, and there was room for them because all the academic men had been removed. Some of the images were of very direct steps to remove problems, for example by group assassination of the oppressive figures.

The Follow-up

Unlike other therapies, the product of this visual process of uncovering the inner world can be retained, worked on later, and reworked on (Case and Dalley, 1990: 3). Most women took their pictures away. About half of the women stayed on for another two and a quarter hours after the workshop ended, discussing both feelings and strategies for change. Some planned not only to have lunch together the following day, but also to ensure they were present in force at the next year's Women's Studies Network (UK) Conference (and they were). Others discussed strategies for challenging pretence in their own academic institutions, working from a recognition of their own feelings, understanding the structural causes and celebrating the possibilities for creative change with a sense of 'We are many, they are few'.

I felt such pleasure afterwards in walking round an academic conference with traces of paint deliberately left on my hands. The magenta stains reminded me that I was visually creative, that I was there as my whole self. It was a similar pleasure to that of having soil-grimed nails from gardening in the centre of a city, indicating that I am in touch with what grows in the earth and am not just a user of buses and buildings. That sense of all my own dimensions made it possible to enjoy what was fundamentally a gathering of women sharing to different degrees. Meeting other women from the 'Thickos' workshop throughout the next day intensified that joy of being a more embodied and valued conference participant. It also reminded me of the kind of women's studies conference I would like to go to: one that uses creative methods and is founded on principles of equality and mutual respect, holism and understanding of the need for linked action for political change in oppressive structures. Picturing our knowledge/power, as in 'Feeling OK about being a working-class woman in academic situations', is a one-off expression of what might be. 'If you can visualize where you want to be, then you're at least half way there' (Badrick, 1994).

Notes

1   Pellin/Contribution Training is a type of Gestalt pyschotherapy developed in Canada by Dave Pellin in the 1960s and subsequently taught in London and Italy by the

founder of Pellin training courses, Peter Fleming. It uses some behavioural techniques and is fundamentally organized around the belief that human beings should be respected and that they can contribute to change (socially and personally) from early experiences of hurt.

2 Dixon, Anne (1982) *A woman in your own right: assertiveness and you*, London: Quartet. She describes an exercise to deal with crumple buttons. With a trusted partner, you hear repeated statements of the phrase that crumples you — in this case it would be 'working-class thicko, prat, cretin, brainless prole' etc — until it loses its power to hurt in the same way.

3 Britain developed a number of regional 'Women Who Love Too Much' groups in the late 1980s after the publication of Robin Norwood's book of the same name.

References

BADRICK, DOROTHY, (1987–1994) My personal notes on various sessions with her.

BRADSHAW, JOHN (1988) *Healing the shame that binds you*, Deerfield Beach, Florida: Health Communications.

CASE, CAROLINE and DALLEY, TESSA (Eds) (1990) *Working with Children in Art Therapy*, London: Tavistock/Routledge.

COATS, MAGGIE (1994) *Women's Education*, Buckingham: The Society for Research into Higher Education and Open University Press.

FLEMING, PETER (1982) *Pellin Diploma Course Notes*, London: Pellin Training Centre.

HARRIS, THOMAS ANTHONY (1969) *I'm OK, You're OK: A Practical Guide to Transactional Analysis*, New York: Harper Row.

HUGHES, MARY and KENNEDY, MARY (1985) *New Futures: Changing Women's Education*, London: Routledge and Kegan Paul.

MILNER, MARIAN (1957) *On Not being able to paint*, Madison, CN: International Universities Press.

RYAN, JAKE and SACKNEY, CHARLES (1984) *Strangers in Paradise: Academics from the Working-class*, Boston, MA: South End Press.

SCHAVERIEN, JOY (1987) 'The scapegoat and the talisman', in DALLEY, T., CASE, CAROLINE, SCHAVERIEN, JOY, WEIR, FELICITY, HALLIDAY, DIANNA, NOWELL-HALL, PATRICIA and WALLER, DIANE (Eds) *Images of Art Therapy*, London: Tavistock.

SENNET, R. and COBB, R. (1977) *Hidden Injuries of Class*, Cambridge: Cambridge University Press.

SHONE, RONALD (1986) *Creative Visualisation: How to use imagery and imagination for Self-improvment*, Wellingborough: Thorsons.

SPENCE, JO (1995) *Cultural Sniping: The Art of Transgression*, Edited by Jo Stanley, London: Routledge.

SPENCE, JO (1986) *Putting myself in the Picture*, London: Camden Press.

STANLEY, JO, with HUNTER, BILLIE, QUIGLEY, MARGARET and WALLACE, JENNIFER (1987) 'Class Conflicts', in CHESTER, GAIL and NIELSEN, SIGRID (Eds) *In Other Words: Writing as a Feminist*, pp. 167–174, London: Hutchinson.

TREVITHICK, PAM (1988) 'Unconsciousness raising with working-class women', in KRZOWSKI, SUE and LAND, PAT (Eds) *In our Experience*, pp. 63–83, London: The Women's Press.

WALKERDINE, VALERIE and LUCEY, HELEN (1989) *Democracy in The Kitchen: Regulating Mothers and Socialising Daughters*, London: Virago.
WALKERDINE, VALERIE (1990) *Schoolgirl Fictions*, London: Verso.
WALSH, VAL (1993) 'Unbounded Women? Feminism, Creativity and Embodiment', keynote paper for the art and cinema section of WISE (Women's International Studies, Europe) in workshop Feminisms in Europe: Cultural and Political Practise, Paris.

Appendix

(1992 handout)

The Educated Working-Class Women's Group

I see the Working-Class Educated Women's group as a think-tank for women to discuss what Higher Education does to our identities. We are working towards sharing our ideas constructively with more women at a later date. I personally would like to see networks and conferences all over Europe — a bit like the way the 'Women Who Love Too Much' network of groups developed.[3]

Origins

The group began because several women met at Pam Trevithick's workshop on working-class women's anger at the Women's Therapy Centre, London during the mid-1980s. What they discovered there made them want to carry on. We meet about every five weeks, usually for a whole day, with shared food, at my flat in Holloway, North London. The meetings are not minuted but people take lots of personal notes.

Current Group Work

In the past, from 1989, we have functioned as a sort of consciousness-raising group. I felt a bit uneasy about that and wanted to quickly set up conferences and workshops, to utilize and share our experiences and ideas for change; the others did not. From 1990–1991 we took it in turns to bring papers/topics to meetings which were often circulated in advance, then discussed for one to two hours. Since the middle of 1991 we have been working on a TV programme which would be a showcase of (funny, sharp, often mixed-autobiographical) scenes bringing out the issues surrounding being working-class educated women. In Winter 1991, we decided to give this project a name — Didn't She Do Well — and Jo Spence arranged headed notepaper. I think it has given us a more cohesive and proud identity — on the quiet. The issues being dealt with in the programme include what I see as the main topics of most of our regular discussions:

- Feeling shame at having a working-class background (e.g. disguising your accent, sewing false designer labels into your clothes, trying to pass).
- Feeling angry at the 'educated' situations that make you feel your class is not good enough, at the way you feel divided from your family.
- Feeling deeply, increasingly opposed to an education system that does this to people — and trying to expose and oppose it ourselves in our practice as educators.

Chapter 13

My Mother's Voice? On Being 'A Native' in Academia

Liz Stanley

On 'Going Native'

'Going native' is a major research sin. It putatively involves crossing the dividing line between 'us' and 'them', between scientists and people, and between 'there' and 'here'; that is, between life and academia. To 'go native' is to become an academic renegade. The significance of this is shown when we remember that 'going native' is the prime sin of colonialism, for it represents a commitment to seeing and living the world from the viewpoint of 'them', the natives who are 'there' and emotionally involved, rather than 'us', the rulers who are 'here' and rationally detached. The notion of detachment is a crucial part of the apologia of colonialism — that 'we' know better and so should have power and control over 'them'. In social science research terms, 'going native' is to become scientifically renegade because it constitutes a betrayal of the scientific community, along with its ideological practices, its networks and its patterns of allegiance. 'Going native' challenges the hierarchies of knowledge that science constructs and enforces: true and false knowledge, knowledge and opinion, scientific and everyday knowledge, truth and belief, thinking and feeling. 'Going native' symbolizes loss of commitment to the academic side of the dividing line, which is constructed between science and life, because it constitutes a betrayal of the canonical scientific precepts of academia: detachment, objectivity, rationality, as counterposed by involvement, subjectivity and emotionality. It also gives the intellectual and political game away: academic research conceived thus is an act of colonialism located within the rule of intellectual imperialism.

Thus social scientists are counselled in textbook after textbook never to 'go native'. Some of the key terms of science indicate the required 'proper' stance for researchers — detachment and not involvement, objectivity and not subjectivity, rationality and not emotionality, and so on. Recently I asked a group of graduate feminist researchers what 'going native' meant and what there was about it that made it taboo.[1] The majority answer was that it was a personal involvement which prevented the kind of detachment they saw as essential to critical feminist analysis. My response was two-fold. First, if detachment really was necessary then no one would be able to think critically and analytically about things in which they are involved, and many people patently *do* achieve this. Second, and perhaps more importantly, feminists are women, and so involved and 'native', and yet at the same time also think critically and analytically about challenging and changing both the category 'Women' and the actuality of women's lives and experiences. 'Going native', indeed 'being native' as an ontological state, prevents neither critical thought nor analysis.

By being conducted by women, and also being 'for women' in the sense of being directed to social and political change, feminism within the academy is at its basis on the side of 'the native'. This is because it represents the re/ turn of the dispossessed, the march of the women into the male establishment of academia, the intrusion of those who are 'other' to the values, beliefs and practices of science. 'The women' — the category 'Women' marked by the actuality of the multiple differences of real women — bring with them feelings, emotions and commitments, values which position the feminist academic on the side of involvement, subjectivity and emotionality and not on that of detachment, objectivity and rationality. The presence of feminist values within the academy is even more seditious than this, however, for it also refuses to see as 'reality' the connected binaries of detachment/involvement, objectivity/ subjectivity, rationality/emotionality, science/life, culture/nature, masculinity/ femininity, male/female. The malestream treats such binaries as central to academic life, but feminist analysis positions them as elements in the gatekeeping practices of a masculinist élite.

There are many feminists who perceive a feminist version of science as a vanguard position that better enables feminist academics to research and theorize the lives and oppressions of 'women' as a category of difference rather than sameness; 'we' research and theorize 'them', and through the practices of science we become detached. This is a supportable position, but it is not one I agree with; indeed it is one, I hope whole-heartedly, that I have attempted to counter throughout my academic career.[2] Insofar as any feminist academic speaks and writes 'for the' women and not 'as a' woman (Miller, 1991), she takes up the speaking and writing position of men, or rather that which men-in-science have articulated as the only way possible to be analytical and theoretical and scientific. I am not interested in a feminist science that is little different from this, other than in its good political intentions — after all, many of the male scientific establishment have perfectly good intentions too. My concern instead is for a different academic feminism, one which does not accept the slide to the 'academic' end of the feminist/academic binary, but which instead refuses the binary altogether. It is this different speaking and writing position for the academic feminist that I now want to discuss.

On Being Native

The research and writing position that interests me — the academic 'voice' I choose to speak and to write in — can be characterized as a kind of ethnography,[3] but one which collects academic and intellectual life and work into the ethnographic frame, rather than drawing this around only specific kinds of activity, those carried out by 'them' rather than 'us'. Elsewhere I have referred to it as 'intellectual auto/biography', that is, the textual process of accounting for the intellectual approach and ideas and the analytic conclusions of the researching and writing feminist. This is an approach which recognizes that the academic feminist's account of her life and work (her 'autobiography') necessarily includes her descriptions, interpretations and analyses of the lives and activities (thus 'biography') of others, and theirs hers of course (thus autobiography and biography are intertextual, indicated in the term 'auto/biography'); and also that this is not merely a narrative — the story of the life of — but rather a critical and analytic account that looks rigorously at the grounds of its own knowledge-claims (thus both 'intellectual' and crucially concerned with questions of epistemology). Feminist ethnography in this sense of the term is critically aware, reflexively constituted, analytically and epistemologically positioned, aware of its own knowledge-claims and concerned to give readers as many textual means as possible of engaging with, disputing, even rejecting, the grounds for these as well as the claims themselves.[4]

There is, however, a crucial difference between feminism and ethnography which needs to be recognized, for ethnography is almost by definition about 'them', while feminism, equally by definition, is about 'us'. The factor which encourages me to bring together these two terms, definitionally in conflict, is the mediating term of 'academic'. As a good many 'movement feminists' have not been slow to point out, by entering academia feminists become hybrid, outsiders becoming insiders. It is this hybrid condition, the liminality of that state of intellectual being we gloss as 'academic feminist', the ontological movement between insider and outsider and the epistemological consequences thereof, that engages me, not least because it is in a fundamental sense 'my life' as well as that of academic feminists generally. By 'becoming academics', academic feminists are positioned as both insider and outsider, both them and us. We are perpetual 'strangers', but *strangers within*.[5] And there is another important difference between feminism and ethnography: ethnographic authority derives from a variety of textual means designed to demonstrate to the reader that the ethnographer/writer has indeed '*been* there', whereas the very factor that discredits 'others' from knowledge and from science is that they '*are* there'. Feminism disputes the scientific assumption that there is no necessary relationship between ontology and epistemology, instead seeing all knowledge as rooted in experience, while ethnography by and large, with shifts and starts and gloomy head-scratchings, accepts it.

I have considerable sympathy with Clifford Geertz's insistence that:

> The basic problem is neither the moral uncertainty involved in telling stories about how other people live nor the epistemological ones involved in casting those stories in scholarly genres — both of which are real enough, are always there, and go with the territory. The problem

is that now that such matters are coming to be discussed in the open. . . .
the burden of authorship suddenly looks heavier. (1988: 138)

I would prefer to use the term 'problematic', however, with its implication that there is both an intellectual problem, and also a set of methodological and procedural strategies for investigating it. However, I read this problematic of 'how to represent' as a useful characterization of what it is to be human, alive and so thinking about the world we live in in order to understand, and perhaps even to change, it. That is, I associate such contrasts as features of the everyday world, the world *of the native*, and the ethnographer depends on precisely these everyday competences. I want to demonstrate something of this by referring to a situation in which I was thoroughly 'a native', being as involved, committed and emotionally engaged as it was possible to be.

Following the death of my father in 1984, my mother and I engaged in many hours of taped talk — mainly her talking and my listening and prompting — which were named in my mind at the time and then more formally on paper later as 'My Mother's Voice', for I listened, first as she spoke and then later to her voice on tape, as intently as that favourite image of mine as a child, the dog listening to 'His Master's Voice' depicted on record labels. The title of this chapter, 'My Mother's Voice', refers to the literal voice of my mother, first in 'reality', then in two representational forms, on tape, and in transcribed words on the page. 'My Mother's Voice' invokes all the complex overlaying of the written and the spoken that I referred to at the start of the chapter, while my narrative about it, here and not there, now and not then, to us and not her, raises all the issues of power and representation that haunt ethnographers and under-pin the 'movement feminist' critique of academic feminism. However, I also use the title in another and more ironic sense, indicated by the interrogatory question mark of 'my mother's voice?' 'The situation' referred to above is not just these taped conversations, but the absolute silencing of my mother's actual voice when she suffered an extremely severe stroke in 1990, which left her so brain-damaged that she lost the ability to comprehend the nuances of spoken language and completely lost the ability to speak. Between 1990 and her death, there was a two-year period of hospitalization, and this included for some months my own daily residence on her hospital ward, and thereafter until her death my regular two- or three-day visits every two weeks. I had been a par-ticipant in some aspects of my father's decline and death, then a major parti-cipant in my mother's attempts to make sense of this. I became the major participant with my Mum in her decline and death, and very directly involved in my own attempts to make sense of what was happening to her and, as the person who became legally and emotionally responsible for my mother's wel-fare, what was also happening to me.

My Mother's Voice?

My mother was Win Stanley, formerly Hickman; she was born in 1913 and died in 1992. She was the daughter of 'poor but honest' parents, as I was too;

her first bout of TB at the age of four years had hospitalized her, and thereafter her mother kept her at home and away from school, partly to protect her, partly to help with younger siblings; later bouts of TB hospitalized her when I was four years old, then later, when I was 11, she had a lung removed. My mother's narrative in the form of taped conversations with me was embarked upon deliberately and consciously as a break from the many months of misery and despair as my father had suffered stroke upon stroke and became more and more brain-damaged. Eventually he was hospitalized when his increasing violence spilled over onto ambulance drivers, and he died a few difficult months following this. From his hospitalization onwards, my Mum attempted to understand and come to terms with such a dreadful end to nearly 40 years of marriage to a dearly loved husband (Stanley, 1990b). The taped conversations were a part of this process of her trying to 'understand and come to terms with'. They described people and events and feelings around which she thought about a set of immensely practical issues: the relationship of the past to the present and the role of memory; how she had changed from the 3-year-old infant on her potty, whose first memory was the ceiling plaster collapsing on her, to the exhausted old woman without a future, only a past; what people are really like and by what evidence this can be known; whether people can in some fundamental sense change their selves; what a 'self' is and when it begins and ends. As I have discussed elsewhere, a number of these issues also came to preoccupy me during the two year period from my mother's stroke in 1990 to her death (Stanley, 1994a). Here I want to focus on what it was that produced this commonality in our concerns, the impinging necessity of tragic events, those of decline and death, and the equally impinging necessity of attempting to understand them.

The kind of events that I am referring to are 'necessary' in the sense of being irresistible and unamenable to personal or even impersonal control: terminal illness, dying, death; I use the word 'tragic' to describe them because of their inevitability in a particular context, with only one's moral and behavioural stance towards them being controllable. I briefly address four key sets of themes or issues that both Mum and I returned to over and over, I in a 'fieldwork diary' that I wrote from the day of my mother's stroke until her death and after, and she in the taped conversations already referred to.

Past, Present and Memory

My Mum puzzled a good deal about the past. As she said to me 'I like thinking it all over, home an' that, me Mum an' Dad an' that, it's really all I have now Lizbeth'. Her younger brother Fred, a domestic tyrant ruling their parents with a rod of iron, her volatile older sister May and her wild mood changes, the 'puzzle' of sister Ivy in her middle-age with a house full of stolen packets of tea, the car accident at the age of five years that had left her youngest sister Dorry emotionally and intellectually fundamentally changed. One of the things that preoccupied her about all this was how she and others had moved from one point in time, which she associated with youth and a kind of innocence, to their older and changed selves: thus, for example, May's volatile mood changes led her to challenge everyday expressions of class hierarchies, but later caused her nearly to kill a pregnant and unmarried daughter and almost ended her marriage to kindly and placid uncle Bill; and Fred moved from being spoiled and bossy to later alienating everyone he knew and living for most of his life friendless after his mother's death. My Mum too had moved almost imperceptibly through time, from her first memories as an infant surrounded by busy family life, to the lonely woman becalmed at the further edge of life who was in her words 'just waiting for death'. The past and memory exercised my Mum in another way also, not as the source of 'true' memories, but instead of tricks and concealments. My Dad's strokes brought with them increasing tempers and physical violences, and with them harshly contemptuous words about my mother. Mum poured over the evidence for and against her: yes, he had always sneered because she could not read and write, because she had had sex with him before they were married, because she loved him; no, he tried to help but had not known how, had known that her pregnancy was the only means of forcing his mother's agreement to their marriage, had loved her as much as she him, as his letters to her when she was in hospital having her lung operation showed.[6]

My own 'puzzlements' have, over time, cohered around my father rather than my mother, and my parents to the complete exclusion of my brother. In a kind of parallel to my mother wondering what he really felt about her, so I wondered what my father 'really' felt about me: as a baby he had pushed me around in my pram at every opportunity, a working-class man almost alone at that time in doing so; as I was growing up he scrimped and saved for presents, a bike then later a radio; my Mum spoke of his love and pride in me; but effectively all of my memories now are composed by his angers and tempers, whether to risk them, how to avoid them, and later in my teens how to encourage them for the pleasure of feeling contemptuous of him. And yet; and yet when I cleared my mother's house after her death I found letters I wrote to my parents when they were in Germany and when I was working as a children's nanny in London (when I was aged 15–17), letters in which I lovingly teased him, used pet names of him, missed him, looked forward to seeing him. Is the puzzle here his feelings for me, mine for him, the processes of change, the relationship of parents and children, memory, or simply the accruing complexities of life?

Temporal and Ontological Change

For Mum, temporal change, change over time and as a consequence of time changing and moving on, has a puzzling and disturbing quality because emeshed within it are ontological changes, changes in the being, in the character as well as the behaviour, of people. Are such ontological changes an inevitable feature of temporal shifts, or is there something else involved here as well? My mother was clear that sister Dorry had fundamentally changed: 'She was different after, [the accident], completely different, it'd changed her.' Regarding my father, my mother was never sure whether the changes that resulted in his rages and violences were the product of time and the physiological decline of strokes and brain-damage, or whether 'he' had changed in some more fundamental sense, or whether indeed this version of 'him' had always been there somehow beneath the loving surface of days and months undetected by her. She was also concerned with the necessary changes that had occurred to her own self as a consequence — although sometimes she wondered whether as a cause. On the one hand:

> I had to become hard, I had to Lizbeth, or I'd've gone under; he wanted to break me, that's what I think, but I weren't going to, so I made myself hard.

And on the other:

> He didn't like it did he, when you come so I could get to the hairdressers, he thought I should just be there with him never doing anything or going anywhere, just a nothing. And he didn't like it before when I wanted to go to work, tho' he liked the money alright, that's what he bought that little car with, that first black one, d'you remember that car Lizbeth? [but yet again] Well, he was always worried I'd do too much, that the TB would be back, so he wanted me to rest an' not do too much, he always tried to look after me.

For me, the puzzles about such change were focused around 'the stroke', what it does to people, and whether and to what extent it 'changes them' in a fundamental sense or merely removes the inhibitory controls that usually govern our relationships with others. My mother seemed to me, post-stroke, as lovingly kindly as before and with rather less understandable temper than before, although with many other kinds of moods: 'I' became the dead-centre of the interactional universe, and others were merely inconveniences to be brought under my mother's anxious, troubled, but almost uncommunicable will.

'Knowing' People

The ontological puzzles of 'knowing people' — which is the 'real' them — have epistemological reverberations, and these were of perhaps prime concern to my mother. They centre upon how we know, using what evidence, and what we do with contrary viewpoints and evidence. Thus 'Did he change, Lizbeth, that's what I want to know. Nellie says when he was little he always, well his Mum your Granny Stanley, she made him the little dictator, after your

Grandfather pushed off [when my father was about 3, his brother about 2]. It's no good for boys is it, that? It makes them little buggers don't it?'. However, 'He weren't like that with me, but I never stood up to him, I'd've put my head in a gas-oven for him, I loved him that much, it was only when he was ill, I had to Lizbeth, I had to'. But then 'Did he change tho' or was it me, cos I was like that with him?'. Later in the same conversation she related this to the relationship between my Dad and me: 'You an' him, as you was growing up you was always, the two of you, I remember that time he smacked you, his handmark on your leg [when I was about 6]. I said to him you do that again an' we go. An' I meant it Lizbeth. An' he never did it again did he? . . . [Later she said:] You didn't get on with him then did you? [in my later adolescence after I left school, worked, then went to college] an'yet he'd've done anything for you. But he didn't like anyone standing up to him, he never did'.

The same kinds of epistemological issues preoccupied me also, including what relationship all this talk had to the 'real events' that were so utterly unrecoverable, why 'the same' memory could seem both so certain at one point and so completely uncertain at another, and why 'the same' evidences should be differently evaluated as the mind turned and returned to them. At some points during the two years that my mother was hospitalized, these issues cohered around my mother herself and my relationship with her, but also, at various and increasing crisis points, with the nursing and medical staff and their very different interpretation of 'Win Stanley' from my own. Thus 'the hospital' (my gloss for a complex of nurses, ward sisters, doctors and ancillary medical staff) in my view over-stated my mother's intellectual and linguistic abilities, seeing her kindly smiles and nods and apparent agreement with whatever they proposed to her as evidence for this, while I saw these things as smiles and nods with no real understanding of verbal questions and propositions.

The Nature of 'The Self'

There came a point in my father's decline when he was hospitalized; initially, in the aftermath of the violent outbursts which had led to this, my mother treated my father as effectively dead: 'If it would help him Lizbeth I'd go [to visit him in hospital], but it won't, I can't do anything for him now'. Then with persuasion from me and from the consultant in charge of my father's 'case', she began a pattern of visiting which re-established as much as possible the pattern of domestic care for my father, around food and drink and clothes, that had characterized their married life. Some months later, after an even greater mental decline, my father slipped into pneumonia and began to die. As soon as he did so my mother immediately stopped visiting him. I worried about this, at my father dying alone and among strangers, and about how Mum might feel about this later after his death. When we talked about this in one of our by then regular taped conversations, she repeated her earlier words: 'There's no sense in my going Lizbeth, all I could do is sit there, sit there and watch him. If it'd help him I'd go, I'd do anything for him but I can't, so there's no point in my sitting there getting upset, I might as well be here. You can go if you want. . . .' Various domestic disasters loomed over my mother at this point which I think were more important than this death that in a very real sense had already happened; these included my father's poll tax bill and a depended-upon neighbour of more than 30 years thinking of moving, for which she wanted my help. I asked her whether she wanted me to sort out these things or to 'sit with' my father, that is, be with him while he died. Mum was adamant that it should be the former, so I visited my father only in between; he did in fact die 'alone', with only hospital staff with him, something I have always regretted but at the time felt unable to challenge.

For my mother, 'death', the death of my father, was a social death more than a physical one, and, as the social and interactional bonds went, so it seems to me he became ontologically 'other' to her. What on one level was a kind of quiet ruthlessness in placing her emotional survival above his dying, was on another the simple acknowledgement that in every 'real' sense my father was already dead. With all this and my response to it in mind, I spent as much time with my mother as I could following her first stroke, and then from her final stroke during the 11 days of coma it took her to die. While this can be read in a number of ways, how I inscribed it in my notebook, as I sat by her bedside, was in terms of 'self' and when and how self begins, and ends. I watched 'my mother' recede hour by hour from the face and figure in the bed, and I tried to catch the very moment when 'it' happened and her dying finally and irrevocably began. What interested me was whether this 'moment' could be discerned, and then, as I watched and waited, whether it is only ever other people who can see it or whether there are some people who discern it of themselves. That is, if they know the point when they are no longer themselves, if this is actually *knowable*, or whether all that gives knowledge has gone when this point is arrived at.

A Brief Conclusion

It might be objected, against the general argument of this chapter, that in one sense I am not 'a native' at all, for over the last 20 years or so I have been immersed in the world of books and ideas and intellectual debates that characterize academia. Certainly there is no return to 'pre-textuality' for me, to a time when 'the self' was not a matter for analysis and theory (for this was the origin of my interest in sociology), when 'time' and its passing did not interest me (for soon after my academic career began I became involved in historical research and writing), when the representation of lives in diaries and letters and other sources was not of overwhelming epistemological interest (for such an interest gave rise to my becoming an academic as well as my interest in auto/ biography). My mother is a different matter. She came from a poor working-class background, one that had no truck with books and as little with schools as it could manage, and for health and domestic reasons she escaped the net of schooling entirely. Her puzzlings and wonderings and analyses were most certainly not the product of 'book learning' but rather of life and circumstance. And there we both are, in the tapes and the fieldwork notebooks, my mother 'a native', and myself 'a former native' plunged by circumstance into nativity. Therein both of us are concerned with, preoccupied with, and in my view achieve, both rationality and emotionality, both subjectivity and objectivity, both involvement and critical analysis, both immersion and detachment. In saying this I make no claims at all that either of us are or were exceptional: we did what many people involved in the inevitability of tragic circumstances do all the time.

The general themes of this chapter are concerned with knowledge, academic gatekeeping and science and are all pointed up in my discussion of 'the native'. I have proposed that the apparatus of science over-dichotomizes, by treating as binaries, attributes that are much more complexly related in social life, and that one of these false binaries is that of 'scientist/native'. The convention that defines academia at the level of ideology defines it as different, divorced from life, a separate sphere. This convention banishes 'I' as part of a set of gatekeeping practices which make it appear as though Science really does exist, really is entirely and absolutely objective, unemotional, rational, uncommitted, detached. Thus speaking and writing as I have done herein 'as a' (as a woman, as working class, as a feminist) rather than speaking 'for the' (speaking and writing for the women, the working class, the feminists, on their behalves rather than we, I, speaking on our own) constitutes my means of both being and remaining 'native' *and* doing and being 'scientific'. Being involved like this includes rational thought, critical detachment, analytic theorizing, for these are not exclusively scientific attributes but rather human ones. 'Going native' does not disempower academics intellectually, however vulnerable it may make us feel personally, and of course personal vulnerability is precisely what we ask of our 'subjects' all the time. Feminist academics should make full intellectual and analytical use of our 'hybrid' status and reject any attempt to present this as merely a slide into what Hilary Rose (1994: 259) disapprovingly terms 'radical subjectivity'. It is no such thing, but rather a determined and principled bringing together of the binaries of science, thereby showing the defining objectivity of so-called subjectivities.

Notes

1 '"Going native"? Issues in feminist ethnography', paper given to the Dance Research Seminar, Department of Dance Studies, University of Surrey, September (Stanley, 1994b). I am grateful to Theresa Buckland and Janet Lansdale for giving me this opportunity to speak and be spoken to.

2 See here for example Stanley and Wise (1979, 1983, 1993) as well as Stanley (1990a, 1992).

3 By which term I mean, to quote Agar (1980: 1–2), 'Ethnography is an ambiguous

term, representing both a process and a product. As a product ethnography is usually a book ... as a process ... [it is how] an ethnographer attempts a comprehensive understanding of some human group'. The group in question can be a whole society, or a much more specific and limited social setting, and it can be located 'at home' as well as 'abroad'.

4 See here Abu-Lugod (1990) for an approach in many ways similar, although less concerned than I am with the relationship between writers and readers of feminist texts, with feminist textual politics.

5 Michael Agar's (1980) introductory text invokes this central ethnographic symbol in its title of *The Professional Stranger*. The title is more accurately applied to academic feminists, for we never, ever, leave 'the field', for our 'strangeness' is a compound of being women, being feminists, as well as being academics.

6 These letters were cremated with my mother. After losing such a tangible 'proof' of his love, I too started to wonder about his feelings for her. And both before and after, I wondered at the committal of these feelings to the written page, for my mother at this stage in her life could neither read nor write and was dependent on her sisters reading to her in my father's absence.

References

ABU-LUGOD, LILA (1990) 'Is there a feminist ethnography?' *Women & Performance*, **5**, pp. 7–27.

AGAR, MICHAEL (1980) *The Professional Stranger: An Informal Introduction to Ethnography*, New York: Academic Press.

GEERTZ, CLIFFORD (1988) *Works and Lives: The Anthropologist As Author*, Cambridge: Polity Press.

MILLER, NANCY (1991) *Getting Personal: Feminist Occasions and Other Autobiographical Acts*, New York: Routledge.

ROSE, HILARY (1994) *Love, Power and Knowledge*, Cambridge: Polity Press.

STANLEY, LIZ (Ed.) (1990a) *Feminist Praxis: Research, Theory and Epistemology in Feminist Sociology*, London: Routledge.

STANLEY, LIZ (1990b) 'A Referral was Made: behind the scenes during the creation of a Social Services Department elderly statistic', in STANLEY, LIZ (Ed.) *Feminist Praxis*, pp. 113–124, London: Routledge.

STANLEY, LIZ (1992) *The Auto/Biographical I: Theory and Practice of Feminist Auto/Biography*, Manchester: Manchester University Press.

STANLEY, LIZ (1994a) 'The knowing because experiencing subject: narratives, lives and autobiography', in LENNON, KATHLEEN and WHITFORD, MARGARET (Eds) *Knowing the Difference: Feminist Perspectives in Epistemology*, pp. 132–148, London: Routledge.

STANLEY, LIZ (1994b) ' "Going native"? Issues in feminist ethnography', paper given to the Graduate Feminist Seminar, Department of Dance Studies, University of Surrey, September.

STANLEY, LIZ and WISE, SUE (1979) 'Feminist consciousness, feminist research and experiences of sexism', *Women's Studies International Forum*, **2**, pp. 359–372.

STANLEY, LIZ and WISE, SUE (1983) *Breaking Out: Feminist Consciousness and Feminist Research*, London: Routledge.

STANLEY, LIZ and WISE, SUE (1993) *Breaking Out Again: Feminist Ontology and Epistemology*, London: Routledge.

Grievance

The pain in my voice hurts people.
It makes bureaucrats withdraw into their briefcases,
medicos reach for their pads
it hurls even my psychotherapist halfway across the room
upon the oiled wheels of her systems.

Tell me, my friend,
what is the worst thing you can imagine?
being tortured?
being forced to witness the torture of your children?
being powerless to stop the torture of your friends?

The big boys are doing bad things in the room behind closed doors
and the clatter of their instruments is more terrifying
for being unseen.

Their laughter goes through us like a machine gun
and it is all part of a normal day's business.

They are efficient, for they can,
with one quiet word
draw into their little bowl
all the malignancy,
stir our blood round with sticks
and, naming our mangled parts
trap us in isolation.

We are efficient, for we name ourselves
little, unworthy, quite beneath contempt
and we will name ourselves
in threat of torture
mad or misguided, too thick to understand
guilty in error, simply impotent;

we will walk round baring our wounded stars
hanging our own labels
asking, please, for enough rope.

Each week I am asked
to tell them precisely how
they can torture me and my children,
display our wounds and scars
disclose our soft openings and betray
the precious entrances
to our safe places.

I am asked to tell them point by point
help them to phrase it

I am asked how to spell grievance.

Dinah Dossor 9.6.90

194

Contributors

Barbara Brown Packer was born in Southern California. She received a bac-
calaureate degree with honors in political science from the University of California, Santa Barbara and a master's degree from Stanford University. After
teaching at the high school level for two years, she began her career in college administration. She received her doctorate in Administration, Planning and
Social Policy at Harvard University. In 1994 she founded Catalyst Educational
Consulting Services, a consulting company working closely with colleges and
universities. She frequently speaks and writes on her area of research, women
and higher education.

Avril Butler, CQSW, MA Women's Studies, works as a Senior Lecturer in
Social Work at the University of Plymouth. Her research interests include confidentiality, empowerment in work with families, women's mental health, autobiography, feminist perspectives of teaching and learning in Higher Education.

Celia Davies took up a post as Professor of Women's Opportunities in the
University of Ulster in 1987, and established the Centre for Research on Women
in 1988. Hers was the first such professorial post in the UK and was later
retitled Professor of Women's Studies. Celia is a sociologist whose research
interests have centred on women's employment and equal opportunities, particularly in relation to the NHS. Her most recent book is *Gender and the
Professional Predicament in Nursing*, Open University Press, 1995.

Dinah Dossor is Director of Learning Resources for the School of Design and
Visual Arts, Liverpool John Moores University, after many years teaching Fine
Art Theoretical Studies. She has been a long-time NATFHE activist, with particular concern for Equal Opportunities, most recently as Chair of the University branch and as member of NATFHE National Executive Committee. She is
an occasional writer of poetry and academic papers, and 'lifelong' single parent
of two daughters.

Debbie Epstein lectures in Women's Studies and Education in the Centre for
Research and Education on Gender at London University's Institute of Education, thus bringing together her commitment to feminism and to the practice of
teaching. As well as working on issues of equality in education, she is also

working on a feminist analysis of the *Oprah Winfrey Show*. Recent publications include: *Changing Classroom Cultures: anti-racism, politics and schools* and *Challenging Lesbian and Gay Inequalities in Education.* A forthcoming title (with Richard Johnson) is *Schooling Sexualities: Lesbian and Gay Oppression, Identities and Education.*

Mary Evans is Professor of Women's Studies at the University of Kent at Canterbury, where she has taught since 1971. A graduate of the LSE and the University of Sussex, she is the author of numerous books, including, most recently, *Battle for Britain* (with David Morgan) and *The Woman Question.*

Penny Holloway is a Sub-Librarian at the University of Ulster. She has long been an active member of the Association of University Teachers and has been a member of the National Executive since 1989. She is currently Chairperson of AUT (Ulster). She takes a particular interest in issues of sex discrimination and pay. She has published articles on these topics in *AUT Woman*, and jointly coordinated a seminar on performance-related pay for trade unions in London in February 1994. She is the AUT representative on CUCO.

Lesley Kerman is an artist and writer who has been a Head of Department of Humanities, Performance and Media, Head of Department of Art, Design and Media, and a Principal Lecturer in Charge of Art and Design History. She has worked in various institutions of Higher Education and acts as an external examiner in Fine Art, Art and Design History and Women's Studies. She has served as a member of the National Executive of the Association of Art Historians. Her published writing has been reviews of Art Exhibitions in the *Guardian, Arts Review, Aspects.* She is a Graduate of Kings College, University of Durham, Fine Art Department, where she studied with Victor and Richard Hamilton. Her own work was first exhibited in the Young Contemporaries 1963/4. Recent shows have been in Swansea Art Gallery, The Brewhouse Taunton, Howard Gardens Gallery Cardiff and the Pitt Rivers Museum, Oxford.

Mel Landells works as a researcher and is currently studying British women farmers and identity. Her past research has included organizational change in social services and confidentiality and empowerment in work with families. She is co-editor of the *Women's Studies International Handbook.*

Louise Morley is a Lecturer in the Faculty of Education and Community Studies at the University of Reading. She teaches Women's Studies, Education and Interpersonal Skills, with research interests in equity, empowerment and the micropolitics of Women's Studies in Higher Education. She is Course Director for the MA in Equity and Change in the Public Services, and coordinates her department's international programme. She has published widely on feminist pedagogy and women in organizations. She is Honorary Secretary for the

Women's Studies Network (UK), lives in West London and likes to dance, travel and listen to opera.

Tracey Potts's first degree was in English and Women's Studies from Wolverhampton Polytechnic. She is currently engaged in postgraduate research at Warwick University where she also completed an MA in Interdisciplinary Women's Studies. Her research is involved with issues around feminist literary politics and the reading of Black women's testimonial fiction. Since being diagnosed as having ME in 1987, she has become increasingly concerned with the encounter between academic feminism and 'lived experience'.

Janet Price is affiliated to Liverpool University, though unemployed due to ill-health. She teaches on feminist health issues, and is undertaking research on the colonial constitution of women's health. She has had ME for 6 years, and the experience of this has led her to become increasingly involved in addressing where and how bodies fit into feminist theorizing and practice.

Naz Rassool was born in South Africa and now resides in the UK where she works as a Lecturer in Education at Reading University. Her research interests include language and cultural relations in the pluralist nation-state, the sociology of technology in education and the sociology of education. She has published in the field of the sociology of technology in education policy issues in bilingualism for ethnic minority groups in the UK and is currently working on a study on education policy issues in relation to ethnic relations in post-Communist Bulgaria.

Heidi Safia Mirza is a Senior Lecturer in Social Science, at South Bank University. She has taught Afro-American Studies at Brown University, USA, and Sociology at the University of London. As a researcher she has worked on the Daycare Project at the Thomas Coram Research Unit, Institute of Education, and the Drugs Information Project at Goldsmiths College, University of London. Her current research interest is the experience of black women in Higher Education. She is the author of *Young, Female and Black* (Routledge, 1992).

Jo Stanley is a freelance writer and cultural worker, particularly involved in exploring older women's life-history in creative ways. Her most recent book is *Bold in her Breeches: women pirates across the ages* (Pandora, 1995). She also edited the late Jo Spence's collected works, *Cultural Sniping, the art of transgression* (Routledge, 1995). Originally from a Liverpool working-class family and trained as a designer, she now lives in North London and is trying to let herself work visually and write more fiction.

Liz Stanley is a Reader in Sociology and the Director of Women's Studies at the University of Manchester. Working class by birth, a lesbian by luck, and a Northerner by choice (for as all its denizens know, Manchester is the centre of the known universe), she lives with Sue Wise. Greatest interests and pleasures are books, cats, food, wine, music, in changing permutations of that order.

Val Walsh trained as an artist, designer and teacher, before qualifying in Sociology, Art Education and Women's Studies. After 21 years full-time as an academic, in 1993 she went freelance to develop interdisciplinary and multimedia materials and events which promote women's co-creativity and mutual empowerment. She also started to train as a Shiatsu practitioner. She is researching women's experience in art education and as artists, and completing a book on feminism and women's creativity. A parent for 16 years, she lives in Liverpool.

Index

Academic Board 139–41
access 4, 15, 169
  black women 149–51
accountability 10
adjunct professors 48
affirmative action 32–3, 47
agency 82–3
anger 2
  black women 153
  working class oppression 171, 173
anti-feminists 43, 49, 94
anti-racism 4, 5
  black women 150–2
  New Right 62–8
anti-sexism 166
appointments 13, 140–1
art
  school 135–8
  subject hierarchy 135–6, 138
  therapy 5, 175–9
Asian-Americans 24, 26, 29, 31
Asians 24, 31
assessment
  performance indicators 7, 9–10, 15–17
  research 9–10, 14–16, 116
  sexual harassment 166
  teaching 10, 78
assistant professors 51
associate professors 33–4, 53
auto/biography 5–6, 185, 191

behavioural sciences 42, 46, 51
Black Consciousness Movement 23
Black Studies 78
black women
  higher education 5, 145–53
  marginalization 5, 22, 27, 31, 39, 89, 150

motivation for education 146–7
as 'other' 22–39
passivity 3, 22, 31, 39
role models 36–7, 145
transgression 89–90, 95
universities 4–5, 25–39, 145–51
USA 3, 23, 25, 28–9, 31–5
writing 34, 121, 123, 152
Brent 63, 64–6

career advancement 3–4, 42–3, 45–55,
    78–81, 94, 172
  black women 25, 27, 30–9, 146–8,
    152
  creativity 116–27
  disability 157
  glass ceiling 50, 137–8
  lack of women in senior posts 5,
    12–13
  lesbians 90
  qualifications 74
  sexual harassment 161
  women in management 5, 131–42
  see also promotion
casualization 3, 15
childcare 77, 79
  black women 34–5, 152
  researchers 14–15
civil rights 32, 43, 45–6
class oppression 2, 5, 86, 171, 173
  black women 24, 26, 28, 37
  see also middle class; working class
colonialism 5, 75–6
  black women 24, 26, 28, 38
  going native 183
Commission for Racial Equality 11
Commission on University Career
    Opportunity (CUCO) 13

199